AIDS, ART & the origins of the CULTURE WAR

Praise for

AIDS, Art & the Origins of the Culture War

"Written mostly as the AIDS crisis crested, Atkins' collected essays bring us directly to the specificity of the AIDS experience: The profound integration of ART, the Art World, and the political crisis. The deeply personal details of dying, surviving, and witnessing. Atkins' work eclipses subsequent cliches and makes the reader see the visual life of this disaster, resisting its waning memory."

—*Sarah Schulman, writer and activist*

"*AIDS, Art & the Origins of the Culture War* is an IMPORTANT and NECESSARY book. Robert Atkins' writing in the Village Voice (and elsewhere) defined an urgent and turbulent time during the 1980's, 1990's and beyond. But his writings chronicle more than history: They foretell the current culture war battles about free expression and censorship raging across the planet."

—*Antonio Muntadas, artist*

"Unapologetically partisan, passionately engaged and deeply immersed in a long history of activism, Atkins' collection of essays cannot be more timely. There are frequent comparisons between the ideological climate today and the culture wars of the 1980s and 1990, yet the political evolution of censorship in the last 40 years needed to be traced—until now. This book brings to life the main actors, the political manipulations, and the creative resistance."

—*Svetlana Mintcheva, writer,*
National Coalition Against Censorship

"The worldwide HIV pandemic is obviously not over. Memory, history and heart must be mobilized to eradicate AIDS. This book, loaded with all three, is a potent weapon."

—*Jeff Weinstein, writer and editor*

"Critic, activist, and historian, Robert Atkins' bulletins from the culture war fronts remind us of the deep roots of our current social malaise. His pointed prose illuminates the strategically-provoked prejudices that have hoodwinked so many. Looking at the actions of artists and cultural groups to push back, this book suggests ways forward while honoring our progressive past."

—*Steven Watson, cultural historian, Artifacts*

"Anyone seeking to understand America's culture war would be hard-pressed to find a clearer, more compelling account of its development from the racist/homophobic attacks on freedom of expression to the organizing strategies and artworks that arose in response. These attacks of the late twentieth century also laid the groundwork for contemporary assaults on nearly every form of constitutionally protected expression. *AIDS, Art & the Origins of the Culture War* is both an invaluable historical resource and a roadmap for the resistance we so desperately need today."

—David M. Roth, SquareCylinder

"Atkins traces a through-line from the little known 19th century *Kulturkampf* to JD Vance's recent claim that Christian nationalism "remains America's creed," reminding us of stupidity's current triumph. The essays string odious ornaments—Anita Bryant, Pat Buchanan, Clarence Thomas—onto a lethal necklace choking our civic life. Despite this strangling of intellectual inquiry and free expression, Atkins' book offers hope. It affirms that art's exchange of ideas and community building is our path forward, the primary vehicle for human adaptation."

—Gordon Knox Arizona State University Art Museum

"Robert Atkins' granular account of the suffering and the censorship that occurred during a time of crisis and destruction should be required reading for anyone interested in American culture."

—Cynthia Carr, writer, Candy Darling: Dreamer, Icon, Superstar

"According to James Baldwin, ideas re-emerge when they are needed. Robert Atkins has written a book that examines the AIDS crisis of the 1980-90s--and provides strategies that may be relevant again in the present. Thank you, Robert, for staying in the trenches, fighting the good fight for freedom of expression then, and effective means of preserving our freedoms now."

—Martha Wilson, artist, Franklin Furnace Archive, Inc.

"As someone who has worked at the intersection of art and AIDS for over 20 years, I was struck by [Atkins'} book's range."

—Ted Kerr, writer and activist

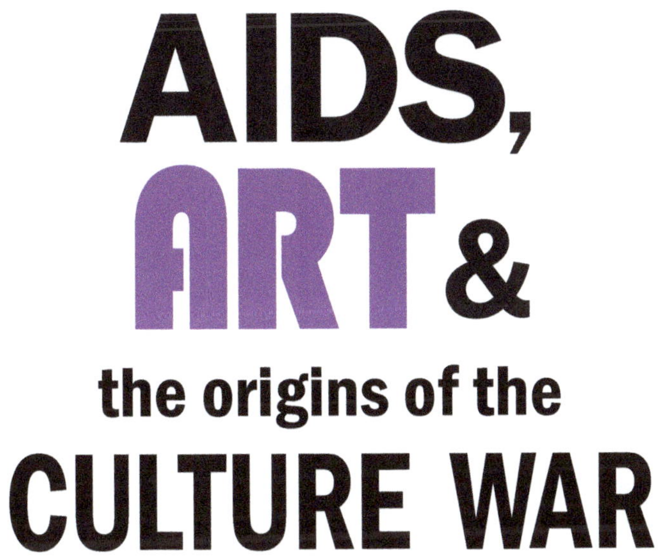

AIDS, ART & the origins of the CULTURE WAR

selected writings of Robert Atkins

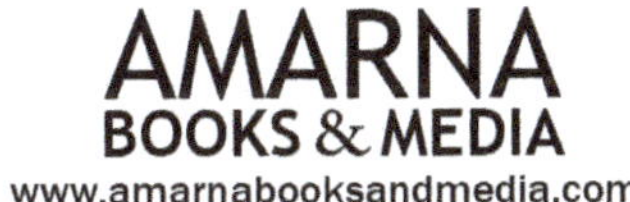

AMARNA
BOOKS & MEDIA
www.amarnabooksandmedia.com

ISBN (paperback): 978-1-961869-09-7
ISBN (hardcover): 978-1-961869-16-5

Library of Congress Control Number: 2026936212

Book design by Thomas Edward West of Amarna Books & Media
Front and back cover photographs by Kermit Berg

First print edition March 2026

Amarna Books & Media
Philadelphia, PA
www.amarnabooksandmedia.net

Acknowledgements

This book comprises writing from many years, as do these acknowledgements. First and foremost, thanks to the editors Nancy Grubb (of Abbeville Press), Jeff Weinstein (*Village Voice*) and Steven Watson, my in-home advisor during the 20 years I lived in New York. Each of them helped sharpen my writing and thinking.

Many agencies and organizations—including the National Endowments for the Arts, the National Endowment for the Humanities, the University of Hawaii, Manufacturers Hanover Bank, the Penny McCall Foundation, Microsoft, Carnegie Mellon/STUDIO for Creative Inquiry, and the Blue Mountain Center—throughout the years have provided welcome support that have directly or indirectly helped bring this book to fruition.

Special thanks to the late Thomas Sokolowski, my art-world co-conspirator. His dry wit helped create an abundance of fond memories, many of them during our co-founding of Visual AIDS and co-curating of *From Media to Metaphor: Art About AIDS*, the first show of AIDS-art to travel abroad.

I also wish to extend heartfelt thanks to my friend Kermit Berg, for his permission to use his photographs for the book's covers. Although my selection of a photo of an elevator control panel for the book's front cover may seem odd, in retrospect this one seems almost pre-ordained: This is the elevator in the Berlin building where Kermit and his husband Malte own an apartment, in which I've stayed. Kermit's comment that the colloquial German translation of elevator is *aufzug*—up and down—resonated with me as a description of the unpredictable passage of life, especially for those with HIV.

And of course life ends. I want to acknowledge here the recent death of my brother Richard. Loving and generous, he sadly died too early to celebrate this book's publication.

Finally, I wish to express my gratitude to those who since the 1980s have resisted the official cruelty, popular prejudice, and genocidal threats—both existing and some not yet even imagined—to the survival of those with AIDS.

—*Robert Atkins*

Table of Contents

PART THREE

PART FOUR

FOREWORD

AIDS Life

By Jeff Weinstein

Editors learn terrible things from their writers, typically about the planet's vast and thriving garden of stupidity, greed, and wanton death. In the late 1980s, I asked Robert Atkins to start a column dubbed *Scene & Heard* for New York's weekly *Village Voice*. An out art critic and temperature-taker of social mores, he reported, in peripatetic and telegraphic form—as if he were everywhere—the meetings, discussions, and actions of activists and art-worlders who were shocked and then roused by the viciousness of government, religion, and so many others toward gay men who died, as they said, "from AIDS." Also from neglect and hatred. Right away, when so few were awake to what was really going on, Robert got it.

I was Robert's editor, but on this topic, in many ways, he edited me.

I'm 78 years old and still recall my hybrid scream-sigh when I heard Pat Buchanan, communications director for the White House's Ronald Reagan, say that AIDS was "nature's revenge on gay men." Two-term Reagan, as many know or should know, did nothing, literally nothing, to acknowledge our danger, misery, and rapid deaths. We now understand all too well that anyone, queer or not, can get HIV, but medications and funded social initiatives prevent infection—yay to the recently developed pre-exposure prophylaxis, PrEP!—and if you have HIV, mute it profoundly. Still, we must continue to fight back, as Robert constantly implores in his wide-reaching introduction, because viruses, microscopic and human-size, don't evaporate like cinema ghosts: they persist and infect. According to U.N. AIDS, 1.3 million people worldwide became infected with HIV and 630,000 died from AIDS-related illnesses in 2024.

The worldwide HIV pandemic is obviously not over. Memory, history, and heart must be mobilized to eradicate AIDS. This book, loaded with all three, is a potent weapon.

As I'm writing, it's an icy start to December and I've been humming and singing the old standard, "I'll See You in My Dreams." Here's why. When I finally get to sleep I do dream… of lovers, friends, and colleagues, some of whom Robert knew, who died so shatteringly young of HIV-1 complications 30, even 40 years ago.

College boyfriend Michael sickened with pneumonia and vanished quickly as the epidemic, then named GRID, began to take hold. Vito, diagnosed in 1985, knew what he had and, affectionate and brave, marched and put his body on the line with ACT UP, the AIDS Coalition to Unleash Power, and co-founded the Gay and Lesbian Alliance Against Defamation (GLAAD). Queer writer Chris went dancing right before he left us, laughing, twirling, and punching back. Dear partner Joe, out of the Navy during the Vietnam War, left a hoarse message on my primitive answering machine: "Jeff, time to say goodbye, goodbye." I had no idea he was dying.

I see and hear them in my dreams.

In 1988, the World Health Organization at the United Nations established December 1 as World AIDS Day, to "raise awareness" of the pandemic and provide a rubric for local and international fundraising. In this necessary book, we read that Robert, that same year, was a founder of New York's Visual AIDS, among the first groups to memorialize artists who succumbed. The little group strove to access the public and private power of museums and galleries to spur AIDS awareness and promote humane treatment of those infected with HIV. From its origin, Visual AIDS has preserved and then taken and digitized images of dead (and living) artists' work, creating the largest archive of such work anywhere.

Robert and other critics and curators at Visual AIDS immediately advanced the idea for a "A Day Without Art," in which museums and galleries would, on World AIDS Day, take down or hide their wares to envision, collectively, just what loss looks like. Earlier anti-Vietnam War petitions and demonstrations directed at New York's Museum of Modern Art were part of its inspiration, offered by art-critic member John Perreault.

"A Day Without Art" was launched fast in 1989, and more than 800 art institutions participated in varying ways: the Guggenheim Museum, for example, hung a huge black shroud from top to sidewalk. The group itself also created works including "Night Without Light," when skylines across the U.S were darkened, an exhibition and competition for a PSA to screen on TV, prevention-oriented broadsides designed by artists, and in 1991, "The Ribbon Project" or *Red Ribbon*. Happily, by the mid-nineties, anti-retrovirals were prolonging and saving lives, so "A Day Without Art" became "Day With(out) Art," an opportunity to show art for more than one day by ill artists who had passed or a wider range of AIDS- and HIV-related artworks.

In his elaborate May, 1990 piece in *ARTS Magazine* about "A Day Without Art," we see how industriously Atkins, just before the internet, wove together stories large and small about what was being done across the country. A participant as well as journalist, Robert was never trapped by impossible "neutrality." In it, he cites the ever-growing *NAMES Project Quilt*, soon to become the largest community artwork in the world:

The *NAMES Project AIDS Quilt* "has been criticized by some activists as an inappropriate concession to grief and a paralyzing deterrent against political action," he wrote. "Such simplistic thinking persists..." For the *Voice*, in 1987, Robert described the *Quilt's* roll-out on the Capitol Mall: "Like the Vietnam War Memorial, the *NAMES Project Quilt* is shocking for its concreteness; especially when it's the way you learn about the death of an acquaintance."

I too viewed the *Quilt* in Atlanta and wrote about it before it first came to New York. I completely agree. The *Quilt* also carries names into the future, a particular handkerchief for grief and a large, beautiful goad to action. Grief is sorrow and celebration, all at once.

Both the introduction, "When the Culture War Became the Culture," and second part of the book concern the concomitant period when National Endowment for the Arts funding for shows about AIDS and sexuality were bludgeoned by pre-Trump right-wingers. They didn't altogether win. Robert's thesis proposes that the so-called Culture War is a single ongoing struggle between repressive censorship and freedom. It's a cogent argument.

This past December 2025, for the first time since 1988, no huge red ribbon commemorating December's World AIDS Day was hung on the White House, a fought-for memorial to the millions who have died of AIDS-related illness. Life-saving funding has withered, like HIV-infected bodies.

Guess who. Guess why.

I asked Robert what he thinks about this knife into the heart of our recognition and safety:

"I'm appalled at the end of 2025 that the Trump administration is withdrawing U.S. recognition of World AIDS Day. Symbols are important, we know. But perhaps worse is that HIV drugs are being priced beyond the means of people who need them."

Grief involves sadness, celebration of dead friends, and worldwide action. Please use this book.

Art and Action

Art generates so many questions: How can it be both so powerful and so misunderstood? Why do we believe it contains just two chief powers—either to provide pleasure or therapeutic relief? Aren't these mundane attributes for what many regard as the highest form of human endeavor, its most exalted expression? And, by extension, why are artists seen only as either wily tricksters or suffering fanatics?

Art is among the most complex and the least understood forms of knowledge. At its best, it elicits a multi-faceted response, a blend of intellect, emotion and even physicality. Its complexity may derive as much from the invisible process of its making, as its completed form as an art object. Experiencing art demands a sympathetic relationship between the artist's making and the viewer's looking. Although akin to the relationship between an author and reader, it lacks the shared verbal or written language of its making in which to communicate.

This book is a hybrid that some readers may initially find confusing. Its varied, sometimes overlapping parts are comprised of essays, articles, reviews and an historical overview that function like collage elements set around the central subject of the Culture War. It is social history, an attempt to describe a cultural landscape. That multiple perspectives are needed to describe the origins of so significant a political shift—that is to historicize it—should come as no surprise. More surprising, perhaps, is the refusal to treat this historic episode as just that—and instead to blame the current malaise as primarily a result of the development of social media. Minimizing the magnitude of this change is of course a strategy to more seamlessly replace one version of the status quo with another. Social media is in fact, just one of the Culture War's many causes, one which did not even exist at its start. To put it another way, to explain a complex subject like this one demands encircling it.

Cultural historians—even those interested in simply expanding or updating knowledge of the Culture War—are currently discouraged from pursuing any such inquiry. In an increasingly politicized climate that threatens "offending" universities and media outlets with economic punishment, this crackdown operates both systemically (or publicly) and also invisibly (or privately) through self-censorship. Censorship of all kinds is the modus operandi of authoritarians. By contrast, the m.o. of historians is increasingly "intersectional," utilizing an approach to the past that digs deep and wide, acknowledging the variety of social and cultural causes that broaden traditional accounts of history, too often focused only on political and governmental actions.

Comparing today's political climate with that of the 1980s—really any era—requires both an open mind and critical acumen. It flies in the face of the increasingly propagandistic and oversimplified character of education, reinforced by the removal of books from school libraries ranging from classics such as *The Diary of Anne Frank*, despite the current administration's lawsuits over alleged anti-Semitism on college campuses, and Nobel Prize winner Toni Morrison's *The Bluest Eye* for its depiction of sexual assault and incest. Distinctly unpredictable, the keys to understanding history are often found in shadowy areas that surround the mainstream, and exist apart from the notoriety and media coverage that helps create the so-called "conventional wisdom."

Some readers will be able to relate to the origins of the Culture War due to their resemblance to current conditions. The diminished faith in the efficacy of the government to deliver beneficial change about HIV disease to its sufferers, for instance, bring to mind today's renewed conflict about health care funding. Few, however, will have specialized knowledge about everything that transpired during the past half century, more than a decade before the Culture War had even been named.

Consider this startling example from 1990, the year the most progressive healthcare bill in U.S. history was passed by Congress and signed by President George H.W. Bush. Named the Ryan White Comprehensive AIDS Resources Emergency (CARE) Act, this revolutionary legislation requires not only the free provision of treatment options for HIV disease for the uninsured and under-insured, but the establishment of state centers to educate citizens about HIV disease and its transmission. All Americans—straight and gay, infected with HIV and not—have benefited from this.

Who was Ryan White? Born in Indiana in 1971, he was a hemophiliac who contracted HIV in 1984 from a contaminated blood transfusion. Barred from attending public school. his outspokenness about living with HIV transformed him into an attractive symbol of AIDS prior to the development of the so-called AIDS "cocktail." (This mid-1990s' drug regimen replaced the ineffectual drug treatments that preceded them and are still in use today to effectively treat people with AIDS.) White died in 1990, years before the release of the "cocktail," but just months before the passage of the Ryan White Act commemorated by the photograph of his smiling face on the cover of *People* magazine.

The transmission of the virus via blood product rather than sex made the young activist an "innocent AIDS victim," according to right-wing thinking. This differentiated him from the so-called "guilty" victims of HIV, injecting drug users and especially gay men who were supposedly the vector of HIV disease. White's appearance on the cover of *People* magazine demonstrated the media's ability to valorize White and demonstrate their concern about HIV while simultaneously condemning queers throughout the magazine and others owned by same media company. This is the "blame game" that Culture Warriors play in order to divert attention from actual problems, such as their refusal to provide affordable medical insurance to US citizens.

Bear in mind that 1990 was two decades before the tortuous passage in 2010 of Obamacare. No bill like it would pass muster today in Washington's paralyzed legislative branch or neo-imperialistic executive branch. Alarmingly, many current recipients of the AIDS Drug Assistance Program (ADAP) in Florida, for instance, will lose their coverage in 2026. This is due to the program's drastically lowered income caps, the removal of the most-prescribed HIV treatment regimen from their formulary, and the lack of financial support for clients purchasing health insurance. But it's not only red states where the legislative mandate of the Ryan White Act of 1990 is being flouted. Once again a diagnosis of HIV disease will become a death sentence for many, and likely not just for the uninsured and underinsured

Prior to 1990, artists in New York, Los Angeles, and San Francisco had watched a shocking number of their colleagues die, and/or suffer the indignities of being turned away from hospital emergency rooms, evicted from housing, and lacking job protection. They had watched with frustration the Reagan administration's indifference to the discrimination against those with HIV. With only healthcare professionals speaking out, they took action on behalf of their friends, themselves, or both. Their actions assumed varied forms, both direct and indirect. Individuals collaborated with other individuals to create action-oriented organizations and artworks, all of which put media and art-related methods and ideas at their cores.

During the late 1980s, art and artists became the most powerful force in the U.S. working to ameliorate the suffering of people with AIDS and to educate varied publics about its transmission. By "art" at this time, I'm mainly referring to the public art that rolled out prior to the passage of the Ryan White Act in 1990, beginning with the *NAMES Project AIDS Memorial Quilt*, which had its public debut on the National Mall in Washington, D.C., on October 11,1987 as part of the Second National March on Washington for Lesbian and Gay Rights.

The San Francisco-based *Quilt* began its seemingly endless rounds of touring and fundraising following its debut. Meanwhile in New York during the mid- and late-1980s, two organizations emerged from their founders' lengthy conversations: *The Silence=Death* Project created the well-known graphic that would stand for ACT-UP (the AIDS Coalition to Unleash Power). Its designer married two elements: the text and the pink triangle, the Holocaust symbol for homosexuals, which they inverted. The third organization of the 1980s that garnered a huge response to its projects was Visual AIDS. Founded by three curators and a writer (me), in New York the group staged *Day Without Art*, its first public event, on December 1, 1989, to coincide with the World Health Organization's second World AIDS Day. Nearly 800 organizations participated. Numerous educational initiatives followed, along with the *Red Ribbon*, which debuted on the televised Tony Awards on June 7, 1991.

Some will question whether these works of public art are art, rather than emblems, "visual slogans," or symbols. But if contemporary existence teaches us anything, it is that something can be more—or mean more—than just one thing at a time. In the case of public art, reaching large audiences is a key marker of success. These public artworks drew huge pop culture-sized audiences. Although many viewers were unaware that they were looking at art, they were exposed to vital information about AIDS treatment and transmission. These works also affirmed the thinking of Hans Haacke, a key artist of the late 20th century who referred to art as part of the "consciousness industry," like advertising.

The "Queer Expressions and Icons" section of this book is largely devoted to essays about art that differs from public art in its appearance and production. Such works were often produced in the mediums of painting, photography or video and revealed a personal aesthetic that enabled viewers to identify their makers at a glance. In other words, they were "art," or the now rarely-used term "private art.

Hundreds of such works appeared in numerous explicitly queer shows that began to appear in the late 1980s in New York. Until then big-name artists, like their big-name actor-counterparts in Hollywood, remained in the closet, fearful of coming out and facing possible financial consequences. Curator Dan Cameron's *Extended Sensibilities: Homosexual Presence in Contemporary Art* at the New Museum in New York, in 1982, was both the first museum show employing the lens of sexual identity for its organization and the last of the pre-AIDS exhibitions, undone by its inability to persuade well-known queer artists to participate.

The good news about these community mega-shows was their regularity, they were frequently staged to celebrate Gay Pride month in June. The (possibly) bad news about them was that their volunteer-raised budgets were not large enough to produce expensive catalogs that documented participating artists and their art. This limitation, however, promoted cooperation and consensus among organizers, rather than competition and conflict. These shows were followed by the opposite of such exhibitions, that is the retrospective show devoted to a single, often baby boomer artist that traveled from museum to museum during the early twenty-first century and demonstrated the centrality of queer artists of this era, to art of all sorts.

As with most art writers, reviewing books was part of my purview—and happily so. I've included a few in this book, from a survey of contemporary lesbian art to self-serving accounts by National Endowments for the Arts chiefs attempting to justify their failures running their admittedly beleaguered agency. My book ends with a review of Benjamin Moser's Sontag: Her Life and Work (2019).

Sontag first received widespread attention for the provocative "Notes on Camp" (1964) and compiled such remarkable essay collections as *On Photography* (1977) and *AIDS and Its Metaphors* (1989). A novelist, filmmaker, and president of American P.E.N., she vociferously deplored the censorship of Salman Rushdie's *The Satanic Verses*. Appropriately, she wrote her final, controversial essay "Regarding the Torture of Others" (2004), about the shocking photographs taken by American GIs at the Abu Ghraib prison in Iraq. To many of us queer writers of non-fiction, including me, Sontag was an inspiration.

Production deadlines for this book during early 2026 have coincided with the ramped-up political emergency emanating from the White House. To meet these deadlines, I have been immersed in a world of ribbons and quilt squares, and spent too much time pondering the destruction of our health-care system and the ICE-produced detentions, kidnappings and murders of US citizens and un-documented immigrants alike, rather than the "worst of the worst," the misleading rationale offered for the onslaught of citizens and militarization of American cities.

Completing a book is a moment for considering its effect on its author. Although my book contains numerous references to the AIDS public artworks I've discussed, I have also come away newly impressed by them. Each is different in tone and physicality, yet seems to reach more than a single audience. Among them are audiences of activists, people with AIDS, art and history buffs, mourners, Buddhists, advertising *aficionados*, Christians and students, as well as those who don't fit into at least one of these categories.

They also share something else: they are virtually impossible to misinterpret. This is a really BIG DEAL in an age of so-called "alternate facts." They are, in fact, *facts*, and powerful means of altering consciousness. They are also—I believe—singly, jointly and unquestionably not just art, but possibly great art. You decide.

Robert Atkins
January 14, 2026

PART ONE

When the Culture War Became the Culture

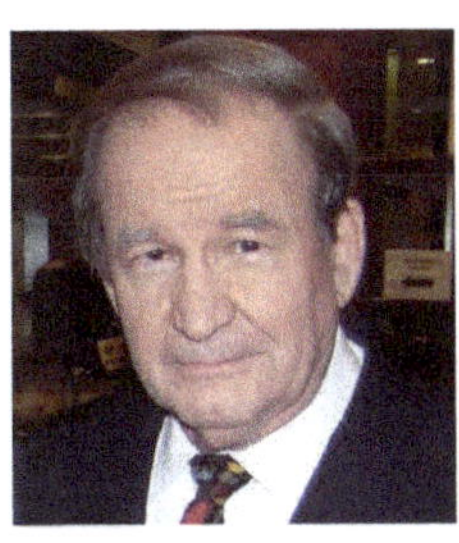

There is a religious war going on in this country. It is a cultural war...for the soul of America.

Presidential candidate Patrick Buchanan addressing the Republican National Convention, August, 1992

Our mantra is: You must use your agency... It's a spiritual war. The divine providence works through your agency.

Steve Bannon describes how to proselytize for Christian nationalism, quoted in a 2024 interview in *The New York Times*

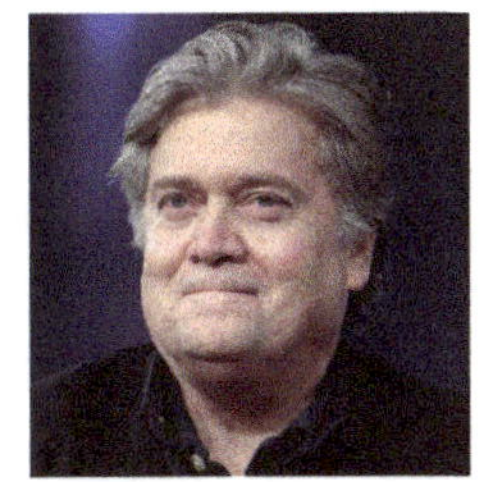

By the time Presidential candidate Pat Buchanan spoke at the Republican National Convention in 1992, the cultural conflict he evoked was already well underway. Voters had repealed Dade County-Miami's gay rights ordinance in 1977. The National Endowment for the Arts (NEA) had eliminated art critics' grants in 1981 and later in the decade penalized institutions for presenting supposedly blasphemous works, as with the New York Film Festival's screening of Jean-Luc Godard's *Hail Mary* in 1985 and the Southeastern Center for Contemporary Art's 1989 presentation of an NEA-supported exhibition that included Andres Serrano's photograph *Piss Christ* (1987). The Cincinnati Art Center was charged with obscenity in 1990 for its presentation of the Robert Mapplethorpe retrospective exhibition, *The Perfect Moment*, which displayed images of homosexual sex and evoked the artist's AIDS-related illness. The Attorney General's Commission on Pornography (a/k/a the Meese Commission) began its assault on the First Amendment in 1985 by targeting convenience stores for their distribution of "men's magazines'" based on a shoddily researched report it issued linking sexual imagery and violence.

Buchanan had received his coveted speaking slot at the quadrennial convention because he won an unexpectedly large number of votes against incumbent President George H.W. Bush in the Republican primaries earlier in 1992. His populist message was anathema to elite, right-wing figures in the Republican Party, but apparently not to ordinary voters. Buchanan's apocalyptic tone and seeming allusion to suspect German history—"cultural war" sounded to many liberals like Nazi *kulturkampf*—was as alarming as his message. By the mid-nineties, the neutral-sounding *Culture War* had come to signify the frequent and aggressive conflict between religious conservatives and social liberals. Its appearance on newspaper front pages, in op-ed pieces and in the monologues of late night talk show hosts became, and remains, ubiquitous.

Ironically, the original, nineteenth-century culture war—or *kulturkampf*—occupies a largely forgotten place in European, even German, history. The Catholic Church waged the non-military offensive against Protestant Prussia's control of education in an unsuccessful attempt to help regain the power the Vatican lost as a consequence of the 1870s unification of the German and Italian states. Until recently the term was virtually unknown In the U.S.. It is hardly an exaggeration to say that over the past four decades the Culture War has become not just an unpleasant aspect of U.S. culture but the culture itself. It has normalized a disagreeable and obstructionist public discourse transforming everyday matters into sources of contention, often employing hot-button social issues to pit Americans against Americans.

Looking back, harbingers of the Culture War were evident before 1977. The belligerent disingenuousness typical of the Culture War has frequently roiled U.S. politics. In 1950, Senator Joseph McCarthy kicked off a campaign to uncover never proven, large-scale infiltration by Communists of the U.S. State Department and Hollywood film industry. He convened hearings in which citizens were encouraged to inform on one another to divert suspicion from themselves, similar to the Cold War era conduct of the East German *Stasi*, or secret police. Those who refused to "name names" to the House Un-American Activities Committee or the Permanent Subcommittee on Investigations McCarthy chaired in the Senate were placed on a so-called "Black List" that made future employment a pipe dream. Suspected homosexuals were subject to especially harsh treatment, mirroring their tenuous legal status. Although McCarthy's unhinged attacks on vast numbers of citizens resembled the histrionics of later culture warriors, unlike them his targets were accused of betraying the government and divulging state secrets to foreign powers, acts traditionally regarded as treasonous. Later Culture War assaults on private beliefs or behaviors with only domestic relevance became a key characteristic of Culture War conflict for which Americans attacked Americans. Following a televised committee hearing about alleged communists in the military in 1954, the senator was driven from public life following lawyer Joseph Welch's stinging question: "Senator, have you no sense of decency, sir, at long last?"

President Richard Nixon shifted McCarthy's attention from uncovering alleged national security breaches by foreign agents, to fomenting division among American citizens. Those whose conservative views echoed the administration's were dubbed the "Silent Majority" while Nixon's petulant responses to questions about his Watergate involvement were met only with proclamations of the near-dictatorial—later known as "unitary"—power of the Presidency. The scandalous events that began with the illegal break-in at the Watergate Apartments culminated in Nixon's resignation in 1974, a year after Vice-President Spiro Agnew had resigned following charges of corruption. Despite the diminished moral authority retained by the administration and the Republican Party, the supporters of the Silent Majority's moralism and Anita Bryant's successful Miami campaign helped pave the way in 1979 for Baptist minister Jerry Falwell Sr.'s founding of the Moral Majority. Like so many conservative Christian advocacy groups, it shut down a decade later because of squabbling among televangelist preachers including Pat Robertson and Jim Bakker, as well as frequent accusations of sexual, sometimes homosexual, misconduct by church leaders themselves.

Readers may wonder how far back in history to seek precedents for the origins of the Culture War. We live, after all, in a society long afflicted with tribal prejudices based on religion and race. The Puritan settlers who established the Massachusetts Bay Colony re-created a society beset by the same virulent intolerance they had faced in Europe. Religious prejudice drove the Mormons, founded in the 1820s in upstate New York, farther and farther West until they reached the Great Salt Lake in today's Utah. A century later, Father Charles Coughlin, a/k/a the Radio Priest, broadcast weekly programs promoting fascism and antisemitism to audiences that numbered a full quarter of the U.S. population. Racial animosity, too, has existed in the U.S. from the outset of the European occupation of North America. The colonists annexed territories overseen by the indigenous First Peoples and began, in 1619, to import and enslave West Africans. Racial exclusion was the *raison d'etre* of post-Civil War legislation including the Chinese Exclusion Act of 1882, the Jim Crow laws that mandated racial segregation after the Civil War, and the internment of Japanese-Americans during World War II.

Despite such horrific infringements on Constitutional rights, the twentieth century also saw expanded suffrage and individual rights, often through landmark decisions of the Supreme Court. In 1954, for instance, the year of McCarthy's televised meltdown, the Supreme Court issued the *Brown v. Board of Education* ruling that required racial equality in education. By contrast, the twenty-first century has been markedly different. Since 9/11 and the overly expansive Patriot Act passed in response to it, progressive change has slowed to a trickle. Long-established freedoms and judicial precedents have been ignored to eviscerate voting rights, consumer protections, and campaign contribution limits. The notable exceptions of the Affordable Care Act (2010) and *Obergefell v Hodges* (2015) supporting same-sex marriage were made by Supreme Courts far more ideologically balanced than the current version. Former Republican Senate Majority Leader Mitch McConnell's hypocritical refusal to hold hearings for President Barack Obama's appointment of Merrick Garland to the high court in 2016 deprived it of a needed centrist and enabled Donald Trump to appoint three justices, creating the court's current ultra-conservative majority. Its partisan lurch to the right was soon signaled in rulings eliminating the federal right to abortion in the *Dobbs* decision (2022) and the decision in 2024 expanding presidential immunity from prosecution for illegal conduct.

At the end of the eighties and throughout the nineties, many Americans were too busy and/or disengaged, and the events too recent, to connect the dots between allegedly blasphemous art, queers acting up in response to homophobia and AIDS, rampant censorship, and the vilification of artists and the arts. The early nineties saw not just Buchanan's declaration of war, but congressional demagoguery in Newt Gingrich's bellicose "Contract With America" and the Republican impeachment of Bill Clinton for sexual impropriety, which backfired on the GOP. Two developments of that day did lower tensions between Washington and its queer constituents, but without resolving the issues they addressed: The

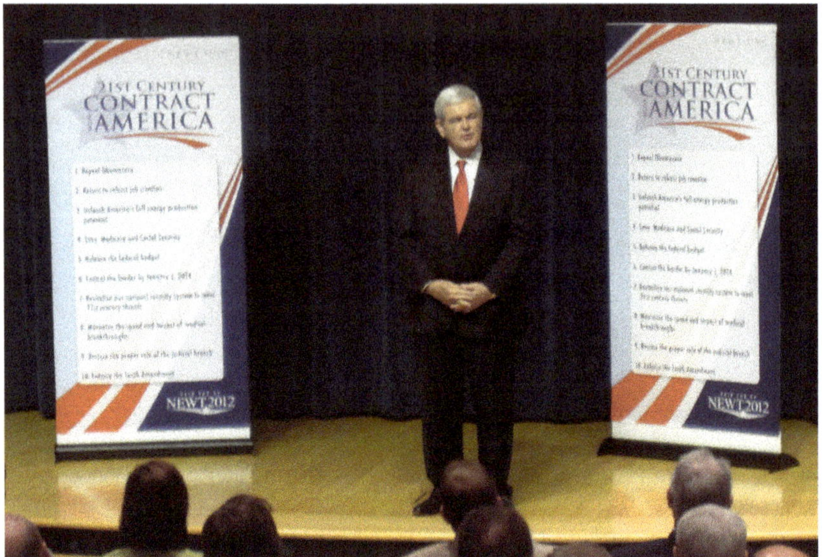

*Former Speaker of the House Newt Gingrich campaigning
for President in 2011 with the "Contract With America"*

enactment of the problematic "Don't Ask, Don't Tell" policy of the
military that continued to require service people to hide their sexual orientation, and the discovery of the so-called HIV cocktail—a
drug maintenance regime, not a cure—that, helped mitigate the
HIV-AIDS crisis in the U.S. and other First World countries. Unlike
the U.S, these more egalitarian societies had not transformed HIV-
AIDS from a health problem into a rancorous, Culture War- crisis.

*   *   *

The tumultuous decades of the 1980s and 90s constitute the
origins or initial phase of the Culture War and provide the
temporal frame for this book. The introduction you are reading is intended to provide a large, if broad-brushed, cultural history presenting a backdrop of public events against which the Culture War was enacted and is better understood. The book brings
together my eyewitness journalism, mostly for the *Village Voice*,
as well as more reflective considerations of Culture War-related

matters for other sorts of publications. In both cases, they also encompass my interest in resistance by individuals and advocacy groups as evidenced in the founding of new organizations devoted to freedom of expression and/or concern for people with AIDS. Some examinations of the ongoing careers of artists and artworks at the center of some Culture War conflict, usually in retrospective exhibition form, are also included and provide a sort of twenty-first century coda to earlier events.

The end of the Culture War's initial period—both a hiatus and broadening of it—came after 9/11 and the Patriot Act of 2001, hastily passed in response to it. This overzealous legislation narrowed citizens' rights of association and expression, and hampered journalists' ability to do their jobs. It did prompt, however, a surprisingly straightforward discussion about sacrificing constitutional freedoms for enhanced security. In the face of the horrendous attacks, traditional American bellicosity won out over diplomacy. Despite George W. Bush's principled attempts to remind Americans of their Constitutional obligation to respect Muslim-American religious beliefs, the events of 9/11 were framed in xenophobic, Culture War terms as a clash between religions and civilizations, rather than among U.S. citizens holding different religious beliefs.

This nativist hostility to difference took overtly racist form in the 2008 election. Obama's presidential candidacy required him to act on the demeaning need to be validated by "trusted" African-Americans such as General Colin Powell and Oprah Winfrey. He was also forced to endure the so-called "Birther Campaign" and its false allegations of his being born in Kenya, which would have made him ineligible for the presidency. Once inside the White House, humiliation followed humiliation: Michelle Obama was even "slut-shamed" for wearing a sleeveless dress.

For many citizens, Hillary Clinton's 2016 election loss provided a stunning wake-up call about Trump's takeover of the Republican Party through unprecedented Culture War tactics that challenged long-accepted precedents. Unfortunately, Clinton received insufficient electoral college votes to win the presidency, despite garnering millions more popular votes than Trump. The title of her account of that election, *What Happened*, suggests the historian's aims of describing and clarifying reality, of presenting, expanding and (re)interpreting the current boundaries of the so-called "conventional wisdom" or what is generally regarded as what happened.

Some historians suggest—wrongly—that Culture War conflict is merely politics as usual, or that the so-called pendulum of history will reverse itself in its next dialectical swing. Yet the supposedly disconnected Culture War skirmishes of the past half-century are remarkable for their recurring character, predictable causes and effects, and for their appeal to increasing numbers reached through social media. My use of the singular *Culture War*, rather than the plural *Culture Wars*, is intended to underline—rather than undermine—the connectedness of nearly all Culture War conflicts. At their most fundamental, they are parts of a larger Christian Nationalist project to create a government favoring not the traditional, charitable outlook of many Christian institutions, but instead reflecting the lust for power of the wealthy "messengers" of God who founded the numerous mega-churches that sprang up at this time. One tradition they did not support was the Constitutionally mandated separation between church and state.

*   *   *

Among the first identifiable skirmishes of the Culture War was the Anita Bryant-instigated repeal of Dade County-Miami's gay rights ordinance in 1977, fifteen years before the Culture War had a name. Miami's extension of civil rights for homosexuals contrasted sharply with the increasingly harsh laws enacted against homosexuals beginning long before the British colonies declared independence in the late 18th century During the 17th century, Lesbian sex was often linked with witchcraft, and punishment was meted out by religious groups. Homophobic legislation culminated in twentieth century laws outlawing queer immigration and government employment. Courageous resistance to such laws was mounted by two underground California organizations starting in the 1950s and 60s: the Mattachine Society for men and Daughters

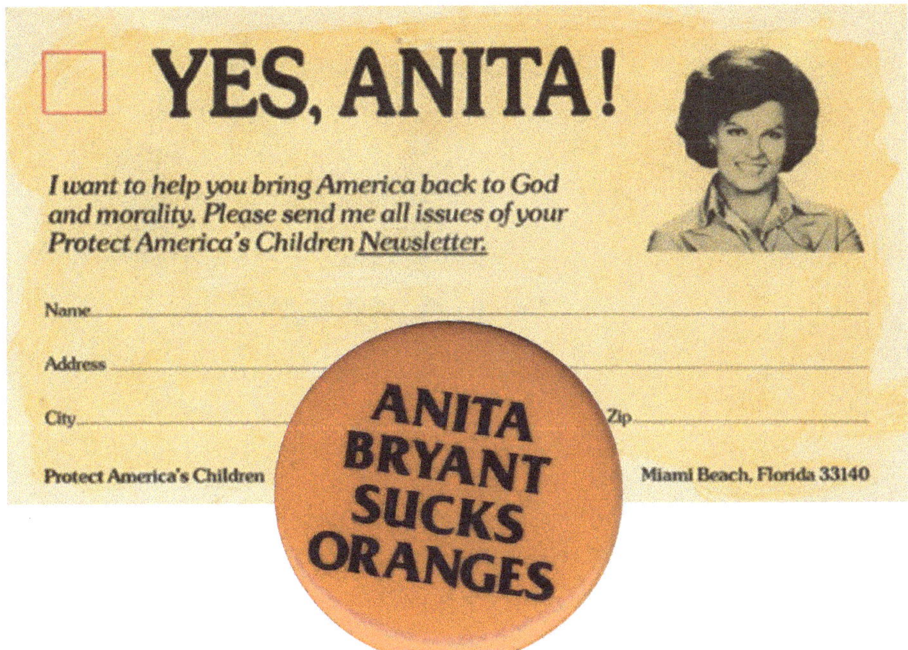

of Bilitis for women. The Stonewall Rebellion in 1969 in New York is often regarded as Gay Liberation's founding, or at least founding of its public face. Yet homosexuality remained a subject that was only beginning to be discussed in 1977, much less understood.

U.S. courts have never taken into account the diversity of attitudes toward homosexuality over time and among different cultures: from its acceptance in ancient Greece and Rome to the practices of Navajo and other First Peoples who dubbed homosexuals *two spirits* and the possessors of shamanic powers. Homosexuality was decriminalized by the revolutionary regimes of the French (1791) and Bolshevik (1922) Revolutions. Yet judicial (and general) understanding seems even to lack the basic information that the very concepts of *homosexual* and *heterosexual* did not exist until the end of the nineteenth century. The meaning of the term *homosexual* expanded beyond its conventional and exclusive use then as only an adjective modifying behavior, as in homosexual acts. It was first used at the turn of the twentieth century to identify an individual as *a homosexual*. This assertion of identity transformed the fluidity of sexual expression into a rigid binary that enabled the policing and persecution of homosexuals.

Bryant's campaign to overturn the Dade County ordinance succeeded largely on her assertion of the unfounded association of homosexual teachers with pedophilia. The alleged danger was implied in the title of her 1977 book *The Anita Bryant Story: The Survival of Our Nation's Families and the Threat of Militant Homosexuality*. Her campaign's success is a reminder that the general perspective on homosexuality was based on a selective and simplistic reading of Judeo-Christian scripture. Bryant's triumph had mixed consequences for her, however. Despite the referendum's nullification of the earlier policy, the Evangelical Christian, former Miss Oklahoma was widely seen as a self-promoter whose anti-gay activism led to a boycott of Florida oranges and the loss of her job as a spokesperson for the Florida Citrus Commission. But Bryant's homophobic campaign revealed an opportunity for expanding conservative Christian influence on a national stage. Her pioneering approach to putting the policing of sexuality and later gender in the hands of voters remains effective today, as was evident in the outsize anti-trans emphasis of Republicans in the presidential campaign of 2024.

Bryant's campaign coincided—not surprisingly—with a moment of gay men and lesbians' unprecedented attention and acceptance, a dividend of both the emerging Gay Liberation movement triggered by the Stonewall Rebellion and earlier liberalizing attitudes about sex and sexuality from extra-congressional developments and court rulings. These included the blockbuster, often positive, coverage of the return of Christine Jorgensen from Sweden after her sex change in 1953, the publications of Alfred Kinsey's widely-discussed *Sexual Behavior in the Human Male* published in 1948, and its counterpart about females in 1953. Ultimately, the most essential element in this realm was the development of the birth control pill in 1960 that enabled women to safely and easily avoid pregnancy. Early gay liberation initiatives such as "coming out day" by homosexuals helped spur recognition of pioneering queer accomplishments, particularly in the realm of popular culture. If this influence was often embodied in "straight" actors and consumers of LGBTQ culture—as with Bette Midler's sold-out performances at the Continental Baths or President Carter's chief of staff Hamilton Jordan's alleged use of cocaine in Studio 54 in 1979—it at least provided relief from the drumbeat of queer immorality that was beginning to subside.

Yet opposition to such progress found its way into the 1980 campaign for the presidency. Suffused with religiosity, it was decidedly different than its more secular predecessors. Incumbent president Jimmy Carter foregrounded his relatively tolerant, born-again Baptist beliefs that are better remembered than his then widely known rock 'n roll fandom. Candidate Ronald Reagan took a page from Bryant's book: He engaged in a *quid pro quo* with fundamentalist Christians trading right-wing support for his "evolution" from a governor who supported abortion rights to a president and right-to-lifer whose administration would shatter prevailing secular norms.

The political honeymoon that queers experienced during the late 1970s was short-lived, as well. In addition to the Miami repeal in 1977, the assassination a year later of Supervisor Harvey Milk, the first openly gay elected official, in San Francisco City Hall was all too reminiscent of the tragic shootings of Robert Kennedy and Martin Luther King a decade earlier. But it was the appearance in 1981 of the AIDS-causing HIV virus that ended any possible recognition of LGBTQ+ Americans as those needing civil rights. Instead, homosexuals were primarily regarded with fear and loathing as vectors of a deadly disease and stripped of humanity. As the governor of Texas quipped on a hot microphone following a public appearance: "If you want to stop AIDS, shoot the queers."

For religious conservatives, AIDS was just reward for homosexuals' "immoral" lifestyles. For the media, it constituted a sexual panic open to being sensationalized in crude, tabloid-style coverage. For queers, it was an existential threat to survival in the face of more than a decade of prejudice and insufficient support. The Reagan administration's moralism and inaction were an extraordinary failure of leadership, obviating its duty to ensure greater public understanding of HIV and its spread. By the time Reagan left office, more than 46,000 Americans had died of HIV and the President had yet even to constructively discuss the problem.

*　　*　　*

The story of the Culture War gained momentum during the early eighties. At the end of the seventies, Bryant had proven that homophobia made for effective politics. Yet even in hindsight her discriminatory campaign did not constitute a trend. It was not until the early-1980s' conflation of AIDS and homosexuality, of homophobia and AIDS-phobia, that the contours of the Culture War began to take shape.

The discovery of HIV/AIDS in 1981 was a landmark event: It was the first in a series of lethal viruses that would include Ebola, SARS, Zika, and Coronavirus. It resulted in the deaths of more than 700,000 in the U.S.—nearly as many fatalities as from Coronavirus— and helped undermine the triumphant narrative of medical progress that led to the doubling of Americans' life expectancy during the twentieth century. It instead unleashed unnerving dystopias that seemed straight out of Hollywood. The record of the first 15 years of AIDS, from its discovery in 1981 to the availability of life-saving antiretroviral treatment in the mid-1990s, also provides a cautionary tale: it is a story of a series of missteps that transformed a health problem into a political crisis. Four decades after the AIDS epidemic began in the U.S., its consequences continue to reverberate across the planet, especially in sub-Saharan Africa. Unfortunately, its lessons seem to have been lost on many politicians and policy makers as they began to struggle with Coronavirus in 2020.

One telling signifier of the unfortunate conflation of homosexuality and AIDS came in the form of the initial name for the HIV virus itself. Following its discovery the National Institutes of Health coined the unfortunate moniker *Gay Related Immune Deficiency* (and its accompanying acronym *GRID*). This was a consequential blunder, suggesting a difference between hetero- and homosexual immune systems and a belief that this misleading binary encompasses all sexual activity by Americans. It not only revealed the

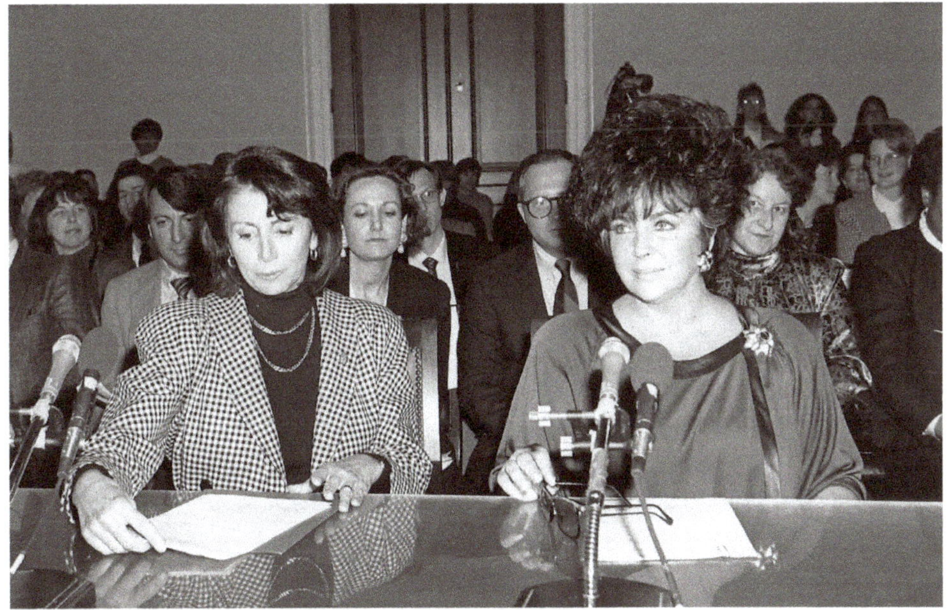

Nancy Pelosi and Elizabeth Taylor Testifying Before the House Budget Committee on HIV-AIDS Funding

agency's structural homophobia but endangered those men who mistakenly believed that avoiding sex with homosexuals (as if they could know) would prevent HIV infection. This doubtless cost the lives of an unknown number of them during the early days of the epidemic.

It also helped create an atmosphere of hysteria and misinformation that subjected anyone infected with the HIV virus to abuse. Conservative pundit William F. Buckley suggested that HIV+ be tattooed on HIV-infected men's buttocks in order to identify them and presumably keep them at arms' length. Reminiscent of the identifying numbers Nazis tattooed on concentration camp prisoners' arms, his proposal was, thankfully, regarded as disturbingly out of touch. Worse, however, were the frequent refusals of service to the HIV+ in hospital emergency rooms during the epidemic's early days. Conservative demonization of People With AIDS and homosexuals were part of a sometimes unspoken attempt by the Catholic Church and fundamentalist Protestant denominations to reverse the effects of the sexual revolution of the sixties. (Some fundamentalist Protestants continue today to promote the outlawing of homosexual activity and identity to African governments.) Their attitude derived from the quixotic belief that the genie could be put back into the bottle; as if the invention of the birth control pill, the codification of women's reproductive rights, the spread of feminism and activism of gay liberation might be reversed.

Although artist Andres Serrano was neither gay nor HIV-infected, he created the paradigmatic visual artwork of the Culture War in 1987, *Piss Christ*. The celebrity of his five-foot-high, color photograph depicting a plastic Crucifix submerged in urine was extraordinarily widespread, second only to Picasso's *Guernica* among twentieth century art works. While its title evokes shock, without it his picture might have remained little known and even celebrated for its beauty. Serrano has noted that it alludes to the contemporary cheapening of religion but professes himself a Catholic uninterested in creating shock or controversy. The notoriety of his picture, however, remains undiminished: In 2022 a print was destroyed *inside* Australia's National Gallery by hammer-wielding teenagers. A year later Pope Francis blessed Serrano in the Sistine Chapel.

After it was exhibited in 1989 at the Southeastern Center for Contemporary Art in Winston-Salem, North Carolina in the NEA-funded *Awards in the Visual Arts* exhibition, it came to the attention of Republican Senators Al D'Amato and Jesse Helms. They would become the two chief Culture War antagonists in Congress. Their outbursts on the Senate floor over the financial support the show (and others like it) received resulted in drastically reduced agency funding and in legislation later directing the agency to consider "general standards of decency" in awarding grants. Organizations and institutions would remain supported but not living artists working in all media, who apparently embodied rebellion. This exacerbated public tension around the censorship of well-known artists and prompted the universally-admired musicians Stephen Sondheim and Leonard Bernstein to refuse grants and speak against the decency oath.

As the sole federal agency exclusively devoted to the arts, the NEA quickly become a political football. Agency directors regularly came and went and frequently found themselves in untenable positions between artists, legislators, and the courts. Attempting to follow the spirit of the so-called Decency Standard, the NEA inadvertently initiated a Culture War skirmish that drew in the clashing constituencies of John Frohnmayer, the agency's new chair, who had assumed his position in 1989. It revoked a grant to a New York gallery for an exhibition that embodied several of the intertwined causes of Culture War conflict in AIDS, homosexuality, and religious attitudes toward them.

The exhibition *Witnesses: Against Our Vanishing* was devoted to AIDS and presented at Artists' Space, a downtown Manhattan "alternative" gallery. Showcasing a variety of personal responses to the AIDS crisis, it was curated by queer artist Nan Goldin. (Many years later she would lead the campaign pressuring art institutions to cut their ties with the Sackler Family whose wealth derived from its Purdue Pharma opioid fortune.) *Witnesses* was accompanied by a catalog featuring a fiery essay by artist David Wojnarowicz. It targeted those the artist considered AIDS villains, chief among them the powerful Catholic Church, terming its New York leader, Cardinal O'Connor, a "walking swastika."

The views of the combatants appeared on the front pages of *The New York Times* for nearly a week. After several days of haggling between the NEA's director Frohnmayer and members of New York's art elite, including Kitty Carlisle Hart, the revered director of the New York State Council on the Arts, a compromise was reached: as with the NIH's GRIDS moniker, *Piss Christ*, and even the academically-oriented defense of Mapplethorpe in the upcoming obscenity trial against the Cincinnati Art Center, words rather than images became the focus of contention. Support for the catalog and support for the exhibition were un-linked. Artists' Space retained the NEA's exhibition support but returned the modest $15,000 it had received for the catalog. The compromise was widely regarded as a victory for Artists' Space and a defeat for Helms and D'Amato. It came at an inflection point when new progressive forces, including some within the NEA, were finally choosing to support the unwell in the battle against AIDS.

A month later the alliance between artists and those battling AIDS—and many who were both artists *and* people with AIDS—became public in the form of the first *Day Without Art* on December 1, 1989. (In 1998 it was re-named *Day With(out) Art.)* This event was organized by Visual AIDS, the group of New York arts professionals that would also conceive the *Red Ribbon Project* in 1991. The more than 800 observations produced throughout the U.S. for the first *Day Without Art*, have been followed by three decades of *Day With(out) Art* observations each year on December 1st, timed to coincide with the World Health Organization's World AIDS Day. They continue to remind us, especially those of us outside of major urban areas, that AIDS continues to lack a cure and remains a deadly scourge in many parts of the world.

The first *Day Without Art* riveted attention on HIV/AIDS as nothing since the debut of another public artwork, the *NAMES Project Memorial Quilt* (a/k/a the *Quilt*), had two years earlier. Visual AIDS also coordinated a meeting on December 1 between a delegation of artists from New York and the NEA's staff that elicited a pledge for more AIDS support from the agency and enabled Bill T. Jones/Arnie Zane Dance Company to cancel their Kennedy Center performance that night without more onerous union penalties it might have incurred. *Day Without Art*, the *Quilt* and *Silence=Death*, a Holocaust-derived spur to AIDS activism designed by a committee of ACT UP (the AIDS Coalition to unleash Power) members, filled a communications vacuum left by the Reagan administration's inaction. By time Buchanan spoke of a "cultural war" at the end of the first Bush administration, hundreds of strikingly effective, usually conventional-format artworks in all media from performance art to photography, and painting to video had been recently produced. They helped comprise the most influential body of socially engaged art in U.S. history.

It had also become apparent that the homophobia and AIDS-phobia spewed by congress people and evangelists generated mega-money in fundraising campaigns. The network of right-wing groups and fundamentalist religious organizations included the Christian Coalition, Donald Wildmon's American Family Association, Pat Robertson's Christian Coalition and those of such televangelists as Jim and Tammy Faye Bakker. Not only were a surprising number of these Evangelical leaders involved in sex scandals that ended their careers, but the "issues" they raised were often as nonsensical as the assertion that Barney, the purple dinosaur on PBS, was gay and "grooming" children for illicit homosexual contact.

The surge in conservative political activity of the eighties and nineties was met with the emergence of a number of powerful advocacy groups supporting First Amendment rights. Their focus on free expression not only broadened their appeal but appropriately responded to the viewpoint suppression that was—and remains—the nearly universal m.o. of Culture War clashes, ranging from the study of Michelangelo's *David* to the Hyde Amendment's prohibition against discussing abortion at any clinic that receives even a dollar of government funding, These groups included People for the American Way, founded by liberal television impresario Norman Lear, the National Campaign for Freedom of Expression, as well as the ACLU's Art Censorship Project, the existing National Coalition Against Censorship and the Washington lobbying group, the National Association of Artists' Organizations. Although artists and art organizations often prevailed in First Amendment-related court cases, they frequently required the help of *pro bono* lawyers to offset the lack of cash settlements that rarely accompanied the rulings of supportive judges. My interest in such organizations grew both from the desire to report on their laudable resistance to right-wing groups and to highlight the rarely mentioned satisfactions of group action, as well. That satisfaction was invoked by Philip Yenawine, a Visual AIDS board member, upon accepting a New York Governor's Arts Award for the group in 1990. "The pleasure," he noted. "was in the doing."

*   *   *

The controversies I've detailed here and covered at length when they were current were among the highest profile Culture War spats of the late 1980s and early nineties. Accounts of them bring to mind *Washington Post* publisher Phillip Graham's observation in 1963 that journalism is the "first rough draft of history." Such reports were initially new and appealing both to producers and consumers of the "heritage" broadcast and print news media prior to the advent of social media. But as the outrage generated on both sides of the early Culture War conflicts grew predictable, the focus of these conflicts changed from art and AIDS to matters affecting more U.S. citizens and involving more government agencies. The issues were both "real" and contrived. The former as with the Clinton administration's still homophobic "Don't Ask, Don't Tell" policy regarding queers in the military; the latter as with Newt Gingrich's Contract With America-related turmoil that culminated the impeachment of President Clinton. One day's events, near the beginning of the twenty-first century, however, changed nearly everything: the horror of 9/11 instantly shifted attention from the domestic realm of the Culture War to the more literally war-like arena of foreign policy.

But this still begs the question: Why was the trifecta of contention involving art, AIDS, and homosexuality so central to the shaping of the Culture War? And to perfecting still-currently employed formulas for heightening divisions among citizens, both real and invented? I am not, however, suggesting that anybody produced a strategy for cultural control a la *Project 2025*. Instead, it seems in retrospect that these new and unfamiliar groups were low-hanging fruit, easy to attack because they lacked established profiles and political clout. Instead of being treated with the generosity prescribed in scripture—that is, as homosexuals regarded sympathetically, as people with AIDS treated like family, and as artists respected as adventurous thinkers—the members of these groups were easily transformed into anonymous "others," responsible for a variety of social ills.

It is impossible to imagine a development in the U.S. akin to the political prominence accorded the writers Mario Vargas Llosa in Peru and Lech Walesa in Poland. Visual art barely existed in the early years of the British settlements on the Atlantic coast of North America. As a professional pursuit it took until the nineteenth century and the emergence of a class capable of supporting (and desiring) art and financing the European training it demanded. In earlier centuries, art was what was missing from Protestant churches vis-à-vis the lavish decoration of the Catholic cathedrals of Europe. That art's messaging capacity failed to cross the Atlantic makes this the historical jumping off point for any discussion of art in the U.S.. The traditional relationship with art can be characterized in the single descriptor—*ambivalence*.

A telling feature of Americans' ambivalence about art is an inability to identify something as art in the first place. Rather than acknowledging any exhibited work as art, some viewers place further demands on it for validation. A description like "this dirty Mapplethorpe photo isn't art" is likely to simply reflect homophobia or to mask a more complex response such as this "Mapplethorpe photo is bad art because it presents a private erotic moment." In fact, there is *bad* art, as is true of any variety of cultural production. Conversely, *art* is frequently employed as a positive accolade, as with "This croissant is a work of art."

Following World War II, American ideology promoted the position of the U.S. as the global capital of everything, including contemporary art, music, and literature. But this superiority was an imported phenomenon. Premier artists, writers, and composers such as Piet Mondrian, Thomas Mann, and Igor Stravinsky (who appeared on the cover of *Time* magazine in 1948) were Europeans driven from Europe by Hitler. Pride in their achievements was frequently evoked during the creation of the National Endowment for the Arts. The new agency was enthusiastically supported by President John F. Kennedy and signed into law by Lyndon Johnson in 1965, despite the lack of most Americans' cultural affinity for the arts.

More typical was the sarcasm and derision with which art works—especially avant-garde, visual artworks—have been described by politicians and media figures. After President Theodore Roosevelt viewed Marcel Duchamp's *Nude Descending a Stair-*

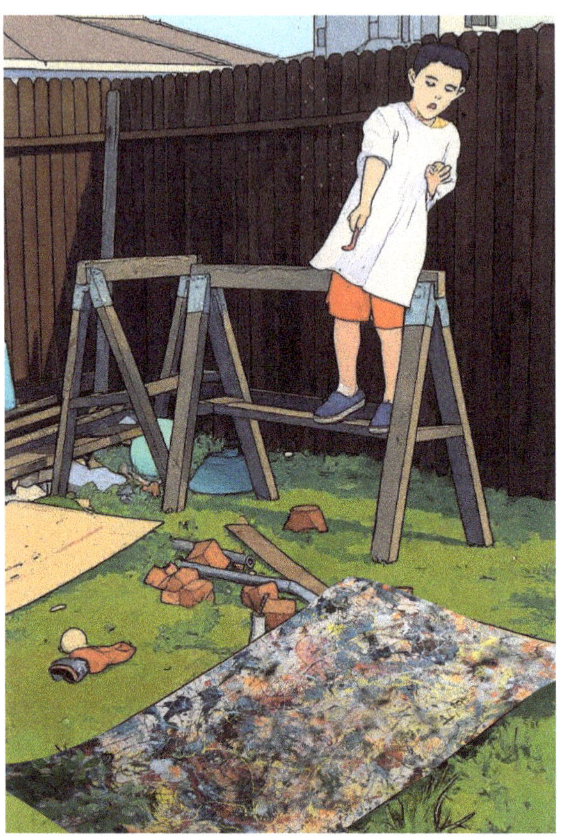

case (1912) in the Armory Show in 1913, he reviewed(!) the show and found the Cubist canvas wanting when compared to a Navajo rug in his bathroom "from the standpoint[s] of decorative value, of sincerity and of artistic merit." (One wonders whether Roosevelt saw Duchamp's "readymade" urinal, *Fountain*, signed R. Mutt, and exhibited in New York in 1917.) Some responses to postwar art were less heartfelt: *Life* magazine regarded Jackson Pollock's "drip" canvases with bemusement and enquired whether a child might be able to produce them. Pop art's hyper-realistic view of the world was aptly seen as a rejection of Abstract Expressionist emotionalism but also dismissed as laughably simplistic.

During the 1980s, art underwent a radical change, too. A new generation of artists' so-called "cutting edge" art was harder for the uninitiated to understand and even identify than previous art.

The ACT UP affiliated artists collective Gran Fury created public, advertising-signage-like works—not paintings or sculptures—that spanned Lower East Side streets or even represented the U.S. at the prestigious Venice *Biennale*. One of their street-spanning banners in New York read "All People With AIDS are Innocent," erasing the distinction between gay men who contracted HIV from sex and hemophiliacs who received infected blood products. In Venice, their works attacked the Pope as a "dick", which nearly got them arrested. Approaching art as a vehicle of political engagement and commercial clarity was a new freedom pioneered by artists of the day.

AIDS also dealt the single photographic image—that is modern photography and photojournalism itself—a crippling blow as a result of its inability to convey the complex meanings of HIV/AIDS. Neither the maxim that a picture is worth a thousand words nor the traditional view that a photograph must be shot at a single "decisive moment" helped generate insights into the syndrome. One radical solution was the serial photographs of the same person with AIDS by Nicholas Nixon, supplemented by interviews.

The relevance of these new understandings reminds us of an often-unique characteristic of the visual arts. Unlike music or literature, film or novels, visual art may require only an individual (or small group) to produce: No publisher, performer, publicist, profit or any other sort of goal or assistance is necessarily needed. On one hand, this has helped account for some artists' revelatory, progressive achievements that were often at odds with the conservatism of the wealthy patrons that collect and support contemporary art. On the other hand, how many of the best known or most esteemed artists can the average American name, much less defend from censorship? Educator and public intellectual Henry Louis Gates recently articulated the paramount importance of free expression with his sardonic observation: "Censorship is to art as lynching is to justice."

*   *   *

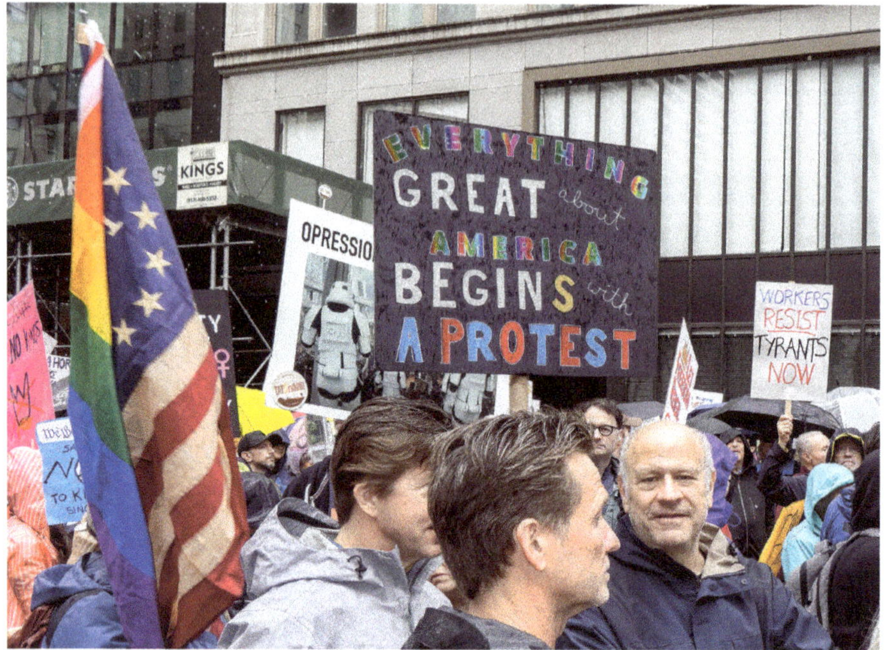

No Kings Protest, New York City, 2025

Unlike its origins in the 1980s and nineties, the causes and effects of the Culture War are now pervasive. Culture War strategies today are about as subtle as the "re-education" campaigns perpetrated in the Soviet penal colonies in Siberia. To say that it is nearly impossible for a conventional political party, the Democrats, to compete with the disingenuous and cult-like character of the Republican Party is to be guilty of understatement The aggressive rejection of the traditional belief in fact and fair play symbolized by Kellyanne Conway's stunning assertion in 2017 that lies are "alternative facts" was a landmark moment in the official Republican embrace of misinformation and disinformation. But it was by no means the first. A tipping point may already have been reached in the victories of George W. Bush for the presidency: First in the apparent politicization of the Supreme Court that resulted in Bush's defeat of Al Gore in 2000 and then in the 2004 re-election campaign won by Bush due to the fabricated Swift Boat Veterans' campaign that de-railed John Kerry's candidacy.

Nor did the Culture War of the late twentieth century employ a well-coordinated attack as outlined in the prescriptive *Project 2025*, prepared by the Heritage Foundation for the Trump campaign in 2024. The conflicts fostered during the last quarter of the twentieth century were instead more often generated by individuals who recognized opportunities for enhanced political power and financial gain. Politics is often a dirty business and in the twenty-first century it got dirtier. Admittedly, neither major political party in the U.S. was guiltless. In the realm of the confirmation of Supreme Court justices, for instance, the charade to mask views about abortion was employed by nominees of both. But McConnell's outrageous refusal to allow Obama's appointment of Merrick Garland to proceed in customary fashion was matched by the inadequate FBI vetting of Trump's court appointments and hastily arranged confirmation hearings. The swiftness of the *Dobbs* decision in 2022 to overturn *Roe v. Wade*'s federal guarantee of women's right to abortion was predictable bad behavior by the time the long-established right was overturned. Same-sex marriage, too, began to be discussed in the context of *Dobbs* seven years after its legalization in 2015, as well. In his unnecessary coda to *Dobbs*, Justice Clarence Thomas penned a road map for its overturning, linking abortion and gay marriage as both wrongly decided on the basis of an imagined constitutional right of privacy. The corruption and ethical lapses of Thomas and Justice Samuel Alito have also helped decimate Americans' faith in the fairness of the court.

The twenty-first century brought increasingly frequent and strident attacks on education, too. Ironically, this returned the Culture War to its *kulturkampf* origins in nineteenth century Prussia. Florida has recently been at the forefront of educational subversion under Ivy-League educated governor Ron de Santis. It has variously prohibited discussion of Michelangelo's *David*, eliminated advanced placement courses and adopted curricular guidelines with kind words for the treatment of the enslaved, and even forbidden use of the term *gay*. The picture for institutions of higher education has been no less bleak, whether evidenced in increasingly frequent attacks on the tenure system, diversity programs, and Congressional pressure on college presidents to resign due to purported anti-Semitism. Local school boards' inclination to censor has frequently meant the banning of beloved books by the Nobel Prize–winning author Toni Morrison, Anne Frank, F. Scott Fitzgerald and many others that seemed to err simply by taking up themes of gender, race, or the Holocaust. Such actions remind us that "protecting" children—or adults in the case of the Naval Academy—has often been an excuse for censorship by adults.

Assaults on education, free expression, and full-throated debate leave a vacuum filled by prejudice, propaganda, and stupidity. Sentiments that were unlikely to have even been voiced until recently are now openly discussed, often in mainstream conservative circles that afford them exposure in well-funded publications and online media programs. This is hardly an underground trend, witness the interest of some Supreme Court justices in revisiting the landmark *Sullivan* ruling that enabled the *Washington Post*'s revelation of the Watergate scandal or the *thinking* of Curtis Yarvin, a "neo-reactionary" blogger (whatever that is). A favorite of Vice President J.D. Vance, Yarvin rejects our republican form of government in favor of something more authoritarian and capitalistic: "A government is just a corporation that owns the country... [We should delete them as] we do with all corporations that have failed... Americans need to get over their fear of dictators."

History is a record of the clash of social or regional forces, values and outlooks, variously predictable or unimaginable. It is frequently as difficult to predict as the weather and more open to interpretation. Nor does it repeat itself, no matter the maxims suggesting the opposite. Do the comparisons between the oppressions of Hitler's Germany and Mussolini's Italy a century ago and the fascist tactics of Vladimir Putin and Trump hold water? All of their mindsets and resulting actions resemble those of ancient Roman emperors or Egyptian pharaohs who appropriated the heroic accomplishments of their predecessors by having triumphal carvings from the past re-carved with their own likenesses. As a species, *homo sapiens* is far too young to have evolved in physical form or the tribal psychology we term "human nature." This is why the millennia-old philosophy of Lao Tzu and Renaissance thinking of Machiavelli remain relevant to the study of governance today

The romantic appeal of great leaders such as Alexander the Great and Cleopatra masks the reality that historic changes have tended to derive from new tools and technologies. Consider the development of war on horseback, the printing press, or the production of the atomic bomb. *Vis-à-vis* Culture War conflict, social media have increasingly facilitated and enabled it. That it too originated during the 1980s is coincidental. Yet its effects on the development of the American mindset demands additional scrutiny dating back a half century. In brief, the origins of digital social media can be traced back to two mid 1980's government actions: the granting of U.S. citizenship to far-right monopolist and media mogul Rupert Murdoch and the Cable Act that enabled the creation of 96 relatively unregulated cable television channels to supplement the original 4 broadcast channels, tightly controlled by the FCC since their origins. Cable television led directly to inexpensive, participatory programming and the interactive online commercial media that algorithmically promotes the misinformation and disinformation, superstition, and half-truths ubiquitous today.

It has become clear that no single leading man or woman will come to our aid. It is up to U.S. citizens to preserve, even rescue, constitutional nationalism from Christian nationalism and the current administration—by any legal and ethical means necessary. For inspiration we might look to Cory Booker's 25-hours-long speech in the U.S. Senate on April 1-2, 2025. One rationale for his historic address was his belief that the U.S. is no longer approaching crisis but has reached an inflection point in determining whether our post-war security, prosperity, global prestige, and democratic ethos will survive. While the beginning of the Trump administration has brought unprecedented cruelty and narcissism, inauthenticity, and incompetence, Booker's speech provided its stunning opposite, generating a global online audience of hundreds of millions of viewers and listeners. In its creativity and originality, it resembled the new, straightforward art of Gran Fury, ACT UP, the *NAMES Project AIDS Quilt, Day With(out) Art,* and *Red Ribbon* that emerged at the end of the 80s and early 90s to combat AIDS. Booker's filibuster was similarly performative and ritualistic, operating within the hybrid parameters of what is simultaneously art and politics. (Black Lives Matter, too, was coined by art-world denizens.) Art does not exist only in objects visible in galleries and museums.

Let me suggest another example of hybrid social media and art that would similarly interrogate the universe it inhabits: The Presidential Inaugurations at which the President swears to protect the Constitution was until recently a quadrennial reminder of the centrality the Constitution provides for our society's shared identity and character. Most of us born in the U.S. are unaware, however, that new U.S. citizens swear a similar oath to *defend* the Constitution as the final step of their aptly-named naturalization process. Perhaps it is time to witness this far-from-humble act online.

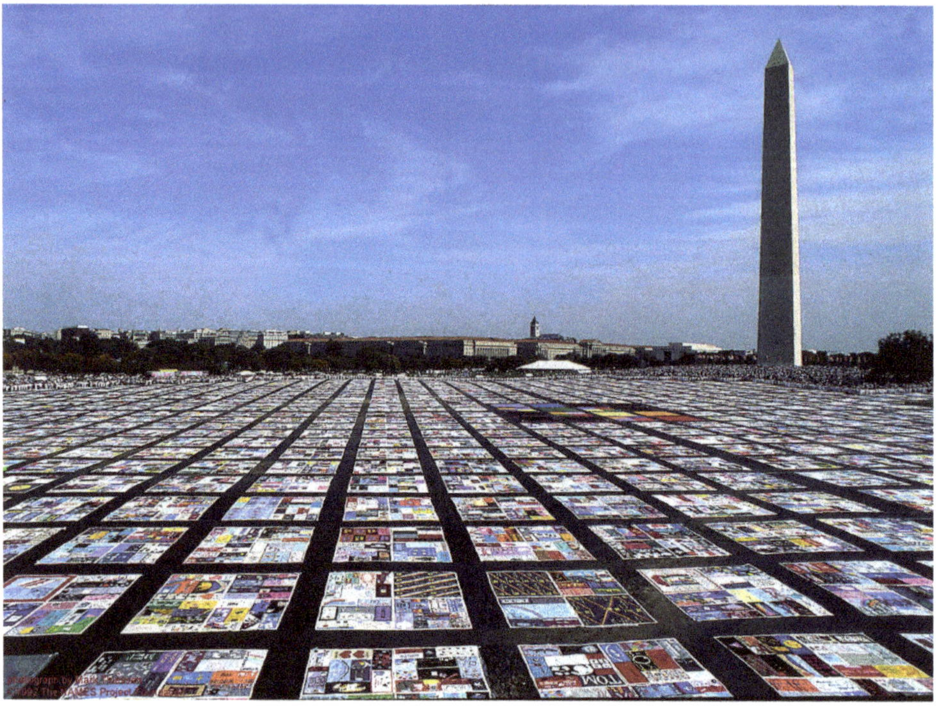

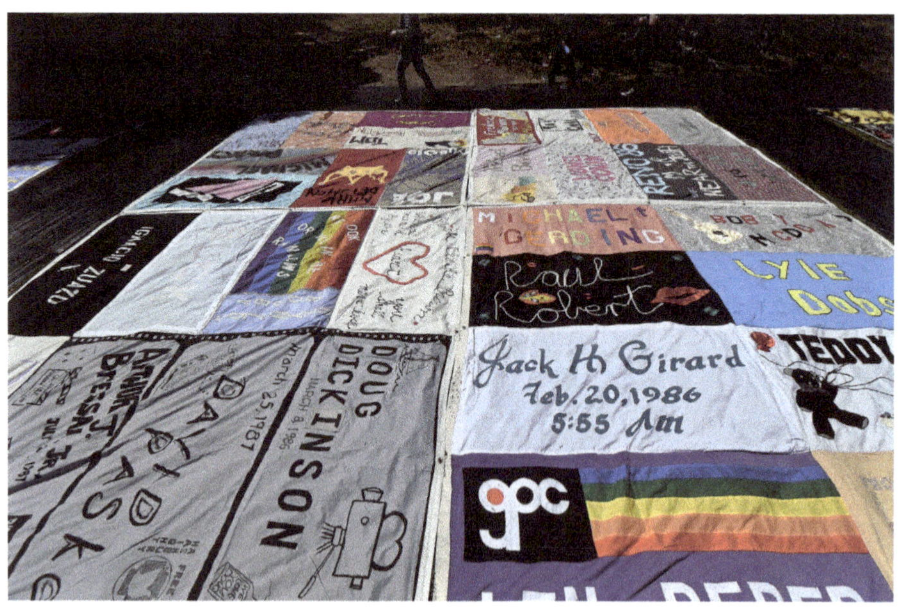

NAMES Project AIDS Memorial Quilt (1987)

PART TWO

AIDS: the Body Politic Under Pressure

Remarkably, the iconic images or symbols of this plague are not made-for-TV movies, photojournalistic pictures, or schmaltzy pop songs, but the NAMES Project AIDS Memorial Quilt, a community artwork, and two artist-conceived emblems, Silence=Death and the Red Ribbon. Their effectiveness is testimony both to the power of art and the limits of popular culture.

Robert Atkins, *Artery: The AIDS-Arts Forum* website 1989

THE LOOK: The NAMES Project Quilt Debuts

Village Voice, October 27, 1987

At 7:20 a.m., shortly after sunrise, eight volunteers begin to slowly unfold each 32-panel section of the *NAMES Project Quilt*. A roll call of those dead of AIDS and commemorated in this pliant, fiber memorial is solemnly intoned. An occasional name catches in an emotion-constricted throat and renders our collective self-control a shambles. As the sun rises higher over the Capitol Mall, two images recur: a flower blooming and a flag unfolding; a symbolic beginning and a ceremonial end. Both seem appropriate. Our grief is not just tangible, but public.

Two hours later, the several thousand present at this pre-march ritual are able to view the panels close-up. There are 1920 of the three-by-six-foot rectangles arranged in 60 sections bounded by white canvas walkways. We see panels (or find them by consulting a directory) for the celebrated likes of Rock Hudson and Liberace, but mostly they are dedicated to the unsung, often identified only by first names, initials, nicknames.

The panels are spectacularly colorful and varied, whether quilted or appliqued, drawn on or cut into, bejeweled or collaged. Images of pets, military medals, and drag queens lovingly and sometimes gorgeously coexist with slapdash calligraphy, campy humor, and heart-rending tributes from loved ones. Like the Vietnam War Memorial, the *NAMES Project Quilt* is shocking for its concreteness; especially when it's the way you learn about the death of an acquaintance. Unlike the Vietnam Memorial's haunting testimony to the facelessness of death, the *Quilt* passionately embodies the specific and personal nature of each remembered life.

From the center of the double football-field-sized (!) work, one felt afloat in a sea of images, surrounded by a variegated garden of color and texture, enveloped by a patch-worked crazy quilt complete with surprising intimations of cozy domesticity. (Yes, domesticity.) Blades of grass visible between the panels and the walkways suggested life, as well as verdant sites of graves.

This associative richness is part of the *Quilt*'s considerable power and the reason it will remain a potent symbol of a national tragedy. It is also what makes it art. The anti-formalist artistic climate of the 1970s, responsible for feminist ritual, art that exults narrative and autobiography, the elevation of fabric and clay to the materials of art, "Bad" painting, the large-scale environmentalism of Christo et al., and Judy Chicago's *Dinner Party*, create an artistic context and perhaps a model for this work of mega-art.

Although the quilt is hardly the stuff of the commodity-oriented magazines, it is—as its organizers point out—the "largest community arts project in the nation." In 1988, the expanding quilt will embark on a national tour, where it will gain yet another identity, this time as a "fundraising mechanism" and "educational tool." Tragically, the *Quilt* is also likely to enjoy the distinction, for the near future, of being the fastest growing artwork in America.

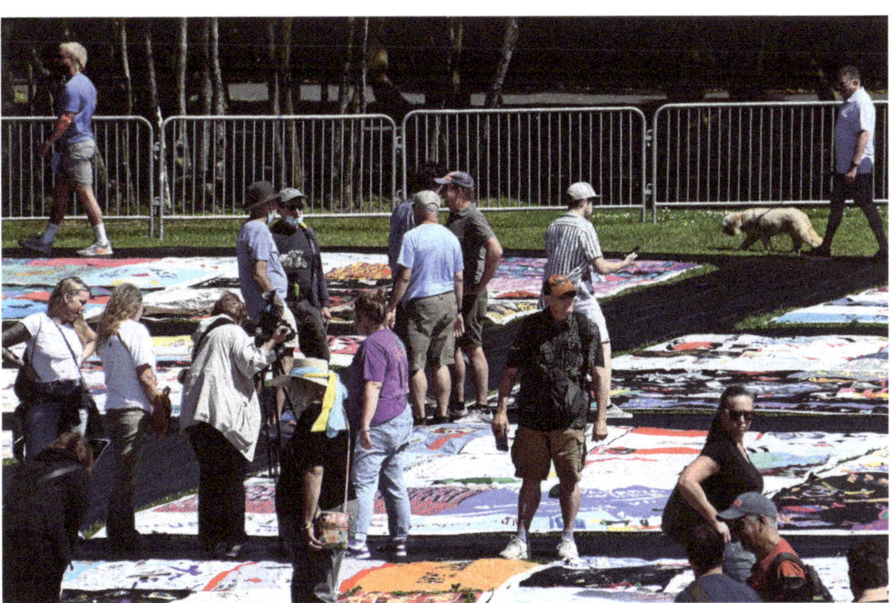

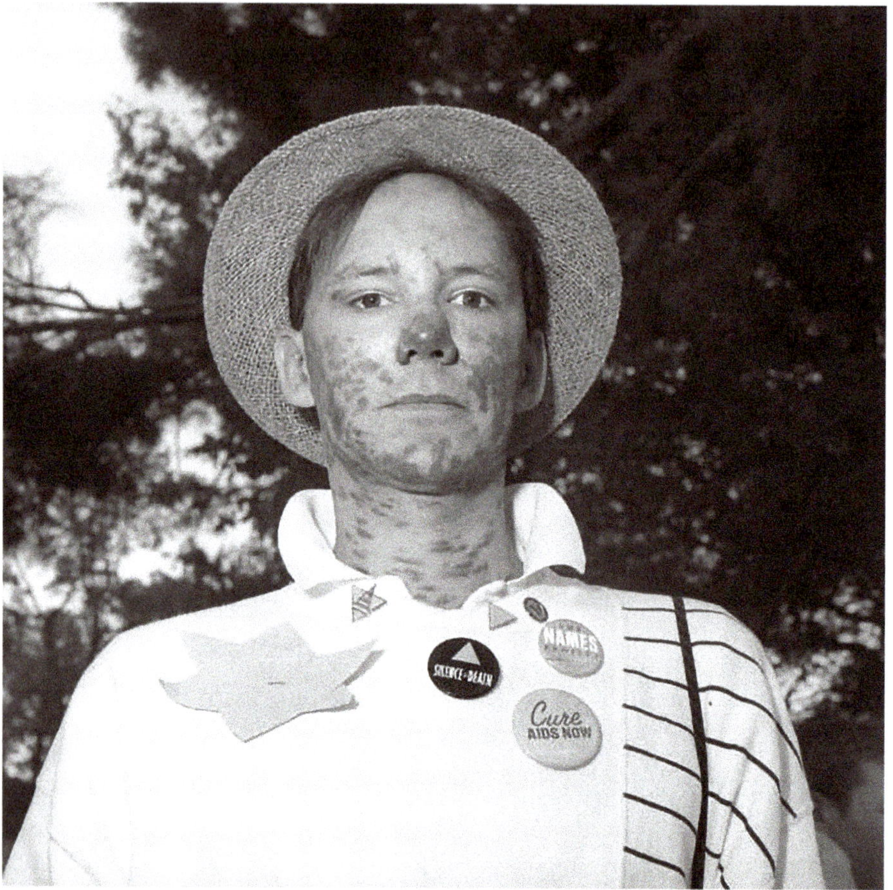

Rosalind Solomon (1988) from the series "Portraits in the Time of AIDS". The subject suffers from Kaposi's sarcoma, an unknown disease among young men prior to AIDS.

Difficult Subject: Photographing AIDS

Village Voice, June 28, 1988

Photographing AIDS is like photographing God: the visible manifestations are ambiguous; the mystery and meaning are frequently unavailable to the eye. Gazing at photographs of persons with AIDS (PWAs), we look for signs. But since AIDS is a syndrome and not a disease, there are no typical cases and no unique visual symptoms. The lesions of Kaposi's sarcoma come closest, and many photographers are drawn to them. It's shocking to discover that KS, though literally stigmatizing, is among the least life-threatening infections a PWA might contract. Like almost everything having to do with AIDS, its representations require careful decoding.

Last month, Rosalind Solomon's and Tom McGovern's exhibitions of PWA portraits opened at the Grey and the Neikrug galleries, respectively. They are simply the tip of a photographic iceberg moving into New York. That it is photographers, rather than painters, who've made the majority of AIDS-related images shouldn't be surprising. With its mechanical grounding in the appearance of reality, photography seems like an efficient way to grapple with the threat of the unknown. That this is largely illusory is what makes AIDS so obdurate a photographic subject.

*　　*　　*

In 1988, every AIDS photograph operates within the interpretive context of photojournalism. Never has a phenomenon like AIDS been so radically "mediated": that is, knowable only *through* the media (except for those with personal experience) and constructed by the media as far more than a matter of public health.

The moralistic media construction of "good" and "bad" AIDS "victims" (hemophiliacs and children, gay men and drug users, respectively) clearly suggests both the complicity of pictures in establishing this image and, more palpably, the nature of photojournalism itself. Newspaper images cannot bear any intrinsic meaning; they float freely, anchored only by their texts and contexts.

This context can be extraordinarily complex. One of *The New York Times*' most sympathetic gay-AIDS stories to date—a heartfelt piece about AIDS and the San Francisco Gay Men's Chorus [May 14, 1988]—encouraged readers to identify with gays, but it was followed, a few pages later, by a story (about the gentrification of Hamburg's red light district due to AIDS-related brothel closings) that actually managed to find a silver lining in the epidemic-cloud. Normally, the *Times* simply renders gays and lesbians invisible, as in a front page story [April 22, 1988] headlined "Researchers List Odds of Getting AIDS in Heterosexual Intercourse," which was no more about hetero- than homosexual risk. Illustrating the chorus and Hamburg articles were pictures of musicians rehearsing and a man on the street; these meant little apart from the contextualizing words.

Can "art" photographs be distinguished from photojournalistic "documents" simply on the basis of a more overt formalism or a more pronounced appearance of subjectivity? Such qualities vary widely. What counts most, as with journalistic pictures, is context.

Consider, for example, the all-too-frequent exhibition disclaimer to the effect that "not every person pictured in this AIDS exhibition is a PWA or even gay." (This point reveals both contemporary litigious instincts and the employment and housing discrimination PWAs face.) Or consider how the same photo/word amalgam functions in a small edition shown in a gallery, or offset for wheat pasting on the streets. Based on such considerations, I've set up some loose and overlapping paradigms for thinking about AIDS-related photographs: the modern picture, the Conceptual Art-derived photo-image, and the activist model of AIDS photography.

*　　*　　*

Rosalind Solomon's *Portraits in the Time of AIDS* (at New York University's Grey Gallery, 33 Washington Place, through July 2) embodies many of the virtues and pitfalls of the modern documentary approach to art photography. Her black-and-white pictures belong to the twentieth century photographic mainline that links August Sander and Walker Evans, Lisette Model and Diane Arbus, Garry Winogrand and Larry Clark.

They also make us aware of the difficulties of photographing an epidemic; of the complete irrelevance of the media model of starving Ethiopian babies, and of the absolute necessity of the show's title to tell us who these often ordinary-looking people are. They educate by reminding us that PWA demographics blur the boundaries of race, age, and sexual preference and that PWAs live at home more often than in hospitals. The sheer quantity of large prints (subjects in close-up are nearly life-size) confronts us with the urgency of AIDS. "There's no escape," this exhibition announces, only a pressing need to engage the crisis.

Such commendably "correct" sentiments do not guarantee effective art; to the contrary, they frequently get in the way of well-intentioned photographers. In the best of Solomon's photographs, such sentiments are necessarily back-grounded. A middle-aged PWA stands in front of his parents. Their eyes averted, they seem to be contemplating the unnatural prospect of burying their child. Or a PWA—or so we assume from the show's title—holds a double portrait of himself and a man we take to be his deceased lover. These poignant and complex meditations on loss convey the emotionally filigreed texture we associate with literature.

But Solomon's photographs can sometimes lose their thematic bearings. Is the sour-looking black man on the fire escape angry at AIDS or the photographer or himself? Like a photojournalistic picture pulled off the page, this image drifts without a sufficiently explanatory context to anchor it.

The emotional complexity of Solomon's pictures usually prevents such drift. What is sacrificed, however, is the appearance of artless transparency, the illusion of spontaneity and adherence to fact that underlies the modernist tradition. Nicholas Nixon retains that crisp factuality in his 8x10 contact prints made from identically sized negatives, but jettisons the "decisive" moment of the single image in favor of the serial portrait. (In September he will be the subject of a retrospective, *Pictures of People*, at the Museum of Modern Art.)

Literally works in progress, Nixon's images of PWAs are shot at roughly weekly intervals, from which he culls six to 12 images for each portrait. We see the ups and downs of individual PWAs' lives and frequently the context of family and friends. (One disturbing series focuses as intently on a PWA's much younger brother as on the PWA himself.) In the intimacy of his images, the passage of time stands for the process of living as much as dying.

Another way to assault the limitations of the modernist single image is through words. This may also allow the crucially important

PWA viewpoint, typically absent. Nixon is planning to pair his images with interviews, but they will appear only in book form. (This separation of word and image is typical of many photographers, including Ann Meredith, who photographs women with AIDS, and Sage Sohier, who photographs gay and lesbian couples.) Portraitist Gypsy Ray saves her texts from functioning as footnotes to images by insetting her subjects' typed or handwritten commentary directly into the mats of the prints. Her photo-works also bring word of the AIDS "culture": a doctor who "struggle[s] for the energy" to serve his PWA patients; an elderly volunteer who writes that "the closeness I feel with my AIDS clients is touching me in a way I find no words to describe. To truly care is to allow my clients to remain independent and in control of their lives."

While giving the syndrome a human face is vital, Ray's pictures remind us that AIDS images don't necessarily have to be embodied in PWAs. Those who've moved away from portraits to other AIDS-related subjects—the scientific and medical industries and the body as the site of psychic and representational conflict are two obvious examples—often rely on Conceptual Art-derived strategies. Anti-photographic in modernist terms, these approaches include the coupling of words and images, the fabrication of studio setups, and the use of found images, historical approaches, and traditionally non-art subject matter (such as the role of medicine in defining "normality" and gender).

Nancy Burson pairs microscopic images of diseased and healthy cells as objects for visualization; her images of the HIV virus may soon appear in billboard format. Linda Troeller's scrapbook like photographs juxtapose her mother's TB with AIDS. Joe Ziolkowski evokes (homo)sexual desire in ghostly, metaphorical images of male nudes, sometimes with nooses. Richard Hawkins' installation of 24 photographs and paintings coupling Kafka and Tom Cruise is an Apache dance of desire in the media/AIDS age. Each of these artists raises issues of power and social control and demonstrates the quality of analysis required to combat the Right-wing politicization of AIDS. Such "deconstructing" strategies tend to relate more closely to pioneering feminist/Conceptual works of Martha Rosler,

Mary Kelly, or Victor Burgin than to the mass media-oriented post-modernism of Richard Prince and Cindy Sherman.

For Gary Borgstedt, making the personal political means turning to the historical model of John Heartfield's anti-Nazi photo-montage. His viewpoint is explicit in the titles of his painted photographs—including *Held Hostage to Moralism* and *The Police Wore Rubber Gloves*. For *AIDS Patient on AZT*, Borgstedt collaged the face of a young masked man with a wire fence and snippets of text that read: "AIDS patient on AZT doing well wishes to share rent with positive people only. Enjoys life, takes care of self. $300 limit rent. Please leave message. Honest sincere people only." Not only are the underground status and limited resources of this PWA (and by inference the high costs of AZT treatment) revealed, the viewer must also imagine how he or she would respond to such an ad. Will the tenant's health decline, making him unable to take care of himself? Would you choose to get involved?

Not every artist creates work for gallery contexts. Some artists take their work directly to the streets. Steve Evans—who primarily makes Constructivist-looking installations that include images of the Nazi treatment of gays—decided last year to put his artwork to activist purposes. Then living in Atlanta, he designed color posters that collaged found images and phrases. Pictures of a laboratory, a face, and a crowd were paired (respectively) with phrases that read: "A situation many could profit from," "Know who is what," and "You live near a center for control." (The Centers for Disease Control is in Atlanta.) The ambiguity of the last phrase enabled Evans' poster to migrate from the streets onto official bus placards: Evans believes that it was approved because some higher-up assumed it referred to drug control!

Evans's forceful work can be slightly oblique, and that's not a luxury an activist group intending to reach a diverse audience is allowed. Gran Fury is a collective of 12 to 15 artists, designers, and filmmakers associated with ACT UP (the AIDS Coalition To Unleash Power); it's named for both their anger and the Plymouth Fury. (ACT UP/Gran Fury will take over the White Columns Gallery, 325 Spring Street, during July.) Gran Fury's work may be familiar: the window at the New Museum of Contemporary Art (*Let the Record Show*), the "Silence = Death" logo/symbol it's helped popularize, or its eye-catching informational posters about AIDS. (A widely circulated one brought us the horrific news that one in 61 babies in New York City is born HIV-positive.)

Gran Fury also designs posters for ACT UP demonstrations. The most striking of these were two that announced the Kiss-In, the kickoff event of nine days of AIDS-related demonstrations in April and May. One showed sailors kissing in a '40s-style image. The other showed one woman on her knees in front of another in what appeared to be an Edwardian photograph. The message "Read My Lips" bisected each.

These posters tip their hats to Barbara Kruger's word-image works, which are, in turn, derived from advertising. But where Kruger offers analysis, Gran Fury advocates action. The message is spelled out on the posters themselves: "We kiss as an aggressive demonstration of affection...We kiss so that all who see us will confront their homophobia." Both gay and non-gay audiences are addressed.

As frustration and anger about the mismanagement of the AIDS crisis grows, people are responding with increasing energy and ingenuity. Last February, photographer Diane Neumaier shot a remarkable series of images that merge photojournalistic document, Conceptualist strategy, and activist methods.

Her subject was an action in the New York subway by the Metropolitan Health Association. The guerrilla group plastered bilingual how-to information on using condoms and cleaning drug "works" on subway ad placards along with messages like "find a cure" and "action = survival." Their interventions were quickly removed; according to Neumaier, Upper West Side trains were returned to a pristine state of commercialism in just 12 hours!

Neumaier does not consider her photographs of this action her own work, in the usual sense. "I've given them to people who speak about AIDS. They have been seen in a show...But basically I'm not concerned about authorship."

Not merely documents, her images of the strategically placed messages are also spirit-lifting testimony to the pleasures of radical disjunction. A double mug shot of Koch and Cardinal O'Connor reads: "Don't let anyone tell you what they said. Hear them say it! Money for AIDS, not for war." Or out of the mouth of a glossy beauty smiling seductively at her tuxedoed boyfriend: "Find a cure. Find a cure. Find a cure."

John Giorno, poster—one of several commissioned by Visual AIDS—for Day Without Art (1993)

A Day Without Art: A Day of Mourning & Action in Response to the AIDS Crisis on December 1, 1989

SCENE & HEARD *was my bylined, bold-faced column in the **Village Voice** that appeared at least once a month to enable either follow-ups to issues I'd been addressing in the weekly newspaper or short thematic commentary about matters that seemed to not be receiving the attention they deserved.*

SCENE & HEARD *Village Voice, December 25, 1989*

What may prove to be the most significant event of **A Day Without Art**—the December 1 day of public actions and events by 800 art institutions and groups in response to the AIDS crisis—took place in private. **National Endowment for the Arts** chairman **John Frohnmayer** met with a 16-member, multi-cultural delegation organized by **Visual AIDS**, the organization (which I helped found) that sponsored A Day Without Art. The ad hoc group was a rainbow coalition of artists, arts administrators, curators, AIDS activists, and people with AIDS.

After rejecting a broadly conceived, multipage position paper with questions addressed to him, Frohnmayer—in a handwritten, faxed memo—insisted that discussion be limited to "the AIDS crisis and how we can better inform the public of this disease...and how I and the [NEA's] AIDS working group can be more effective in addressing the crisis." Video artist **Branda Miller**, who had documented the **Artists Space** brouhaha as part of her engaged art practice, was told that she could not videotape the meeting. Press was barred.

In conversation with a dozen note-taking participants, including NEA staffers, a virtual transcript was pieced together. The 90-minute meeting began with a presentation by the NEA's AIDS working group—the symbolically important, but largely ineffectual, committee organized in 1988. Dancer/choreographer **Bill T. Jones** blew away the chitchat with a bombshell: his company had decided to reschedule its sold-out 7:30 pm performance at the **Kennedy Center** in observance of A Day Without Art. "This day should be to us like **Memorial Day**," he said. "What [AIDS] means is that the light is no longer there; the stage is dark. We'd like to do the performance at 12:01." If this were done, however, the company would not only lose thousands of dollars but would also be in breach of numerous contracts with the Kennedy Center and labor unions, and Jones wanted the NEA's support that day in negotiating the potentially treacherous legal thicket.

By all accounts, Jones's stirring announcement helped to set the tone for a frank and forthright meeting. **Creative Time** executive director **Cee Brown** moderated what **LACE** (Los Angeles Contemporary Exhibitions) executive director **Joy Silverman** characterized as "an informational exchange, an education for Frohnmayer about AIDS, contemporary art, and their relationship." Among the points made crystal clear by the delegation were: the ubiquity of AIDS in the art world and the inevitability of sexually charged AIDS imagery in contemporary art; the reality of the double-marginalization of gay or lesbian artists and artists of color dealing with AIDS; the uniquely American nature of the NEA's peer-panel process and the necessity of maintaining its integrity; the history of legislative repression of safe-sex information by **Jesse Helms** and company; and the model role the NEA might play in such areas as health insurance for artists.

Although Frohnmayer primarily listened, most observers found his responses thoughtful and sensitive—in vivid contrast to his handling of the Artists Space affair. "I see no evidence that things will quiet down," he was reported to have said. "This is an intolerant society...and the NEA position is untenable...The stakes aren't just the NEA... [The real question is] will this be a repressive society or will it be one of a confrontation of ideas?" He made it clear that he favors the latter.

Only a few specific suggestions were made on December 1: that the NEA draft a stronger message to all grant applicants about AIDS than the one currently received only by grant recipients; endorse the 1990 Day Without Art; include community arts-AIDS specialists in the NEA's AIDS working group; and respond to Bill T. Jones. Toward the end of the meeting, Frohnmayer was said to have observed that "major policy statements and speeches will be coming in mid-January. I hope we would start implementing some of these ideas in a very short time and that we would be a major supporter of this activity [A Day Without Art] next year." Was the meeting worthwhile? As **Downtown Art Co.** partner **Cliff Scott** noted, "It was successful from several points of view, but the true test lies in the future. If Frohnmayer acts on what we suggested, then it will have been a success."

Within the NEA, one staffer characterized December 1 as the "most encouraging day since he [Frohnmayer] began as chairman." Its newly energized AIDS working group met three times between December 1 and 6 and has divided into issue-specific subcommittees including health insurance coverage. **Bill T. Jones/Arnie Zane and Company** hit the Kennedy Center stage at 12:01 am, December 2, with much of the NEA's program staff in attendance. They had provided moral support, but not "active intervention," during the preceding day's negotiations, according to a dance program staffer and **Sheldon Schwartz**, the Kennedy Center's administrator for artistic projects. Jones/Zane company manager **Johari Briggs** reports that the company stands to lose up to $15,000 for the December 1 postponement. (The NEA chairman could provide the money through a "chairman's action" grant.) Whatever the ultimate results of the meeting, Frohnmayer's final reported comment couldn't have been more apt: "We've all got our work cut out for us."

* * *

"Friday was a Day Without Art," announced auctioneer Ernest Quick. "Tonight [Sunday] we're going to sell art to support activism." **ACT UP**'s "Auction for Action" proved a phenomenal success for the hell raising AIDS activists. **Sean Strub**, who co-organized the December 3 event with **Steve Petoniak**, reports a net of around $310,000 to $315,000 on a $325,000 gross. "It was such an emotional evening," he beamed. "When **Keith Haring**'s *Totem* went for $70,000 [against estimates of $25,000 to $35,000], the audience broke into cheers of 'Act Up, fight back.'" An autographed copy of **Jesse Helms**' book(!) *When Free Men Shall Stand* was bought by discoteur **Chip Duckett**, who, according to Strub, promptly took it to **Mars** (the club, not the planet) and placed it in a urinal...**Art Positive**, the art collective affiliated with ACT UP, has released its $13 "Militant Eroticism Calendar." For information call 582-5590 or 353-3866.

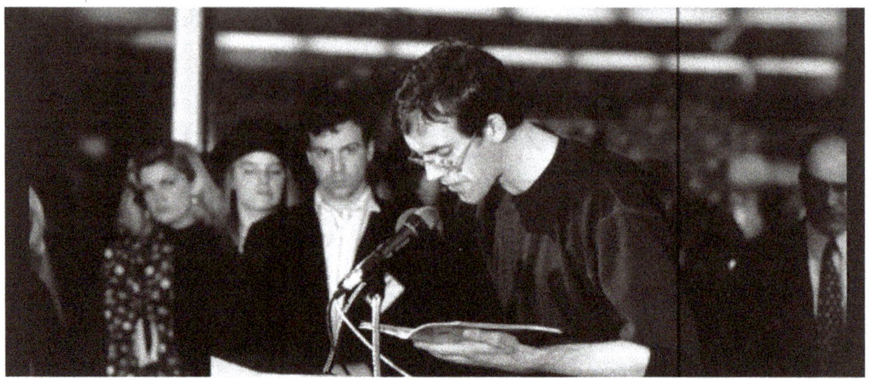

David Wojnarowicz speaking at "In Memoriam:
A Gathering of Hope, A Day Without Art" on
November 30, 1989, Museum of Modern Art, New York

A Day Without Art

ARTS magazine, May 1990

A Day Without Art—the national day of action and mourning in response to the AIDS crisis—proved to be anything but a day without art. From Portland, Maine to Portland, Oregon, at least 700 arts organizations participated in the December 1st event by offering a stunning variety of exhibitions, programs, and actions. Sponsored by Visual AIDS, the New York-based organization of art professionals, this observance of the World Health Organization's AIDS Awareness Day was intended to focus attention on the art community's losses and stimulate discussion about the role artists and art institutions might play in the AIDS crisis. NEA Chairman John Frohnmayer's November 8th announcement that he was rescinding a grant to Artists Space for *Witnesses: Against Our Vanishing*—the Manhattan non-profit organization's exhibition-contribution to *A Day Without Art*—inadvertently kicked off events several weeks early. At that point, Visual AIDS realized that it was also organizing a national network to help combat AIDS-related homophobia, racism, and calls for censorship.

Dubbed "the biggest AIDS event ever," *A Day Without Art* was an unexpectedly visible success: national television network and cable coverage was generous-and vastly exceeded by the hundreds of newspaper articles devoted to the day. Positive attention was focused on persons with AIDS (PWAs) and their supporters at a time when media interest in the syndrome has declined alarmingly. Journalists in Sarasota and Los Angeles who wondered why more local art organizations were not participating initiated sometimes acrimonious public debate. It's difficult to imagine another situation in which middle-class arts professionals might be forced to defend their decision to remain uninvolved in the struggle against AIDS.

But as I meditate on the events of last December 1st, I'm struck most forcefully by the intensity of people's desire to join in. Dozens of organizations became involved at the last minute in a Thanksgiving-week frenzy of activity. Irate members of the theater and dance worlds called to complain that their communities had been excluded from participating. Their more resourceful counterparts acted on their own initiatives; many Broadway theaters went dark for a moment of silence on December 1st and Bill T. Jones/ Arnie Zane and Company canceled its sold-out, Kennedy Center dance-performance just hours before curtain time and re-scheduled it for a minute after midnight on December 2nd.

How to account for the interest and intensity? *A Day Without Art* offered a rare opportunity to do something meaningful within the art world that involved more than fund-raising. Levels of AIDS-induced grief, frustration, and anger have mounted, and *A Day Without Art* was both a reminder of the Himalayan heights to which these emotions have risen and an outlet for their release. Some producers of December 1st programs confided that they hoped that their audiences had found as much satisfaction in the events they had presented as they had found in planning them. Or, as tireless Visual AIDS board member Philip Yenawine explained to Mario Cuomo upon receiving a Governor's Art Award and being asked why he'd devoted so much time to organizing *A Day Without Art*: "The value and meaning were in the doing."

Happily, those widespread feelings of rage and sorrow got translated into frequently moving and effective programs. The beauty of A Day Without Art was that its open structure encouraged mass participation. What follows are snapshot-vignettes that make up a loose and overlapping typology into which many of the activities fall. Although a call for documentation went out, Visual AIDS remains unaware of dozens (hundreds?) of events, especially rituals and performances enacted outside of institutional arenas.

* * *

Many spaces closed for the day; some carried on business as usual behind closed doors, while at others staff members were urged to volunteer at AIDS service organizations. The closures doubtless derived from the fact that Visual AIDS originally conceived of *A Day Without Art* as a moratorium modeled on the Art Workers' Coalition's 1969 moratorium protesting the Vietnam War. Resistance to such an approach came from two directions: mainstream institutions could not envision their boards of directors going along with the shutdown and organizations of all kinds urged that the day focus on art and education-and not just symbolism. The name was retained as a metaphor for the chilling possibility of a future day without art or artists.

Hundreds of organizations and galleries (especially commercial galleries) dimmed lights, shrouded-or removed-an artwork, or displayed the event's poster alongside a wilting vase of flowers. Although it's easy to criticize the dimming of lights as an insignificant response to a crisis of this magnitude, actions frequently reverberate, inspiring other actions.

And taken to dramatic extremes, removals and shroudings proved compelling. The Cleveland and Metropolitan Museums replaced major Picasso paintings (*La Vie* and the Gertrude Stein portrait, respectively) with AIDS information. Crown Point Press removed all the etchings from the walls of its Manhattan gallery, leaving only a single, framed work on the floor that bore the inscription "Witnesses to our losses." Students from the University of California at San Diego gathered at dawn to shroud Niki de Saint Phalle's 29-foot-high *Sun God* sculpture in black fabric and augmented this action with an educational ad and poster campaign.

Many universities and art schools made brilliant use of the

day to educate students about AIDS, racism, and homophobia. The Iowa Arts Council sponsored an AIDS Awareness poster competition for secondary school students and exhibited the winners in the state capitol. Children's museums in Boston, Brooklyn, Manhattan, and Pittsburgh provided programming for children, usually in the form of plays, videos, poster making and discussions.

The Children's Museum of Manhattan presented the performance *What's So Big About AIDS?* to an audience of educators on November 30th, and then to its usual kids-constituency on December 1st. One fifth-grade class responded with serious letters to the museum that belied the "kids say the darnedest things" sentimentality in which adults tend to traffick. "I used to think that there were more ways of catching the AIDS virus. Now I know that there are only three," wrote one student. Or—sadly—"Thanks to you I know how one of mom's good friends died."

With less than six months notice, at least forty-five exhibitions devoted exclusively to art about AIDS were mounted. Solo and duo shows seemed to spring up like mushrooms. Brian Weil's evocative photo-portraits of drug users and mothers and children with AIDS were seen at the Williams College Museum of Art in Williamstown, Massachusetts. The Clocktower in New York presented large-scale exhibitions of work by two artists who had recently died of AIDS: Rod Rhodes' miniature *Tableaux* and Paul Thek's *Technological Reliquaries*. Other artists who were showcased in one-person exhibitions include Luis Cruz Azaceta, Howard Ehrenfeld, Michael Freed, Felix Gonzalez-Torres, Keith Haring, Dan Havel, Lozuise Lawler, Hillary Leone, Paul Ludick, architect Richard Meier, Ann Meredith, Sam Messer, performance artist Tim Miller, filmmaker Rosa van Praunheim, Judite dos Santos, Nicholas Wilder, and Krzysztof Wodiczko.

Major group shows included the Freedman Gallery's (at Albright College in Reading, Pennsylvania) *Art About AIDS*, Artists Space's *Witnesses: Against Our Vanishing*, and the Henry Street Settlement's *Images and Words: Artists Respond to AIDS*. This New York City show confirmed (for the second time in one month) the likelihood of controversy arising over AIDS-related art. The ostensible issue—the location of Gran Fury's outdoor banner-installation proclaiming "All people with AIDS are innocent"—was resolved in time for the show to open on December 1st, although the banner was not yet hanging.

Female Artists Against AIDS presented an evening of dance, music, and art by women at the Hub Club in Boston to benefit a local community health center and to focus attention on the growing number of women with AIDS. In a gutsy curatorial move, First Bank Systems' (now former) arts division director devoted FBS's galleries in Minneapolis, Edina, and Milwaukee to exhibitions inspired by ACT UP (the AIDS Coalition to Unleash Power) Minnesota. In collaboration with the hell-raising political action group, FBS created installations that both disseminated AIDS information and pleaded for activism.

*   *   *

A Day Without Art program organizers frequently made connections with activist groups like ACT UP or with AIDS service agencies. A number of benefits for local organizations were staged, including Artists Television Access's *Silent Knights*, an evening of nearly two dozen silent performances to benefit ACT UP San Francisco. The Howard Yezerski Gallery in Boston presented an exhibition called *Paper Prayers*, based on the Japanese tradition of offering painted strips of paper as prayers to heal the sick, at which visitors exchanged papers for money that was donated to the Boston Pediatric AIDS Project. Larry Kramer, the driving force behind both ACT UP and New York's Gay Men's Health Crisis (the world's largest AIDS social services agency), read his play, *The Normal Heart*, at the John Michael Kohler Art Center in Sheboygan, Wisconsin.

The Kohler Co. had also helped to support the first museum exhibition to document *The NAMES Project Quilt*, which opened at the Madison Art Center in the spring of 1989. Panels from the quilt—and other already existing resources such as Video Data Bank's superb, six-hour anthology of *Video Against AIDS*—were heavily utilized by numerous art organizations and museums across the country on December 1st. *Common Threads*, the HBO-produced film based on the Quilt, was screened at the Boston Center for the Arts and the Museum of Modern Art, where it was introduced by AIDS fundraiser *extraordinaire*, Elizabeth Taylor. At Michigan State University's Museum of Cultural and Natural History, two quilting bees generated twelve *NAMES Project* quilt panels, which were included within an exhibition devoted to the history of needlework produced as vehicles of social change.

The *NAMES Project AIDS Quilt* had been criticized by some activists as an inappropriate concession to grief and a paralyzing deterrent against political action. Such simplistic thinking persists, although it seems to diminished in recent months. At a time when loved ones and care givers are inhumanely deprived of the opportunity to publicly grieve for those who have died of AIDS, the twin impulses to act *and* to mourn must be honored. On November 30th and December 1st, memorial observances were held throughout the country, ranging from candle-lit vigils to a short program at the Museum of Modern Art highlighted by the premiere of an original composition performed by Leonard Bernstein. Among those specifically memorialized in exhibitions and installations were Philip Dimitri Galas, Peter Hujar, Richard Irwin, Nathan Kolodner, Cookie Mueller, John McCarron, Bill Olander, Andreas Senser, Sam Wagstaff, and Nicholas Wilder.

In connection with many events planned for *A Day Without Art*, the mourning-*versus*-action debate seemed invalidated by the nature of the events themselves. A procession organized by artists in San Francisco combined the imagery of death (a casket, candles) with evocatively abstract placards intended to stimulate interest in the bilingual educational materials the marchers distributed. *The Witness Project*, "a census of AIDS in the arts" conducted in conjunction with Visual AIDS, is aptly described by its co-chairperson Simon Watson as "a subtle form of activism." Witnesses fill out a simple form testifying to the often invisible deaths of PWAs; the resulting census information will be available to art historians and curators. Bearing witness is the task of survivors and the responsibility of community citizens. (The Witness Project can be contacted at 241 Lafayette St., New York, NY 10012, 212-925-1955.)

Unfortunately, there will be a second *Day Without Art* on December 1, 1990. Visual AIDS intends to act as an umbrella to publicize AIDS-related activities coordinated by the dance, music, theater, and literary communities. It strongly encourages organizations to work with PWAs and AIDS service providers. The disturbing implications of AIDS cannot be ignored; the attendant homophobia, racism, inequitable health care, and assaults on civil rights must be acknowledged and resisted.

The alternative to such resistance was eloquently characterized by dancer/choreographer Bill T. Jones at a December 1st meeting Visual AIDS organized with NEA chairman John Frohnmayer and the agency's AIDS working group. "What [AIDS] means is that the light is no longer there, the stage is dark," Jones said. "This day should be to us like Memorial Day."

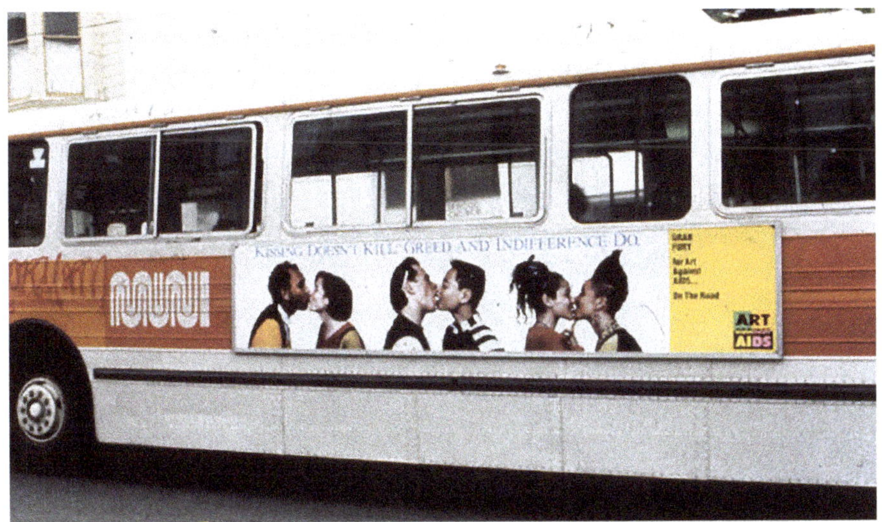

Gran Fury's Kissing Doesn't Kill: Greed and Indifference Do ignites controversy when it appeared on the side of Chicago buses as part of Art Against AIDS' outreach program in 1990

*The **Continuing Coverage** pieces in this book are comprised of excerpts from* **SCENE & HEARD**.

Continuing Coverage: AIDS 1988-1994

California Journal *April 5, 1988*

The first show about women and AIDS: *Until That Last Breath* (at the SOMAR Gallery through March 31) is the brainchild of photographer Ann Meredith and consists of 50 of her large scale photographs, seven sculptural "shrines" created by female persons with AIDS, and audio tapes and texts relating their stories. Meredith's involvement with the project grew from her realization that women are "invisible AIDS patients" and from her work with the San Francisco AIDS Foundation's support/therapy group for women PWA's, reportedly the only one in the country. While the cases of women with AIDS more than doubled between 1981 and 1987 to 7 percent of the total, that figure likely reflects under-reporting. "So many PWAs are single mother heads-of-households who need anonymity," Meredith sighed. "It took months before anyone would allow me to photograph them." The show's title was inspired by the words of PWA Meredith M., a 33-year-old mother of two: "Yes AIDS is a terrible disease. But we still dream. WE still live... The focus of this show is not to show us as emaciated or on our last breath... The purpose is to show that until that last breath entire lives are still going on." Currently working on a video-tape to document these reflections and personal histories, Meredith is hopeful the tape will be finished before the exhibition opens in New York at the New Museum next February. She can be contacted at 460 40th Street, Oakland, CA 94609 or 415-655-7289.

Busing *June 26, 1990*

Controversy swirls around **Gran Fury**––the aptly named art collective affiliated with **ACT UP**—like televangelists around a collection plate. Their pro-condom, anti–**Cardinal O'Connor** text-and-image-works for the current **Venice Biennale** weathered the vagaries of Italian Customs, the ire of Biennale director **Gionvanni Carandente,** and the scrutiny of the Italian legal system. When the art activists returned from Venice in early June, their bus-poster contribution to the **Art against AIDS** campaign in Chicago was being used to transform the Big Potato into the world's art censorship capital. Again.

The work in question is Gran Fury's already widely seen takeoff on a Benetton ad: an image of homo- and heterosexual couples kissing beneath the dictum "Kissing doesn't Kill: Greed and Indifference Do." It was slated for bus-side presentation this month, but the **Chicago Transit Authority** sold the donated advertising space (per its contractual right). Art Against AIDS then politely assured CTA—which cannot legally censor public service announcements—that a later date would be fine.

In the meantime, the work had become a lightning rod for AIDS-phobia and homophobia. Alderman **Robert Shaw**, the same goon who led the 1988 assault on the **David Nelson** portrait of Mayor **Washington**, called the poster a "camouflage" to propagate homosexuality. State representative **Monique Davis** termed it "a subtle seduction of young people on the CTA."

Mayor **Richard Daley** did not succumb to the rampant homophobia, and on June 8 supported the recommendation that the issue be referred to the City Council's Transportation Committee, which is widely regarded as a local burial ground. The real test will be whether the posters go up later in the year. Would that the whole world were watching.

Estate Project *1991*

Artist **Tony Feher** is a 36-year-old Texan who lives in the East Village and supports himself by working for several different dealers. He regularly shows his scatter-style art (most recently at the **Andrea Rosen** Gallery), but he is not represented by Rosen, or by any other gallery. Like so many New York artists, he is infected with the HIV virus.

Feher is one of the subjects profiled in a valuable series of publications produced by the **Alliance for the Arts**'s **Estate Project for Artists With AIDS**. Its fat, book-length report targets institutions; and its free, 32-page guide, Future Safe, was designed for artists.

Healthwise, Feher has been lucky. He's asymptomatic and he has health insurance—acquired from New York Artists' Equity before he was diagnosed and currently costing him an "outrageous" $100 each quarter. Although he admires Future Safe's down-to-earth advice for writing will and cataloguing artworks, he's chosen to devote himself to making—rather than preserving—his art. "It's ironic because I've catalogued **Scott Burton**'s personal collection (Burton died of AIDS) and I'm doing the inventory right now for **Paula Cooper**," he laughs. "You think that someday you'll get a gallery to send over an intern and do all that stuff for you."

But Feher admits that he's been affected by his involvement with the Estate Project, "I am trying to keep track of my work now and I know that I need a will." Before we part conversational ways, Feher draws my attention to Future Safe's subtitle, "Estate Planning for Artists in a Time of AIDS": "The implication [of the subtitle] is that this guide is for everyone." (The Alliance for the Arts can be reached at 947-6340.)... Speaking of AIDS and art, the Public Art Fund's long in-the-works Public Art Issues devoted to AIDS has been published. It's available for $5 at St. Marks' Bookshop.

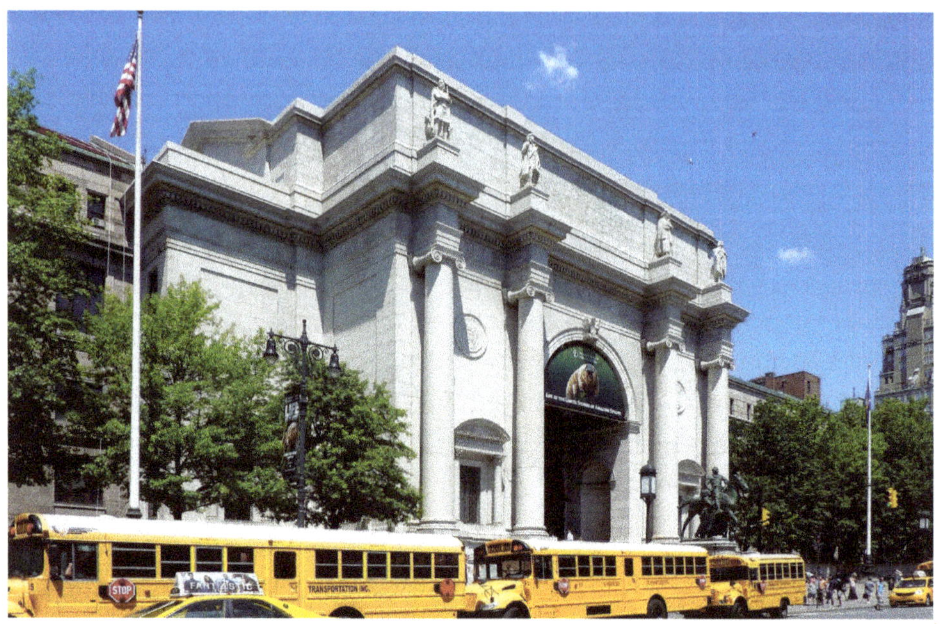

American Museum of Natural History rejects science

De-Evolution *July 27, 1993*

When you enter the **Museum of Natural History**'s lavish new hall of Human Biology and Evolution, bear right at the holograms of the human body. Across from a vitrine labeled "musculoskeletal system" you'll see an oddly empty, inset metal "frame" that's comparable to nearby displays about bodily systems—urinary, respiratory, and the like. It's the only empty frame in the exhibition, and according to four museum staffers, a volunteer, and two creative consultants who helped design the hall—it was built to house information about the immune system, even though the curatorial powers that be had nixed the plan.

Scientific knowledge hardly exists in a social vacuum. "The immune system is currently central to investigations of cancer—especially breast cancer—and AIDS," one staffer told me. Another—all seven informants insisted on anonymity for professional reasons—

noted that far more is now known about the immune system than when planning for the exhibit began around three years ago. But that hasn't stopped other museums from opening exhibitions about the immune system and HIV, among them the **New York Hall of Science**, the **California Museum of Science and Industry** in Los Angeles, and San Francisco's **Exploratorium**. In fact, the Centers for Disease Control encourages their creation through the **National AIDS Exhibit Consortium.** By contrast, the publicly funded Museum of Natural History's chief HIV-related exhibition effort was a 1988 temporary show of historical artifacts called "**In Time of Plague**."

Exhibit curator and anthropology department chair **Ian Tattersall** explained (through museum spokesperson **Jeanne Collins**) that the immune system is mentioned only briefly, in connection with the circulatory system, because it is not an anatomical system. (Then shouldn't it be treated substantively elsewhere?) So why did the frame get built after the immune-system display had been vetoed? Tattersall asserted that the display space is non-functional and that there are no plans for it. (Others dispute these claims, although no one currently working in exhibition construction is talking.) For one consultant involved in the early stages of the hall's planning, "The bottom line is that we have a duty to provide this information... We should be visionary if this display is intended to last 20 years." Or, as **Ellen Futter**, the museum's newly appointed president, told the Times on June 29, "...This museum will take up [the issues of] the environment, biodiversity, ethical questions, human biology and cultural diversity." The just-opened Hall of Human Biology and Evolution is one place to begin.

Nimby Epidemic? *June 8, 1993*

"Soho is a treasure and should be guarded and protected," art dealer **Tony Shafrazi** wrote city Health Systems Agency staffer **Arnold Haber** in an April 27 letter obtained by the *Voice*. The histrionic missive opposing Housing Works' proposed day-treatment facility for people with AIDS is a Freudian's dream: the dealer who splashed paint across **Picasso**'s *Guernica* calls the planned

Greene and Grand Street facility "destructively criminal" and its "placement in this model community...an absolute crime." (Since I am neither **Janet Malcolm** nor **Jeffrey Masson**, I will simply note that Shafrazi's gallery appears to float entirely on the proceeds from the sales of work by the late, AIDS-afflicted **Keith Haring** and his friend **Kenny Scharf**.)

Soho-ites already know **Housing Works**' plan for a badly needed treatment center has split their nabe; non-Soho-ites who've dealt with the Not in My Backyard (NIMBY) crowd certainly won't be shocked by the news. Ironically, central Soho is one of the city's few neighborhoods providing no social service facilities in a community board district with one of the highest rates of HIV infection in New York. A bigger irony is that Housing Works' facility is no poorly (as in city-) run homeless shelter; in fact, it's no homeless shelter at all. Citizens who attended a neighborhood forum at the **Drawing Center** on May 18, learned that the 70-client-per-day program will be open only between 9am and 5pm, that needles won't be exchanged, and that active TB and drug problems are likely to be reduced in Soho because of the treatment center. The facility is designed to centralize medical and social services for PWAs living nearby, in other words, to create—rather than destroy—a community.

The program's opponents—spearheaded by the **Soho Alliance**—seem far less concerned about the divisive effects on the neighborhood of their misinformation campaign and their methods of persuasion. Architects **Larry Bogdanow** reported at the forum that his Greene Street co-op board's contribution of $1000 to the loose-with-the-facts opposition pushed him into the active supporters' camp. Other neighborhood residents at the meeting noted that their boards were asking for three-figure per unit assessments to fight the facility, while two dealers privately complained to me that they've been warned by co-ops not to speak out on behalf of Housing Works if they want their leases renewed. In one sense, the negative campaign is succeeding: it's generated scores of letters to pols like Manhattan beep **Ruth Messinger**, who's uncharacteristically straddling the fence and councilperson

Kathryn Freed, who's broadcasting—let's be charitable—mixed messages. Now the action moves to Albany and City Hall where Housing Works' proposal must be approved by the state's Department of Health and the city's Buildings Department.

Obviously, neither boho-chic Soho nor the so-called art community is a monolith. Despite the views of Shafrazi and his ilk, those dealers, artists, and organization heads supporting Housing Works include **Brooke** and **Caroline Alexander**, **Ida Applebroog**, **Pamela Auchincloss**, **Josh Baer**, **Leo Castelli**, **Paula Cooper**, **Joe Fawbush**, **Emily Harvey**, **Jeanette Ingberman**, **Elizabeth Murray**, and **Ann Philbin**, among many others. For information on how to help—or just plain information—call **Anna Blume** at 925-5805.

P.C. in Paris *February 1, 1994*

I recently returned from Paris where I lectured at the **École Nationale Supérieure des Beaux-Arts** about political correctness, of all things. P.C. threatens to knock **Madonna** and **Michael Jackson** off Gallic media radar screens, but at least M & M have set foot in France. I saw nothing remotely resembling socially engaged art, making the Parisian artworld's newfound p.c. mania something like Poland's anti-Semitism without Jews. (A deeply reactionary editorial in the January issue of *Art Press* conveys some sense of what I mean.) I did see—and heard much more about two poster-works by artist **Olivier Blanckart** currently marring pristine walls in the chic Marais and Bastille gallery districts: One reads *"L'art contre le sida ne sert á rien: mettez des capotes"* ("Art against AIDS serves no purpose: use rubbers") and the other *"**David Hammons** est politically correct"* (likewise **Felix Gonzales-Torres**, **Hans Haacke**, and **Peter Fend**).

Blanckart, an artist with a lust for notoriety rivaling **Jeff Koons**'s, came to my lecture and revealed none of Koons's, well, subtlety. He informed a bewildered audience that he actually yearns for more politically pointed art ("No one talks about AIDS in the French artworld," he bellowed repeatedly) and weirdly dismissed Hammons's work (admittedly never seen in person) as overly African American.

Blanckart also explained that he transformed the gallery site of his most recent show into an AIDS information center, a spectacularly ineffectual gesture since Parisian galleries are drawing practically no visitors during these days of ultra-recession.

He'd have done better locating his AIDS information bureau outside the always bustling **Centre Georges Pompidou**. Inside the Beaubourg, the exhibition "Images pour la lutte contre le sida" (Images Against AIDS) provides a new low watermark in misguided AIDS-arts enterprises. Thirty-seven well-known artists created poster-prints for **Artis**, an organization that its founder, **Bruno Ughetto**, told me recently produced an agit-prop portfolio for **Amnesty International**. Many of the artists in the current show apotheosized condoms, but only one targeted either gay men or drug users!

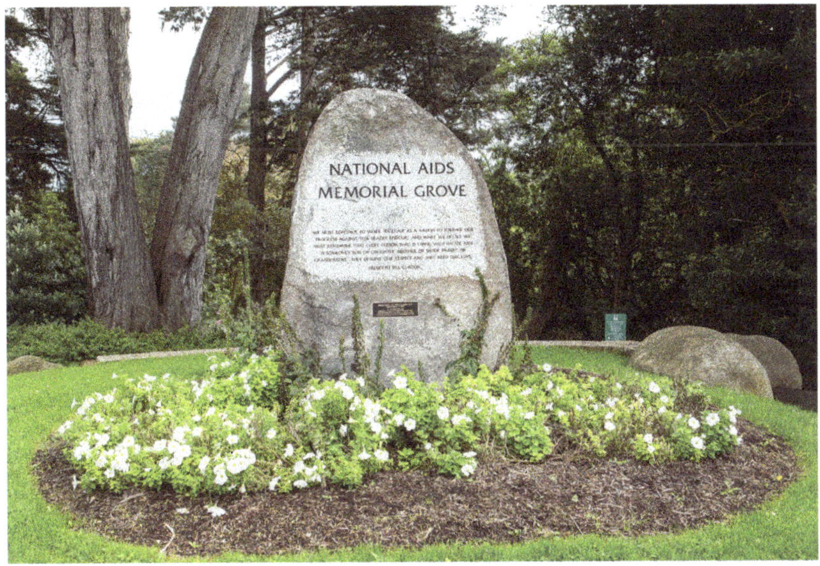

The National AIDS Memorial Grove—10 verdant acres in San Francisco's Golden Gate Park—is the sole national memorial to AIDS

Off the Wall: AIDS and Public Art

Artery: The AIDS-Arts Forum *website, 1999 (an earlier version of this essay appeared on the Queer Arts Resources website).*

Many of the most compelling artworks of the late-80s and early-90s engage the specter of AIDS—in sorrow, rage, and remembrance. Although most critics and curators are well aware of the importance of AIDS-themed works by artists like painter Ross Bleckner or photographer Duane Michals, few have a clue that artists and art-activists created an alternative body of street- and public artworks about AIDS that was far more influential. Remarkably, the iconic images or symbols of this plague are not made-for-TV movies, photojournalistic pictures, or schmaltzy pop songs, but the "NAMES Project Quilt," a community artwork, and two artist-conceived emblems, "Silence=Death" and the "Red Ribbon." Their effectiveness is testimony both to the power of art and the limits of popular culture.

Like everything touched by AIDS, the art it spawned has been relentlessly politicized and ruthlessly "mediated." Art about AIDS is, in part, a moving record of resistance to those who exploit trag-edy for political gain or for the sensationalistic, commercial pur-poses of the media. The story of AIDS-public-art cannot be told without invoking the media: Art about AIDS was initially catalyzed by the excruciatingly "negative" pictures of people with AIDS fea-tured on the nightly news and in the morning papers.

During the first few years of the epidemic—the early '80s—the media offered only images of emaciated AIDS "victims" and "dis-ease carriers." They were not so subtly identified as either "in-nocent" or "guilty." Hemophiliacs and children were "innocent" victims, while gay men and IV drug users were "guilty." Is it any wonder that in such a climate the Gran Fury collective's outdoor art-banner announcing that "All People With AIDS Are Innocent" caused a furor when it was exhibited at New York's Henry Street Settlement for the second Day Without Art in 1990? The first wave of AIDS art was produced with just one propagandistic purpose: to counter such horrific, media representations.

*   *   *

This single-minded response to social crisis brought modern art back to its roots. Two centuries ago, the painters of the French Revolution gave birth to modern art with images like Jacques Louis David's famous *Death of Marat* (1793). There was nothing extraordinary about depicting a martyred leader. But David's de-piction upended three centuries' precedent: He painted a contem-porary figure as he was—a man with an incurable skin disease soaking in a tub. David neither idealized nor allegorized him.

Since then, artists and theorists have debated the role of art in time of crisis. If Picasso's *Guernica* (1937)—the painter's up-to-the-minute evocation of the Franco forces' bombing of a Basque village—is the exemplary, twentieth-century political artwork, it is also an anomaly from an era when painting jettisoned its social moorings in order to explore the characteristics of form and ab-straction. AIDS activists and artists found few role models in mod-ern art. They instead revitalized public art, producing symbols and icons, posters and memorials such as the AIDS quilt. Their public artworks reached millions.

Back in the mid-80s, photography seemed like an effective way to confront both the demoralizing media imagery about AIDS and the threat of the cunningly unstoppable virus. But its mechanical grounding in the appearance of reality would prove to be nearly useless in dealing with a syndrome lacking visual characteristics. What does AIDS look like? Well-intentioned, mostly lesbian and gay, photographers produced hundreds of sympathetic portraits of people with AIDS, images of people with AIDS (PWAs) living with—rather than dying from—HIV disease. But their portraits are often difficult to figure out. Just who are their smiling subjects, these perfectly average looking Joes and Janes?

A furor arose with the first high-profile presentation of pictures of people with AIDS. In 1988, the Museum of Modern Art in New York showed portraits by Nicholas Nixon, who is neither gay nor afflicted with HIV. His serial images of the declining health of people with AIDS offer a sometimes grim record of courage and despair in the face of death. Members of ACT UP (the AIDS Coalition to Unleash Power) protested the negativity they saw in Nixon's work with a picture-side teach-in. (This was one of two anti-MOMA demonstrations ACT UP staged that year; the other protested the exclusion of AIDS-activist graphics from the museum's "Committed to Print" show.)

Nixon's pictures are, in fact, often grim accounts of the virus's murderous capability, but they are also a welcome record of its effect on a diverse, not-always-gay population of heterosexual women-of-color and hemophiliacs. As the first body of work exhibited on an extremely public stage, they also suffered from impossible expectations. Like Jonathan Demme's *Philadelphia* (1993)—the first Hollywood film about AIDS—Nixon's pictures were somehow expected to appeal to everybody: to simultaneously win over bigoted or uncommitted museum goers; and to foment activism and buck up the spirits of people with AIDS. No single body of work could possibly work such magic.

The broadsheets the ACT UPpers distributed at MOMA demanded both "no more pictures without [political] context" and images of PWAs "who are loving, vibrant, sexy and acting up." An abyss seemed to separate Nixon's controversial "negative" imagery from the blandly "positive" portraiture of the photographer-sympathizers. If portraying people with AIDS wasn't the answer, many observers wondered, how could art help change minds and alleviate this crisis?

Gran Fury, an artists' collective that operated as New York ACT UP's propaganda office, offered another "answer"—actually another modus operandi—by creating a strikingly public, non-museum role for art attempting to combat the epidemic. (Gran Fury primarily comprised Richard Elovich, Avram Finkelstein, Tom Kalin, John Lindell, Loring McAlpin, Marlene McCarty, Donald Moffett, Michael Nesline, Terry Riley, Mark Simpson and Robert Vasquez.) Rejecting portraits of people with AIDS, the group instead gave visual form to the shocking statistics emanating daily from the federal Centers for Disease Control and New York's Department of Health. Gran Fury formulated an ambitious agenda to provide the "context" other Act-UPpers had found lacking in Nixon's work. Its members wanted to dispense essential information that the government wasn't. They targeted the street, rather than the gallery, and they recognized that images are far more empowering when accompanied by words of explanation and elaboration.

The collective's graphic street works that began to appear in 1988 married the methods of art, advertising, and education. They cut a wide psychic swath across the AIDS landscape. One print offered the alarming news that one in 61 babies born in New York is HIV positive and another wittily cajoled men to "Use Condoms or Beat It." Gran Fury's first institution-sponsored graphic admonished art world types to fight AIDS, because "With 47,524 Dead, Art Is Not Enough." The toll, of course, continued to mount.

The art world is an eco-system—curators often collaborate with artists, and imagery sometimes travels from street to gallery, and then back again. Gran Fury came into being with the encouragement of activist-curator William Olander, who commissioned to create a piece for the New Museum of Contemporary Art's window on bustling, lower Broadway in Soho. Olander had been impressed by the highly visible work of another collective allied with—but pre-dating—ACT UP called the Silence = Death Project.

This group's six, (anonymous) gay men conceived the graphic emblem that has become synonymous with ACT UP and AIDS activism: SILENCE=DEATH printed in white type beneath a pink triangle, all set on a black ground. To create it, they inverted the pink triangle the Nazis forced homosexuals to wear in concentration camps— and which gay activists of the seventies had already "appropriated" as a symbol of gay liberation. A neon version of the logo was a central element in "Let the Record Show," the feisty installation at the New Museum indicting the Reagan-Bush administrations' inaction on AIDS. It now hangs in the museum's collection.

As Gran Fury's artful propaganda grew more self-assured, it increasingly migrated to more established and better-funded locations. In these public (and often publicly funded) sites, it also generated non-stop controversy. The group's famous Benetton-ad-inspired image of three, interracial, homo- and heterosexual couples kissing above the caption "Kissing doesn't kill: Greed and indifference do," raised hackles across the country as part of Art Against AIDS's "Art On the Road" project in 1990. Their placement on the side of Chicago buses, for instance, prompted one Chicago alderman to call the print "an incitement to homosexuality." Gran Fury's contribution to the Venice "Bienalle" the same year, nearly got the group prosecuted for obscenity.

Bear in mind that the "Bienalle" is the most prestigious of regular international exhibitions: an invitation to participate telegraphs the news that an artist (or, in this case, an art collective) has arrived. Gran Fury seized the opportunity to export its hell-raising methods to Europe. Its so-called "Pope Piece" paired two billboard-sized panels: one coupled the image of the pope with a text about the church's anti-safe-sex rhetoric; the other a two-foot-high erect cock with texts about women and condom use. Italian authorities—including "Bienalle" officials—considered prosecuting the group for blasphemy. Only the intervention of sympathetic magistrates precluded an international scandal.

Gran Fury's spectacular entrance into the public arena coincided with an epochal, once-in-a-century shift in consciousness. This passage from modernism to post-modernism meant that what could be seen only as an artist's protest poster in the context of the Vietnam War, could, 20 years later, be regarded as art. It also linked Gran Fury's work with a number of older, key art-players, such as Barbara Kruger and Hans Haacke. This was hardly an accident. The savvy, art-school-educated members of Gran Fury consciously looked to such art for inspiration, while supportive critics such as Douglas Crimp perceptively and persuasively made the case for Gran Fury's activism-as-art. The same, feminist-derived identity politics that, *en masse*, brought art by people of color and queers into the art world, heightened the visibility of art about AIDS.

In addition to *Silence=Death*, two other public artworks—*The Ribbon Project* (or *Red Ribbon*) and *The NAMES Project Quilt*—have come to symbolize the AIDS crisis. Like *Silence=Death*, the *Red Ribbon* was created by an artists' collective, the Visual AIDS's Artists' Caucus. (The Visual AIDS group—founded in 1988 in New York by Gary Garrels, Tom Sokolowski, Bill Olander and myself—produces the annual *Day Without Art* on December 1, among other educational projects and events.) The Artists' Caucus produced the Ribbon to subvert the onslaught of gooey jingoism unleashed by the Gulf War and embodied in the yellow ribbon. (At the time, the Artists' Caucus comprised Penny Arcade, Allan Frame, Marc Hoppel, Ira McCrudden, Frank Moore, Michael Stohlbach and Jerry Tartaglia.) But what exactly are *Silence=Death* and the *Red Ribbon*? Emblems? Symbols? Logos? Artworks? Or all of the above? Like other conceptual, non-object artworks, *Silence=Death* can't be bought or sold. But art is more than object making; it is also our culture's primary visual means of awareness. (That's why Hollywood and Madison Ave. borrow so much from contemporary artists.) In philosopher Hans Magnus Enzensberger's words, art is a branch of the consciousness industry.

The NAMES Project Quilt (organized in San Francisco by activist Cleve Jones and now headquartered in Washington, DC) is that rare phenomenon in contemporary culture, a genuine community artwork with no initial connection to artists or art schools.

Typically known simply as the "AIDS Quilt," and composed of more than 50,000 three-by-six-foot, quilted, appliqued and collaged rectangles of fabric, it commemorates fully 20 percent of the AIDS deaths in this country. Since 1986, participants have created these quilt components for friends, lovers or public figures like Arthur Ashe, Rock Hudson, and Michel Foucault. Images of pets, military medals, and drag queens coexist with slap-dash calligraphy, campy humor and heart-rending tributes from loved ones. "Love you, Mark" takes on new, poignant meaning when it's signed in glitter by Mom, Dad, and Lover Steve.

Intended to be anonymous, the "Red Ribbon" was designed as a symbol of commitment to people with AIDS and the AIDS-struggle. It debuted on the televised Tony Award ceremonies in late spring of 1991 and six months later you couldn't turn on the tube without seeing it: at the Emmys, the People's Choice Awards, and the Oscars; at sports events like the U.S. Open; at Freddie Mercury's "Concert for Life" in London; and on Presidential candidate Jerry Brown's lapel. The Republican handlers who removed it from Barbara Bush's bodice at the 1992 Republican Convention in Houston appreciated its apparently subversive message. But by then, the Ribbon—like any successful "media" artwork—had already assumed a life of its own. Its apotheosis as the best-known emblem of the early 90s led to its mid-decade oversaturation as a jeweled fashion accessory and computer screen-saver. In the weirdly freeform realm of symbols, it also came to represent the frustration many AIDS activists felt in the wake of the 1992 elections.

The ever-expanding Quilt is too large to be exhibited in its entirety. Its national debut took place in 1987 on the mall in Washington, DC. Like Maya Lin's nearby *Vietnam War Memorial*—whose black granite walls are inscribed with the names of the deceased in the chronological order of their deaths—*The NAMES Project Quilt* is shocking for its concreteness. But unlike the memorial's haunting testimony to the facelessness of death, the Quilt is a passionate affirmation of diversity. Nominated for a Nobel Prize in 1988, the Quilt helped give the plague—and its sufferers—a human face.

Some AIDS activists have criticized both *The NAMES Project*

Quilt and the *Red Ribbon* for their mild-mannered mode of address. But they miss the point. By the end of the 80s, the AIDS crisis had directly affected millions of Americans—PWAs and their families, friends, and caregivers. The Quilt helps attend to the needs of those mourning AIDS losses. The *Red Ribbon* is a bridge to non-AIDS-involved audiences; a gentle first step—its founders hoped—on the road to active support of PWAs. *The NAMES Project Quilt* and the *Red Ribbon* helped transform AIDS from a syndrome that dare not speak its name, to a subject that could be sympathetically raised in *People* magazine and at least acknowledged by those seeing entertainment industry darlings (and role models) strut their stuff at televised events.

In order to shift public opinion, to alter the psychic landscape, such symbolic works must, paradoxically, emphasize their public reach and distance from the art world. This also connects them with Dada-like, guerrilla events: Performance art-inflected demonstrations where protesters drop and others render the contours of their fallen bodies in chalk, or a clandestine action in which Queer Nation encased bible thumping Senator Jesse Helms' suburban Washington home in a giant condom. But there's also a continuum linking these guerrilla actions to mainstream events and observations—such as the annual skyline-dimming *Night Without Light* or the application of a huge Red Ribbon to the Eiffel Tower for a United Nations' AIDS conference—and to art itself.

The Museum of Modern Art's sponsorship of artist Felix Gonzalez-Torres's outdoor photo-billboards of his own empty, rumpled bed completed shortly after his lover's AIDS-related death is an historic, but little discussed milestone of 1992. It suggests how fully AIDS has radicalized art institutions. While works like Gonzalez-Torres's have forebears in conceptual and feminist art of the seventies', before the epidemic major museums had never sponsored such provocative work at the time of its creation.

* * *

The American AIDS crisis will eventually pass, if know-nothing zealots don't undermine every effort to educate and distribute needles, or to support PWAs and needed research. (As AmFAR founder Mathilda Krim noted long ago "each step in the escalation of the AIDS crisis was predictable, and could have been countered.") The suffering caused by AIDS—and those who refuse to treat it as a public health matter—is incalculable. In the not-so-distant future, though, one paradigmatic, public artwork-a memorial nothing like the pedestrian monuments that have been produced in places like Key West—might someday be completed.

San Francisco artist Rudy Lemcke conceived his memorial, "The Garden," as a river of stones flowing over black granite, complemented by bronzed boulders that double as seating. To grace its granite walls he's chosen the touching inscription from Walt Whitman: "... comrades mine and I in their midst, and their memory ever to keep." It's difficult to imagine a more affirming response to an epidemic that's transformed the West Coast epicenter of American gay life.

Lemcke chose Harvey Milk Plaza for the site of his Zen-inspired, place of meditation. Located at the Market-and-Castro-streets entrance to one of the world's preeminent gay ghettos, this plaza is named after the city's first openly gay supervisor, who was the target of a crazed assassin's bullet in 1978. This highly symbolic location reminds us that the struggles of the past must be commemorated and institutionalized.

Although city officials approved the proposal in 1988, (mostly gay) opponents objected, one of the first such instances in the country. They vociferously argued that a memorial should await a cure and that the required $250,000 (to be raised privately) would be better spent on research or treatment. Lemcke countered that "psychological, spiritual, and political health are also real needs that must be acknowledged. The garden is a symbol of life and continuity that will help meet them." Currently helping to midwife the creation of the country's first, municipally funded, lesbian and gay cultural center, Lemcke believes that the garden will eventually be built. The unfinished story of this project—and there are many stories like Lemcke's—is not only an allegory of survival against daunting odds. Creating this memorial is also a defiant act of faith.

New York City AIDS Memorial Park Proposal

Proposal by The Conversation Project—a collaboration of author Robert Atkins & Richard Kamler—for the design competition held in 2011-12

The New York City AIDS Memorial Park is tasked with marrying strange bedfellows: a neighborhood park and a memorial whose purpose seems unrelated to traditional monuments commemorating casualties of wars past. Integrating these twin demands requires re-thinking both the concept of "neighborhood" to include more than geography, and "memorial" to include more than (symbolic) representation.

For this reason, our proposal expands the concept of "neighborhood" to specifically include Greenwich Village's inspirational history of free expression, activism, and social welfare. It expands the idea of "memorial" to a "living" entity that both commemorates individuals and events, and educates diverse audiences about AIDS on-site (and online). It also comprises a non-profit organization, which will produce weekly programming (outdoors when weather permits or indoors in neighborhood facilities when it does not.) These free programs will present lectures or performances of AIDS-related scientific, political, and cultural content and address their social context—the intersection of civil rights, medicine, and healthcare.

The space for this programming—and socializing and picnicking—will be facilitated by the regular Sunday, 11 am–5 pm closing of Seventh Avenue to vehicular traffic from W 12th St to W 11th St. Portable tables and chairs *a la* Times Square will be available to park visitors. In addition, a pair of mechanically powered platforms will rise from their position adjacent to Seventh Avenue, transformed from their regular function as gently elevated, platform-like seating to multi-media-equipped stage or backdrop for programs.

The memorial park's 5000 square foot underground learning center will comprise a small exhibition space, table and chairs for group conversation, and computers providing access to varied kinds of information: submitted names of some of the more than 100,000 New Yorkers who have died of AIDS, a time-line of epidemic-related political and cultural events, information about AIDS prevention, etc. In addition, AIDS-related narratives from neighborhood residents will be solicited as will information about the historical place of Greenwich with Margaret Sanger's campaign for birth control. As suggested in the RFP, one of the two tunnels will provide space for mechanical equipment, the other will be illuminated primarily by a light emanating from a skylight-dome etched with artist Nancy Burson's photo-microscopic images of HIV-infected and healthy T-cells, which appeared on billboards in the area in 1991 as a visualization fo people with AIDS.

Appropriate artists' works will be used wherever possible: Including the late Scott Burton's sculptural stone seating, playground equipment (and seating) based on the pioneering designs of Isamu Noguchi, the Japanese-American sculptor who lived nearby and voluntarily entered a World War II internment camp to register his protest. A cobblestone hardscape will echo that in most NYC parks. Park vegetation will feature hardy, flowering deciduous trees such as calleary pear, flowering dogwood, and a canopy of Norway Maple to symbolize and embody the seasonal cycles of life and death (and rebirth).

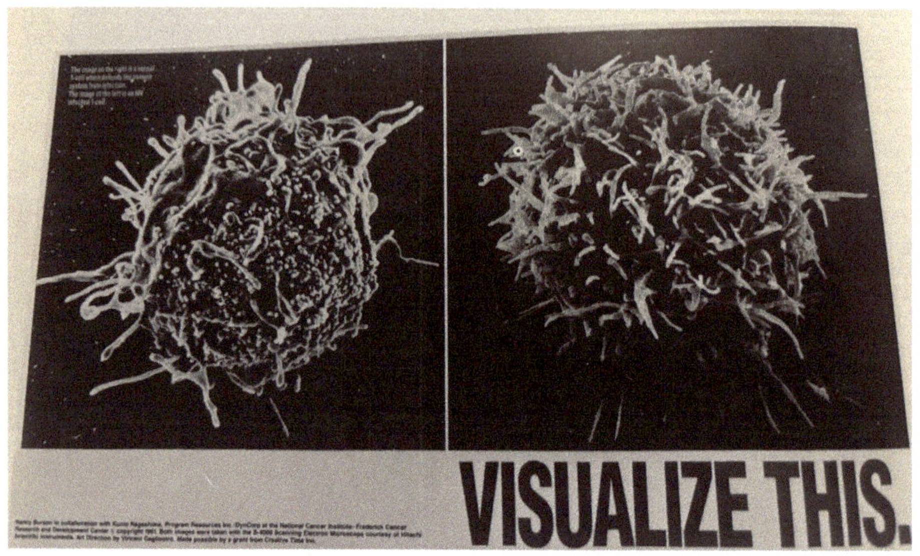

*Visualize This (1990), Nancy Burson
(with scientist Kong Nagashima).Poster and
billboard presenting healthy and diseased T-cells*

From Media To Metaphor: Art About AIDS

Excerpted from the catalog of From Media To Metaphor, the first international traveling exhibition devoted to AIDS. Organized by Robert Atkins and Thomas W. Sokolowski, it visited nine museums between 1991-94, and was circulated by Independent Curators Incorporated, New York.

From Media To Metaphor is an exhibition of artists' responses to the AIDS crisis. Because no single artistic voice or viewpoint is capable of grappling with the complexity of the epidemic, we have selected works, both objects and videotapes, by several dozen artists that *en masse*, evoke the impact of AIDS on American society and psyches.

It is clear that one can not talk about AIDS—or the art it's generated—without raising contentious issues of sex and sexual identity, public health and private morality. To engage these matters, the following essay assumes the unconventional form of a dialogue focused on AIDS and art's responses to the AIDS crisis. Commentary about the works in the show, grounded in both social conditions and aesthetic concerns, can be found elsewhere in this catalogue.

We realize that our dialogue is more likely to raise difficult questions than to suggest easy answers. In the face of an ongoing catastrophe, there is little room for the sonorous voice of authority, including the art historian's often reflexive impulse to categorize. The ebb and flow of our dialogue is intended as an analogue of AIDS-related social conditions that are continually—and messily—in flux. We hope that in conjunction with the exhibited art it will provide information, stimulate action to stem the spread of HIV infection, and foster more humane treatment for people living with AIDS.

Robert Atkins & Thomas W. Sokolowski

ART ABOUT AIDS: TWO VOICES, MULTIPLE CONTEXTS

Thomas Sokolowski: In the Fall of 1987 when I was working on *Morality Tales: History Painting* in the 1980s, an ICI exhibition of large-scale paintings about contemporary social issues, there were very few artists making art about AIDS.

Robert Atkins: Now there are so many—hundreds in the United States who put AIDS at the center of their work.

TS: While organizing the exhibition we certainly had the sense that one artist's work might stand for many who are dealing with similar aspects of the crisis.

RA: When we began thinking about this show in early 1989, we also believed that not only was there too little work about AIDS being shown, but that artists were sometimes penalized for making it: just as artists were fearful of coming out as gay prior to AIDS.

TS: Meaning much of it wasn't—and isn't—saleable. What strikes me about the many projects produced for the 1989 *Day Without Art* is that so many were temporary and site-specific. Some of the first AIDS-related works, then, were specially commissioned installations that no longer exist.

RA: And the corollary is that painters—operating in the most traditional and commodified of art-making media—began to make work about AIDS after the installation artists you've referred to, and three to four years after the first photographers, were making such work. First there was the photo work in the modern, documentary tradition. Photographers tried to combat the horrific representations of people with AIDS (PWAs) made by other photographers, that is photojournalists and the electronic media.

TS: By the way, that's where the "media" of the show's title comes from; it doesn't mean art-making mediums like paint-on-canvas or cast bronze.

RA: Let's present a little history: AIDS was named in 1982; the first wave of photographers wasn't active until at least 1985 and not exhibited until 1988. The entire field of depicting AIDS had been left to the largely unsympathetic mainstream media. Perhaps the major exception was the *NAMES Project Quilt*, which debuted in 1987. Its heartbreaking—and seemingly unthreatening emphasis on memorialization of the dead—helped make the subject of AIDS palatable to those who read about it in *People* magazine.

In retrospect, it's not surprising that so many photographers felt the urge early on to create sympathetic—or what I call positive—images of People With AIDS (PWAs) in conscious opposition the grisly media images depicting them as if they were starving Ethiopian babies. Until the *Rosalind Solomon: Portraits in the Time of AIDS* exhibition at the Grey Art Gallery and the AIDS component of Nicholas Nixon's retrospective, *Portraits of People*, at the Museum of Modern Art in 1988, this photo-work was still underground.

TS: Having organized Rosalind's show, I can tell you that one of the chief responses to these two shows was acrimony. Whether perceived as negative or positive, these pictures occasioned an outcry among some activists. The objectors saw—and still see—Nixon's serial portraits as lacking in social context and creating emaciated monsters out of PWAs. But such exhibitions were rare in 1988 and these photos allowed the faces of individual PWAs to be seen. At least PWAs weren't entirely regarded as statistics.

RA: Yes. These photographs documented the reality of who

PWAs are. Consider the few TV movies about AIDS, for instance. Only *An Early Frost* (1985) and *Our Sons* (1991) featured gay PWA— and none have focused on drug users or their sex partners. Instead we see heroic depictions of 'innocent' victims who contracted the HIV virus through blood transfusions. The divisive media constructions of 'guilty' and 'innocent' victims were precisely what these initial, well-intentioned photographers were confronting.

TS: Solomon's photographs were also more palatable than Nixon's because, in many cases, the PWAs she photographed looked healthy —as so many HIV+ people or PWAs do. Nixon's work was more abrasive. For the first time, in a mainstream art context, viewers saw images of people who were visibly ill. Many people didn't want to see them and accused Nixon of undermining PWAs whose lives are difficult enough.

RA: When a group from ACT UP [the AIDS coalition to Unleash Power] leafletted Nixon's Museum of Modern Art show, their broadside called in part for images of PWAs "who are loving, vibrant, sexy, and acting up." Yet some PWAs found Nixon's work a powerfully realistic representation of themselves. Solomon's and Nixon's works also suffer from inherent limitations of the modern, documentary, black-and white tradition that includes both photojournalism and so-called art photography. As a medical, political, and ethical phenomenon, AIDS is staggeringly complex. In an uncaptioned photograph, it's sometimes impossible to determine what's going on. Is it about AIDS? Or is it simply a generic picture of a young woman in a hospital? The context in which you see the work —in an exhibition, a magazine, or a political demonstration—may largely determine its meaning.

TS: The imaging of AIDS by artists almost immediately brought the conflicting needs of different audiences out in the open. On one hand, there was an ill-informed 'general' public and, on the other, insiders including PWAs and activists. How could there be one kind of image that would serve everyone's needs?

RA: There is more agreement on another matter of representation, of 'positive' imagery —that is, the depiction of PWAs in language. Most we know prefer to be called "people with AIDS" rather than "AIDS victims." Max Navarre said, he was one of the founders of the PWA Coalition, "I'm a person with a condition, I am not that condition." Until the PWA movement emerged out of the 1983 Denver conference, there were no organized outlets for the views of those living with the syndrome.

Photographer Gypsy Ray would later respond to this void by having PWAs write their comments into the mats surrounding her pictures. Nicholas and Bebe Nixon's new book, People with AIDS (1991), includes extensive interviews. Both Ray and Nixon interviewed the caregivers and loved ones of PWAs, as well as PWAs themselves.

TS: There is the cliche that in ten years everybody will be committed to doing something about AIDS because we will all know somebody who is HIV-infected. The present lack of connection between the public at large and PWAs, as expressed through language, is also something the Canadian art collective General Idea has been exploring in their artworks based on Robert Indiana's famous Love icon. Since 1987, they've appropriated Indiana's format and converted the four letters of "love" into the four letters of "AIDS." Some regarded it as a cheap trick; love being the emblematic word and activity of the '60s, and AIDS its corollary in the '80s. In fact, their stated intention was to "domesticate" the word, to communicate that AIDS is an unfortunate part of everyday life and not merely scientific jargon.

RA: One purpose of our show is to present audiences with information about AIDS, as well as contemporary art.

TS: Information about AIDS prevention, treatment, and community resources for PWAs will be available so that if a well-informed visitor comes to the show, he or she will find new information. And if you are someone who had never seen a PWA or considered the dilemmas that PWAs face, then this exhibition will provide information about that, too. Each venue is encouraged to present a local component.

RA: The show suggests a number of possible human and artistic responses to the epidemic. A problem with some AIDS exhibitions is that they have not overtly promoted activism—whether

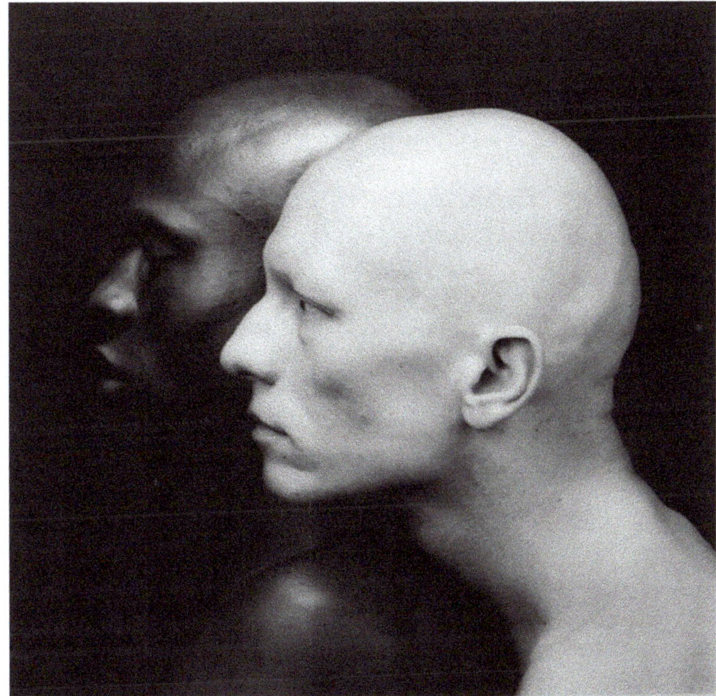

Robert Mapplethorpe, Ken Moody and Robert Sherman, 1984

that means urging the public to contribute money or time for the care of PWAs, or to write letters to Congress, or to demonstrate at the Centers for Disease Control. Because all sorts of people in urban centers are affected by AIDS—people of color, gay and lesbian people, the healthcare community, to name a few—the appeal of a show like this might extend beyond the usual audience for contemporary art. We want to make sure that informational and educational resources are available.

TS: And that the exhibition speaks as directly as possible.

RA: We've deliberately chosen works that are not 'coded' in the sometimes difficult-to-decipher, visual language of historical or contemporary art. We hope that these works will speak directly to varied audiences.

TS: By its nature, this show engages contemporary art that is inextricably and immediately linked to its social context. Much of the art derives from artists' hands-on experience with PWAs—such as Paul Marcus's lengthy involvement with a young mother in the Bronx who subsequently died, or Dui Seid's experience as a home-care attendant for PWAs.

RA: Many of the pieces in the show also generated debate, beyond the narrow confines of the art world, about the representation of AIDS. Nancy Burson's image, "Visualize This," for instance, is an object for visualization by PWAs. She took photo-microscopic images of an HIV-infected and a healthy T-cell and made a diptych that was used as a poster or billboard. Its meaning was debated by funders for whom she sought production costs, and for people who saw the work wheat-pasted on New York walls. Detractors felt that it placed the responsibility for the AIDS crisis on PWAs rather than on the government. This position may be a polarizing example of either/or thinking not necessarily in the best interests of PWAs. Some PWAs employ Eastern and Western medicine, visualize and meditate, and participate in demonstrations as well.

TS: Many of the artists in the show are PWAs; too many others have died of HIV-related causes. Their AIDS experiences, given form in art, teach by example. Being an artist allows you to take your life experiences—positive or negative—and make them a basis of your work. The shock of discovering your HIV+ status—or that of someone close—might be transformed into art.

RA: Or perhaps action.

TS: Wherever the show travels, its local components also allows for a kind of update, an opportunity to create dialogue between artists, care givers, and service organizations.

RA: It can give artists the opportunity not just to exhibit their work about AIDS, but to investigate local conditions. Every community has its own epidemic.

TS: As we conduct this discussion in mid-May 1991, the Whitney Biennial has just concluded. Critics have noted that its thematic undercurrent is the AIDS crisis. The works range from the very pointed *AIDS Timeline* by Group Material [fragments are reproduced in this catalogue], to more subjective and indirect allusions that can be read as an undercurrent of angst, sadness, or anger.

RA: A sort of emotional barometer.

TS: This emotional barometer might be social, as well as psychological. The members of General Idea are Canadian, and they split their time between New York and Toronto. They see their work as very different from American art about AIDS. They feel that they can make art about what Elizabeth Kubler-Ross, in her book *On Death and Dying*, described as the final stage (acceptance) of coming to terms with death, partly because the Canadian government has been so much more responsive to the needs of PWAs.

RA: AIDS is also an emotional barrage. In the face of so much death comes overwhelming grief and anger. Thomas Woodruff spent months painting self-portraits of himself as a crying clown. The texts of David Wojnarowicz's works are shockingly direct in their rage. The emotional range of recent AIDS art seems to be widening. The anger of a work by Donald Moffett that reads "Call the White House and tell Bush we're not all dead yet" is tempered with a defiant and liberating irony. What some viewers might dismiss as mere propaganda is leavened by mordant wit. Moffett's subversive use of media and advertising techniques is also very contemporary.

*   *   *

TS: Warhol is certainly the progenitor of so much media-inspired, activist art about AIDS, whether it's intended for the gallery or the street. He understood that the modus operandi of Madison Avenue might be applicable to SoHo. Gran Fury—whose very name evokes a '60s-model Plymouth used by the police—make their art and politics inseparable. Since so large a part of their audience reads about, rather than sees, the work, the media is a stand-in, a representative or embodiment of the audience One buzzword for the '80s was strategy, and sometimes the strategy became the artwork's concept.

RA: And there are other kinds of strategizing as well.

TS: The art world has rarely displayed such solidarity as it has in connection with AIDS. The commitment has come from artists, critics, and curators. Art is also a useful fund-raising tool. Art Against AIDS auctions donated artworks to raise money for AmFar [American Foundation for AIDS Research] for medical research. At Visual AIDS in New York, art is used as an educational tool. Another group, Visual AID in San Francisco, raises money to help PWA-artists buy art supplies. There are collectives like Art+, in New York, which produce programs, as well as demonstrate. This list only scratches the surface.

RA: Some of the art world's solidarity about AIDS also derives from many attempts to censor art about AIDS, particularly explicitly sexual imagery produced by gay men. Openly gay and lesbian artists are commonplace in the mainstream art world. If the AIDS epidemic had initially hit IV-drug users, it would have been difficult to predict art-world involvement. This is largely a matter of class; professional artists tend to be middle-class. An unfortunate by-product of gay and lesbian leadership of AIDS awareness and activism efforts is that it plays into the hands of those who cynically manipulate homophobia— sometimes by attempting to censor publicly funded art. Art about AIDS frequently invokes political outrage or attitudes toward sexual activity and that's led to some bruising controversies. The first involved an attempted withdrawal of NEA support for *Witnesses: Against Our Vanishing*, the AIDS exhibition that was John Frohnmayer's first crisis after he became a chairman of the National Endowment for the Art in late 1989. AIDS was also the subtext of the Robert Mapplethorpe controversy and trial, although homosexuality was the censor's pretext.

TS: An early and articulate voice in writing about AIDS and sexual repression was Simon Watney, the author of *Policing Desire: Pornography, AIDS, and the Media* (1987). Although the book focused on Britain, the handwriting on the wall is disturbingly clear. A government-condoned sexual panic exacerbated by AIDS has created a climate in which the British government is attempting to recriminalize the activities of sexual minorities.

RA: What's most surprising is that the virulent assault on American freedom of expression has been so effective. It's partly a problem of misleading sound bites and misrepresentations akin to the characterization of a publicly sited AIDS artwork by Gran Fury called *Kissing Doesn't Kill: Greed and Indifference Do* as an "enticement to homosexuality." And painter Kathe Burkhart has depicted Elizabeth Taylor, AIDS fund-raiser and activist *extraordinaire*, defending herself against "charges" of having AIDS—as if having AIDS were a crime and would render her generosity suspect.

TS: The Right understands the power of symbols. Because symbols are richly ambiguous, they are easily manipulated. Look at the Cross: it can stand for the most liberal theology of the Unitarian Church and its virtual opposite, the Ku Klux Klan. Art itself—as opposed to individual artworks—is also symbolic. It partakes of the authority of the gallery or the museum—from a work's literal and figurative location on a pedestal or in a frame. For many people, art is a potent enigma and if it's perceived as an attack on long-held values or beliefs, than it's understandably frightening.

RA: If some want to prescribe what kind of art artists should make, others are likely to prescribe what kind of art this show should present.

TS: It is likely to incite criticism from several directions. For some viewers the imagery may be overly explicit. Others would curate a show like ours with exclusively didactic intentions, an explicit agenda that every artwork about AIDS must overtly concern itself with ending the crisis. This seems too doctrinaire.

RA: How can anyone anticipate the effect and artwork—or a group of artworks—will have on a variety of audiences?

TS: May be this exhibition is unusual because we acknowledge a sometimes blurry divide between art and activism; we don't always see them as synonymous. Good politics do not necessarily make for good art.

RA: Bad political art is bad politics and bad art.

*   *   *

TS: One extraordinary work and the most extraordinary thing about the *Quilt* is the collective quality of the viewing experience as it travels from place to place. Of course, it is profoundly touching to see someone kneeling and crying at a lover's—or child's—quilt-square. But then your own tears might flow, quite independent of the specific thing being seen.

RA: Again, the duality of the personal and the collective.

TS: Susan Sontag suggested a split that cannot be bridged in *Illness as Metaphor* (1977) She wrote, "Everyone who is born holds dual citizenship, in the kingdom of the well and in the kingdom of the sick. Although we all prefer to use only the good passport, sooner or later each of us is obliged, at least for a spell, to identify ourselves as citizens of that other place." When one is in one kingdom, one cannot even contemplate the other. And yet, at some point, our position will shift.

RA: Do you think art can save lives?

TS: Perhaps indirectly. I do think it can help the rest of us live.

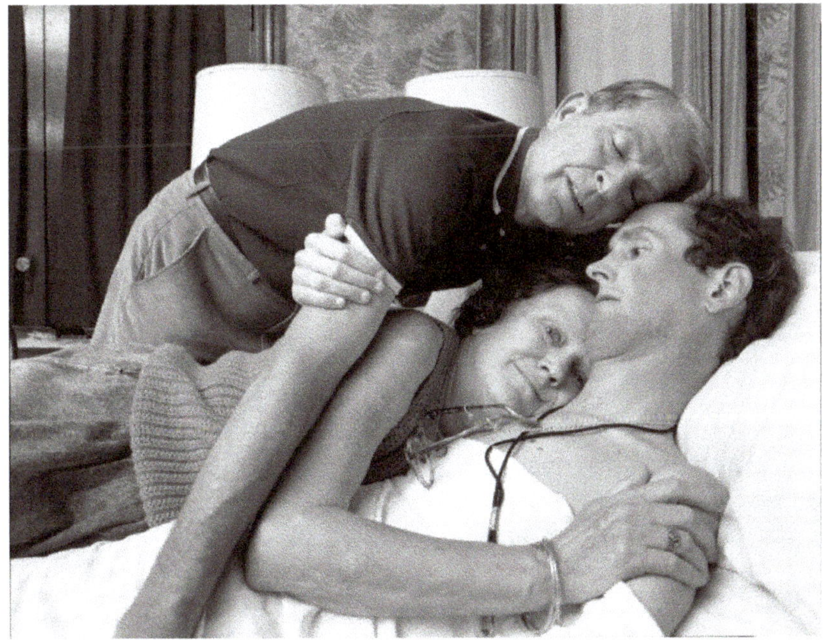

Robert Sappenfield and His Parents, Dorchester, MA 1988 (from the series of pictures of Robert Sappenfield by Nicholas & Bebe Nixon

Moving Pictures

Village Voice, 1991

A review of **Bearing Witness: People With AIDS**, *photographs by Nicholas Nixon and text by Bebe Nixon, Godine,*

What Salman Rushdie was to the Ayatollah Khomeni, photographer Nicholas Nixon is to some AIDS activists. When Nixon's work-in-progress about *People With AIDS* was shown as part of his 1988 Museum of Modern Art retrospective, ACT UP members distributed leaflets calling for positive images of PWAs who are "vibrant, angry, loving, sexy, beautiful, acting up and fighting back." But the often powerfully grisly portraits that they found wanting in compassion and social context at a moment when little art about AIDS was being shown have been partly contextualized by other artists who approach the epidemic from more overtly idealizing or political perspectives. For *People With AIDS*, it is Nixon—and science journalist Bebe Nixon—who have done the contextualizing: they've augmented the pictures with essays based on interviews Bebe has been conducting since 1987 with PWAs and their loved ones.

Photographs and text jointly assume center stage in *People With AIDS*. Shot over time, the black-and-white close-ups—as many as 11 of a single subject—offer the increasingly emaciated bodies of PWAs, sometimes seen in informal poses with care-givers. These photos will be familiar to viewers of Nixon's exhibitions at MOMA and the Zabriskie Gallery, and the re-presentation of the pictures in the book is not likely to resolve the controversy about them. But the addition of words enlarges the emotional and intellectual range of the images and underscores the insufficiency of any documentary photograph to grapple with the complexity of AIDS.

The texts range widely in length and depth, and are sometimes complemented by interviews with parents and lovers. The Nixons' 15 interview-photo subjects came to them through an ad in Boston's AIDS Action Committee newsletter. They constitute a fortuitous cross section of the epidemic's toll: nine gay or bisexual men; three black and one Hispanic women (some of them—or their spouses—used intravenous drugs); a hemophiliac; and one PWA who refused to discuss the source of his infection. Their reasons for participating in the Nixons' project are largely unarticulated and 14 of them were dead by the time the Nixons' endeavor was completed.

In these interviews, they verbalize plenty of what we might expect. Some rant against an uncaring society that has betrayed them, while others find spirituality late in life. Many contemplate suicide. Several intone that frighteningly universal mantra of the universally ill, "I'm not afraid of death, but I am afraid of dying."

These are all essential messages in a culture that regards PWAs as disposable and denies the inextricable relationship between living and dying. Such sentiments pale, however, beside the vivid thematically linked stories that *People With AIDS* presents. Stories about growing up in wildly varying circumstances during the 50s and 60s: Northeasterner Sara Paneto, now a counselor at a Providence detox center, attributes her weakened kidneys to her father's assault on her pregnant mother. "Me and my sisters," she observed, "we were physically, sexually, and psychologically abused from the day we first thought of life." Joey Brandon, by contrast, came from a blissfully supportive Indiana family that provided him with what he characterized as "the last real American childhood."

There are also stories about the energy and urgency that an AIDS diagnosis can catalyze. Donald Perham helped found the New Hampshire AIDS group. Paul Fowler planted a garden. Elizabeth Ramos sued her doctor for malpractice. There may be useful advice here for PWAs, too. Banker Donald Perham and actor Tony Mastrorilli regretted giving up their jobs too soon; George Gannett spoke revealingly about the role of the "perfect AIDS patient" and the denial of feelings it entails.

The most resonant stories in the book are invariably about families—biological and chosen. Parents and lovers put their lives on hold to nurse their children or mates. They describe traumas as different in scale as dining out while worrying about diarrhea or watching a loved one losing control of his mental faculties.

The Nixons' stated purpose was to record these PWAs' stories "with so much candor and so little cant that even total strangers might be moved." Have they succeeded? Their labor of love (proceeds will go to Boston's Hospice at Mission Hill) is immensely valuable: it helps humanize a crisis that hostility and inaction have turned into a global catastrophe and it gives PWAs a voice in articulating matters of personal and social concern. Unhappily, it also misses crucial opportunities to educate its readers.

In her introductory notes about PWA Linda Black for instance, Bebe describes the difficulties Black's doctors had diagnosing her condition. Why not a mention of the Centers for Disease Control's sexist definition of AIDS that excludes so many women like Black? Or a list of simple things people can do to support PWAs and combat AIIDS phobia? No reader is likely to remain unmoved after reading the lengthy comments of Joey Brandon's father, Everett Cloyd, a man who cried about Joey's impending death in the middle of the night, rather than disturb his wife with his tears. But being moved is not enough. Hopefully this affecting book will help spur long-overdue action.

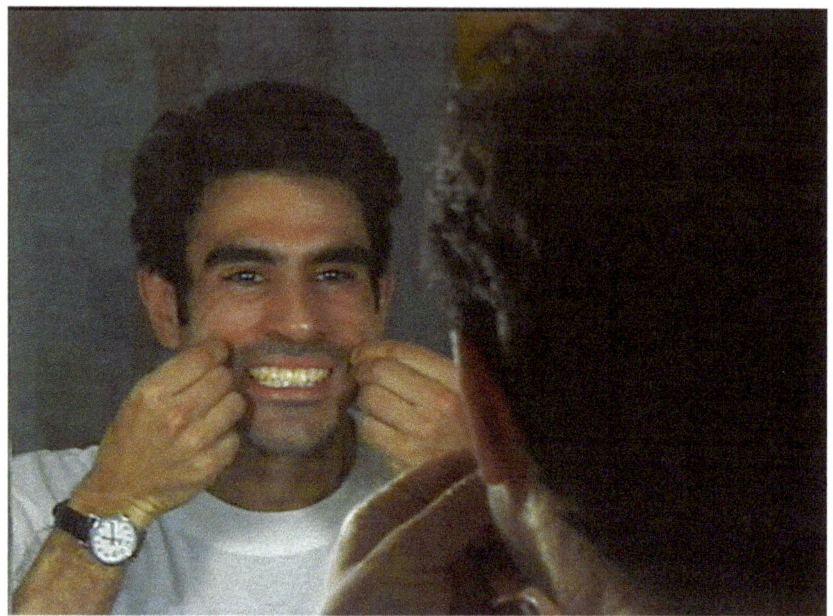

Gregg Bordowitz, Habit, 2001, video still.

Fast Trip, Long View: Talking to Gregg Bordowitz

Artery: *The AIDS-Arts Forum,* 1999

*As a twenty-three-year old faggot, I get no affirmation
from my culture. I see issues that affect my life—
the issues raised by AIDS—being considered
in ways that will probably end my life."*

Gregg Bordowitz

These blunt and riveting lines opened Gregg Bordowitz's essay, "Picture a Coalition," which was published in the "AIDS: Cultural Analysis/Cultural Activism" issue of *"October"* (#43, 1987.) They say plenty about Bordowitz's powers of analysis and his outspokenness, but nothing at all about his capabilities as an organizer and film- and video maker. These are some of the subjects we cover in the interview below.

Outspoken and obviously HIV-positive, Bordowitz's name is nearly synonymous with AIDS activist video in the U.S.. His work spans the gamut from documentaries and educational films, to the first regular cable-television show about AIDS, and imaginative films and videotapes screened at museums, movie theaters, film festivals, and on public television. He has been honored with fellowships by the Guggenheim and Rockefeller Foundations, among many others. He currently teaches at the School of the Art Institute of Chicago and writes a column called "New York Was Yesterday," for the journal "Documents."

Bordowitz is the first subject to be interviewed for Artery's "Artist In the Archives" series. The Estate Project—the parent organization of the Virtual Collection, "Artery" and the artistswithaids.org website—has initiated a program to preserve and archive AIDS-activist videotapes. A thousand hours of fragile tapes by such groups as DIVA TV (Bordowitz was one of its founders) as well as Bordowitz's personal output are already being preserved, thanks to funding from the Royal S. Marks Foundation Fund and the New York State Council on the Arts. This collection will be housed at the New York Public Library and named in honor of Royal Marks.

Robert Atkins
Editor/Producer of "Artery"

Artery (Robert Atkins): In *Fast Trip, Long Drop* you said that accepting your own mortality is the hardest thing. Do you still feel that way? How is your health?

Bordowitz: Yes, I still wrestle with issues of mortality. I am fairly healthy now. There was a period when things looked bleak. My numbers were down and I had a few opportunistic infections. Fortunately, there were treatments for the infections and I was able to maintain my health until the protease inhibitors came out. I went on a cocktail and my health improved. I'm doing well on the new drugs, and now I have to face the fact that I may live for a long time.

But underneath all this optimism is the lingering fear that I'm fooling myself. That the drugs will stop working and I'll become resistant to all available treatments. A likely outcome. So my health, my life, my plans continue to be provisional.

It's difficult for me to talk about my anxieties about longevity. First, because I lost many friends and I feel that I owe it to them not to complain about living. After all, living longer, surviving, does not fall into the category of oppression. I'm lucky, right? However, I tested positive when I was 23. I didn't think I was going to be living in two years. Forget living to see thirty. I spent my entire twenties thinking I was going to die. I didn't prepare for a long life. I gave no thought to money or a career. I didn't think about what I wanted to do with my life, or rather I did—I decided that I would do only what was meaningful to me in the short time that I thought I had.

Now I find myself facing the more abstract questions of existence, like what do I want to do for the rest of my life. I feel like a kid.

Artery: Let's look back by talking about your background. You went to art school?

Bordowitz: Yes, I first attended the School of Visual Arts. Then the Whitney Museum Independent Study Program. In my academic career, I was last seen in the Anthropology Department of NYU studying ethnographic film. Then I went missing from academia, only to return as a full time teacher at the School of the Art Institute of Chicago some ten years later. Currently, I'm also on the faculty of the Whitney Museum Independent Study Program.

I dropped out of school to make guerrilla TV for the AIDS movement and I became a full time activist with ACT UP.

Artery: You helped found two important, activist video collectives, DIVA TV [Damned Interfering Video Activists] and Testing the Limits in the late-80s. Can you talk about them? Why two different collectives? What was different about their work or modus operandi?

Bordowitz: Testing the Limits was formed by five people, lesbian, gay, and straight—David Meieran, Hilery Joy Kipnis. Sandra Elgear, Robyn Hutt and myself—to document emerging AIDS activism in 1986-87. (Jean Carlomusto became a full member of the collective a little later.) The collective was governed by the principle of consensus. All 250-something edits of our first piece, "Testing the Limits," were made by the collective.

Artery: That sounds excruciating!

Bordowitz: It was an excruciating but ultimately a very successful process. I don't believe the work would have been as strong as it was without the endless arguments we had as a group and the burden of consensus. Our differing points of view and nascent understandings of the crisis were fired slowly in a crucible that produced a rigorous and comprehensive examination of the crisis. We borrowed Simon Watney's assertion (from his book *Policing Desire*) that the AIDS crisis must be examined from three perspectives: civil rights, AIDS education and treatment activism. We used the framework of those categories to document the various efforts then beginning in New York. We wanted to show that a diverse number of people were fighting AIDS on a number of fronts. And we wanted to show them as an emerging coalition—that is, the AIDS community. *Testing the Limits* was an organizing tape and a teaching tool.

Artery: How was that first piece distributed?

Bordowitz: It was eventually broadcast on selected PBS stations around the country as well as at museums, the American Film Institute, festivals, schools and, most importantly, community centers where ACT UP chapters and other groups were forming. At that point the members of the collective differed on the direction the group should go.

Artery: What happened?

Bordowitz: I've had some time to think about what happened. So my answer to that question is now informed by hindsight. Part of the collective wanted to become a fundable entity. We'd made the first piece with a few donations and the limited resources we had available to us. A shoe-string really. After the success of the first piece some of the group wanted to open an office and produce a proper PBS type documentary. Others, wanted to continue doing guerrilla video for the AIDS movement. I wanted to do that.

Testing the Limits opened up the possibility of an activist

AIDS-video practice that could provide an instantaneous feedback loop to the movement for self-reflection, self-critique. And there were many other needs for video activism. The movement needed to be documented by people who were directly affected by the crisis—people with AIDS and those who supported us. So I was into producing fast cheap docs with questionable production values to serve those immediate needs. I left Testing the Limits.

Artery: What year was this?

Bordowitz: I think it was in '88. At the time leaving the group was perfect for me. I had just tested positive and I was very interested in what was immediately at hand. I wasn't making long term plans. And I was very addled around money management in my own life. The responsibility of carrying my own rent seemed daunting enough without taking on the fiscal responsibility required of a non-profit organization. Testing the Limits went on to become a respected and fundable organization and eventually produced the very fine, significant documentary *Voices From The Front*. Looking back now both positions—creating a fundable organization and making guerrilla television—were legitimate and absolutely necessary responses to the needs of that moment. Neither one was right or wrong.

Artery: What about DIVA [Damned Interfering Video Activists] TV?

Bordowitz: A large number of videomakers—including Jean Carlomusto, Catherine Gund, Ellen Spiro, Ray Navarro, Peter Bowen, Bob Beck, Steven Zabel, Costa Papas, George Plaggianos, Rob Kurilla and many, many others—formed DIVA in 1989. It was an affinity group of ACT UP devoted to documenting ACT UP's efforts. We sometimes had as many as ten of us covering actions. This did two things: It ensured that activists were producing our own versions of the events; taking ownership of our own history. Very important. And video cameras are also very useful deterrents against police violence.

Damned Interfering Video Activists was organized within a much looser participatory framework than Testing the Limits. DIVA was an open group, organized along an anarchistic, almost syndicalist model of operation. People contributed whatever they could in terms of labor and time. The experienced videomakers trained the inexperienced members. The group was as large as 40 or 50 people at one time. We received some money from ACT UP—all of it went into tape stock which was free to any DIVA member to document ACT UP actions. The availability of cheap consumer video equipment like Hi-8 cameras provided access to the means of production. Enough of us had cameras to create a pool of equipment. Jean Carlomusto and I were working together at GMHC where we had access to editing facilities. A number of others in the group had access to facilities elsewhere.

Artery: How did your partnership with Jean Carlomusto to produce *Living With AIDS* for GMHC come about?

Bordowitz: I met Jean after the first ACT UP protest on Wall Street. David Meieran and I had gone to document the action. We met Jean who was there documenting it for the *Living With AIDS* cable show, which she'd originated for GMHC. Something went wrong with our camera so we called Jean to see if we could use some of her footage. That's how I met Jean. I was hired in 1988 at GMHC and co-produced the cable show with Jean until 1993.

Artery: What sort of reach did the show have?

Bordowitz: With cable you never have hard numbers but you can count on an average of 3000 people catching the show as they surf the dial. There was also a specialty audience of people with AIDS and those who supported us in New York City, which was the epicenter of the epidemic in the U.S.. For many of the works, the show wasn't the final destination. They also circulated through distribution to other AIDS agencies and through the art world.

Artery: Did this activist work get much respect from the mainstream art world?

Bordowitz: To some extent. Galleries and museums showed the work but that wasn't our priority. As an activist one wants one's work shown everywhere, to as many different audiences as possible. The tapes served as educational tools. The art world needed to be educated about AIDS, just like any other audience.

Artery: Have the *Living With AIDS* tapes been collected by the Museum of the Moving Image or the Museum of Broadcasting?

Bordowitz: The New York Public Library has the GMHC collection and the Museum of Modern Art has selected shows.

Artery: Are you involved with the Estate Project's collaboration with the New York Public Library to preserve and archive activist AIDS video?

Bordowitz: Yes, I've donated my tapes to the library.

Artery: *Fast Trip, Long Drop* is a montage of staged and documentary footage. Your subjectivity is foregrounded and you presented what is in part a not-very politically correct amalgam of anger, pessimism and weariness. What was the response like?

Bordowitz: *Fast Trip, Long Drop* was very well received, which surprised me because it is very dark and pessimistic. It was made at a very low point. Video activists were rethinking the previous few years' of work. We had exhausted our strategies, which had been limited to showing positive images of people with AIDS "surviving and thriving." These strategies were legitimate responses to the overwhelmingly prejudicial representations of people with AIDS generated by the commercial media. But by the early 90s, People with AIDS and folks in the communities hardest hit by AIDS needed something else. As a PWA, I needed something else. I needed to openly confront the despair, the hopelessness and the burn out. In '92 I lost someone very dear to me, my friend Ray Navarro. That affected me more deeply than any other of the many losses I had experienced thus far.

Artery: That was also the time of the Berlin AIDS conference.

Bordowitz: Yes, around that same time. Doctors there announced to the world that no cure was on the horizon. (This was before the new treatments became available. Not that protease inhibitors are the cure.) I believe very strongly in the legitimating power of television and media, so it was important to me that a work be produced that addressed the complexity of the AIDS crisis from the point of view of a person with AIDS directly addressing people with AIDS.

Fast Trip, Long Drop shows something no other AIDS doc had shown—a group of people talking amongst themselves about our coming to terms with the possibilities of our deaths. When I made

Fast Trip, Long Drop I was tired of pretending for the sake of others that I would survive. I became preoccupied with the burdens that sick people bear on behalf of those around them who are well. I wanted to get a handle on despair and put it out there as a political problem. To be recognized and discussed. If we couldn't do this, then it all seemed like bullshit. I wanted an honest media produced in the interests of people living with AIDS.

Artery: That's your bottom line, isn't it?

Bordowitz: Yes. *Fast Trip, Long Drop* not only showed people with AIDS coping with the disease, it presumed an audience of people with AIDS. The overwhelming majority of AIDS media up until that point presumed a straight audience of HIV negative people who were threatened by queers and junkies. We were never recognized as members of the general public. The "general public" is a fiction. It's a group of people organized as consumers. Today people with AIDS have been welcomed as consumers by the pharmaceutical industry, which is making huge profits by selling AIDS care to those who can afford it.

It comes as no surprise that we, people with AIDS, became legitimate, credit-card-carrying members of the general public after the appearance of products to sell to us. People With AIDS were scapegoats, then we became a community and now we're a marketing demographic.

Artery: Jean Carlomusto has observed that the documentary footage of demos and actions that was once energizing, is now a source of sadness, a record of images of once-healthy or living comrades. Do you agree with this appraisal?

Bordowitz: Yes, of course I agree with Jean.

Artery: What are activist arenas today?

Bordowitz: AIDS has become an accepted and tolerated ill of society, like homelessness, poverty and cancer. The activist arenas are limited to small group efforts like the Treatment Action Group that still hold the government research efforts and pharmaceutical companies accountable to People with HIV. The AIDS activist movement was a site of conflict, a struggle for power, but it is no longer a vital movement for social change. The AIDS activist movement was the catalyst for the national discussion on health care in the 90s. We were very successful at many things but we were not able to solve the fundamental problem of American healthcare: if you can afford medical care and treatment you'll live longer. If you can't, you'll die. That's the simple truth about AIDS and it's true in the U.S. for many diseases. It's true about AIDS all over the world. That's the big picture. People in situations of crushing poverty in Africa, Asia, Latin America, Eastern Europe—the world over—have little or no access to fundamental healthcare. In European countries and industrialized countries with socialized medicine there are different issues of access but gross inequities exist everywhere.

Artery: In *Fast Trip, Long Drop*, you revealed an enormous amount about yourself: your drinking, your father who deserted you, your unsafe sex of the mid-80s, issues about intimacy and loneliness. What effect did those revelations have on you? And your quest to be the "protagonist of [your] own story"?

Bordowitz: I'm not a confessional artist. I used my own life as material to connect with a larger audience of people. I believed that if those experiences were happening to me, they were happening to a lot people. I didn't and still don't think the experiences I talk about in *Fast Trip* are special or unique. Isn't that the point of coming out? To identify with a common struggle? A common story? So, I included those bits of personal history as a way to tell a story shared by many.

Artery: In *Fast Trip, Long Drop* there are lots of mostly musical references to Judaism. What role does Judaism play in your life?

Bordowitz: My Jewishness was my first experience of otherness in the world. That's why it is mostly represented by the klezmer music on the soundtrack, brilliantly scored and beautifully played by the Klezmatics. Jewishness was the background against which I came to understand queerness and otherness in general. The figure of the person with AIDS was constructed as "other" in the same ways as Jews, people of color, queers, outcasts, etc. have been historically. Prejudice is a corrupt kind of logic, a kind of sick machine that enforces normalcy and profits by it at the expense of diversity and difference. Normalcy is ultimately a fiction like the general public.

Artery: You've worked in both video and film. Do you prefer one medium over another?

Bordowitz: *Fast Trip, Long Drop* was made entirely in video with the exception of the appropriated historical footage, which was originally shot on film. I transferred *Fast Trip, Long Drop* to 16mm film so it could be distributed to film festivals and film theaters, which it was. It also showed on television. I don't prefer film over video, or vice-versa.

I'm not interested in the question of medium. I'm only interested in the question of distribution. Neither "cinema" nor "television" have integrity as separate categories anymore. I don't see why alternative media artists have to pretend that it matters whether they produce an image on a strip of plastic or magnetic tape. Given total freedom of choice—which I have never enjoyed nor expect to have in the near future—I prefer to shoot on film, edit on tape and have the end product broadcast on TV and distributed in theaters.

Ultimately the most important issue for any artist is the set of ideas behind the work. I believe that the ideas behind the work should be much larger than any one medium can contain.

Artery: Can you talk about your most recent films, *The Suicide"* and *A Cloud in Trousers*?

Bordowitz: *The Suicide* and *A Cloud In Trousers* were attempts to address AIDS using already existing texts. Addressing issues of survival more obliquely than I did using methods of documentary.

A Cloud In Trousers is based on a poem by the Soviet poet Vladimir Mayakovsky. The poem was written in 1916. It's a simple film, one actor—David Rakoff playing Mayakovsky—shot in a black box, with a few props. It's a figure study really. It was the first time I worked with a cinematographer—Ellen Kuras. I was also interested in concentrating on directing an actor and working in a focused way with one long text that required a sustained level of intensity. The poem is about the conflict between political commitments and personal commitments, between contending commitments of the heart.

I identified with that conflict. During the years of non-stop, full-time AIDS activism and the media work that resulted from that, I often wondered about the place of my own subjective concerns within my practice. *Fast Trip* came out of that conflict. I was interested in exploring it further with the Mayakovsky piece.

Artery: Is resolution possible?

Bordowitz: I don't think there exists a resolution to the conflict between internal concerns and external concerns, between subjectivity and objectivity. I think the two remain in dynamic and productive tension and its more interesting to bring the inside out and the outside in, as Gertrude Stein suggested.

Artery: What about *The Suicide*?

Bordowitz: *The Suicide* followed *A Cloud In Trousers*. It's a movie based on the play, *The Suicide*, written in 1928 by playwright Nicolai Erdman. It holds an infamous place in Soviet theater history because Stalin banned it and its rehearsal was the official reason for closing down Meyerhold's theater. It's a painfully funny play. It concerns an unemployed man named Semyon who threatens to kill himself because he has no livelihood. When word gets out through gossipy neighbors that he's threatened suicide, representatives of various interests approach him and ask him to kill himself in their name. An intellectual asks him to kill himself in the name of the Russian intelligentsia. A romantic asks him to kill himself for love. A butcher asks him to kill himself over the high price of meat. No one tries to save him.

Artery: So it's an AIDS allegory?

Bordowitz: For me the play was a good vehicle to explore issues surrounding the burdens placed on "victims" by society. People with AIDS were held responsible for burdens on the health care system. We were blamed for the collapse of the nation's moral order. We placed burdens on the legal system. We ruined sex. We were a blank wall upon which many ills could be projected according to the cynical interests of various parties.

People with AIDS were also made the subjects of fantasies from within the AIDS movement. We were turned into angels and heroes.

And so Semyon, the main character of *The Suicide* who is an unemployed man in a society promising full employment, a man without a purpose, becomes a martyr to many causes. In the end he refuses to kill himself and he declares that he wants to live. In his final monologue at his own funeral, Semyon begs everyone to allow him to live.

Artery: What a fantastic image!

Bordowitz: The character in the play, Semyon, was a man who'd seen the revolution and expected to benefit from it. Instead he finds that he has no place in the future society. I identified with that. It's willful on my part, but I saw Semyon as a person with AIDS. A person whose suffering was turned into a political football. And it's a post-protease inhibitor work. My interest in the play and mining it for its allegorical content had to do with the possibility of living much longer than I had expected. I'm still dealing with these issues in my work. I'm finding it very difficult to relax into the uncertainty of that situation. There's a level of spirituality, a kind of serenity that continues to elude me.

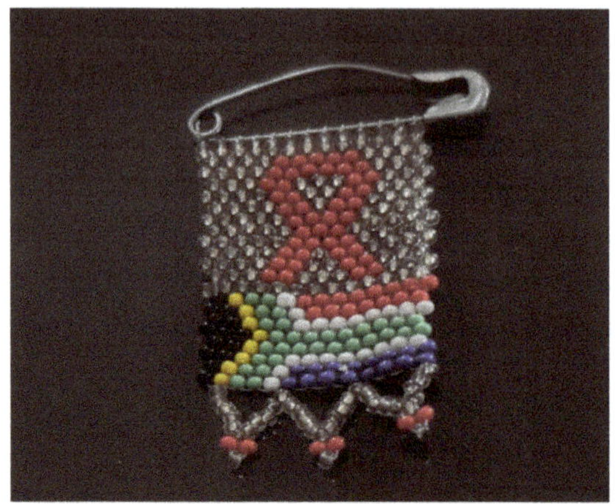

How to Have Art (Events) in an Epidemic: A History of Visual AIDS from *Day Without Art* to the *Red Ribbon* project

*An address delivered at the School of the Art Institute of Chicago on December 1, 1992 and adapted for the book **Disrupted Borders**, edited by Sunil Gupta, River Orams Press, London, 1993*

Visual AIDS formally appeared in the fall of 1988. It was preceded by perhaps six month of informal and sporadic discussions among four gay white men: myself, William Olander (the now deceased, New Museum of Contemporary Art curator), Thomas Sokolowski (the director of New York University's Grey Art Gallery) and Garry Garrels (formerly of the DIA Foundation, and now the Walker Art Center). Between us we'd volunteered and buddied at the Gay Men's Health Crisis, ACTed UP, raised funds for Art Against AIDS, and would continue to do some of these things after 1989. As curators and critics, we were also tracking a growing body of artwork about AIDS and trying to give it visibility.

On 1 March 1989, Visual AIDS issued its first press release, signed by 35 multi-cultural representatives of New York art organizations, museums, and AIDS-service organizations. Entitled *Visual AIDS: The Art World Organizes*, the initial, stated goals were modest, but they laid the foundations for the future. 'Our purpose', we wrote, 'is to support an ongoing effort...to encourage, facilitate, and highlight AIDS-related exhibitions and programs in the non-commercial art world...We hope to increase awareness and encourage discussion of these programs and the pressing social issues that AIDS raises within American society.' We created a slide archive and began to network. That press release ends by noting that: 'an idea involving a moratorium has been proposed to about thirty organizations. [It is] tentatively called *A Day Without Art*.'

Visual AIDS's propensity to stimulate debate occurred a month before *A Day Without Art*. On 8 November 1989, the then-new National Endowment for the Arts Chairman John Frohnmayer inadvertently kicked off *Day Without Art* when he announced that he was rescinding a grant to Artists Space for *Witnesses: Against Our Vanishing*, the AIDS exhibition organized by artist Nan Goldin for *Day Without Art*. Both censorship and AIDS awareness became issues in this tense stand-off between progressive elements of the art communities and Frohnmayer, who was then busily cozying up to reactionary Senator Jesse Helms.

Because the show was conceived for *Day Without Art*, Visual AIIDS found itself well positioned to intervene. After a concerted lobbying effort, Frohnmayer agreed to hold a December 1 meeting organized by Visual AIDS that would include HIV positive artists. The meeting resulted in the revitalization of the AIDS Working Group within the federal agency and NEA directives to its organizational mailing lists about compliance with the Disabilities Act and treatment of HIV-positive staff. It also spurred some ultimately fruitless work by the NEA regarding health insurance reform.

Because Visual AIDS straddled both the AIDS and art worlds, we began to function as a forum, a meeting place for emerging art-AIDS coalitions. We participated in the NEA's 1991 forum on AIDS and again insisted that artists with AIDS be included. We hosted the NEA's 1992 meeting of funders and art professionals that led to the recommendation to implement the second phase of the Estate Project designed to assist artists with AIDS. In 1991, we organized the World AIDS Day Coalition for the World Health Organization and a spectrum of AIDS organizations, although we ultimately felt that the participants saw us only as a vehicle for generating media attention. And of course we worked with the Coalition United for AIDS Action, which organized the AIDS demonstration and rally during the 1992 Democratic National Convention in New York.

Visual AIDS received the New York Governor's Art Award for the first *Day Without Art*. At the black-tie award ceremony at the Metropolitan Museum in June 1990, our acceptor, Philip Yenawine, took the opportunity to chide Governor Cuomo for his lackadaisical approach to the AIDS crisis. At that time, we were also feeling organizational growing pains. Our structure had been democratic-anarchic: we had a steering committee and a meeting chairperson but no officers. Nor were we being offered foundation money. The second *Day Without Art* approached and overwhelmed us as thoroughly as the first had. Our organizational circle had grown so large that producing more than a couple of mailings each year had become prohibitively costly. In 1990, we urged participating organizations to get beyond the 'art ghettos' and out into varied communities. Urging was all we've ever been able to do and unfortunately it's usually hard to know what effect urging has.

Day Without Art 1990 signified a radical shift within the group. Our artist population increased substantially. This made us a livelier, more spirited bunch, but it sometimes gave us less access to useful contacts and our organization constituents. Ideas remained our currency and in 1990 we began producing them at a rapid clip. The boundaries between programs and programmatic artwork began to blur. We operated like an art collective. A half-dozen new projects sprang up: *Positive Actions: the Visual AIDS Competition* was a competition for a temporary public artwork about AIDS to be funded by the Public Art Fund. Entrants were asked to consider these questions: Can art and design make a difference as friends and colleagues confront HIV infection? What can we do as artists and citizens in the public arena to inform, move, inspire, and/or provoke audiences? What sort of physical, social, or political sites would be appropriate for a work about AIDS?

The 'Editors' Project' was a way of getting the normally not very receptive art magazines to do more about AIDS. Ranging from *After Image* to *Artforum*, and from *Contemporanea* to *Shift*, eleven of them published different fragments of Group Material's AIDS Timeline in their December issues. 'Night Without Light' saw the skylines of New York and San Francisco darkened for fifteen minutes and this symbolic observance was repeated throughout the U.S. in 1991 and 1992.

Another project that debuted on 1 December 1990, was the *Electric Blanket*, an outdoor slide-projection event. Information and statistics about AIDS and photo-images of PWAs were projected onto the side of the Cooper Union in the East Village while bands played. Most of the pictures had been gathered in the neighborhood, making this a very local tribute. *The Electric Blanket* has been exhibited inside or outside art spaces from Seattle to Hamburg. It continues to travel and is augmented as often as possible with local images.

Perhaps the 1990 project with the most audience reach was Bravo cable network's *Moment Without Television*, followed by 48 hours of continuous AIDS programming. Bravo's groundbreaking work continues for its third year and inspired PBS and MTV to follow suit.

Visual AIDS has initiated other artists' programs, but I want to turn to one other Visual AIDS-instigated project that's not specifically connected only with *Day Without Art*. It's quite misunderstood and underestimated and its subversive character is also emblematic of the way Visual AIDS has operated. *The Ribbon Project* is what our trademark reads but most people think of it simply as *The Red Ribbon*.

The red ribbon debuted on the televised Tony Award Ceremonies in late Spring 1991, and now you can't turn on the television without seeing them sited on lapels practically everywhere. We knew how subversive the ribbon was, when—a full 15 months after its creation—Republican handlers ripped it off Barbara Bush's jacket at the 1992 Republican convention in Houston. The ribbon has enabled writers who do think and talk about AIDS to write about it. *New York Newsday* ran an article titled 'Red Ribbon to AIDS Kindness' on 6 October 1992, about the apparently red ribbon-strewn Miss America pageant. Bear in mind that the ribbon is hardly news any more. In fact, one might assume that the ribbon is simply mandatory accessorizing at any television event or one might alternately assume that it continues to symbolize AIDS-concern, or both. Certainly people wear ribbons for the 'wrong' reasons, just as some people wore Silence=Death buttons for a variety of reasons (sometimes only in order to get laid). All the same, I am convinced that the red ribbon never deterred anybody from doing something more meaningful to end the AIDS crisis.

In any case, I did learn from 'The Red Ribbon to AIDS Kindness' article that the new Miss America volunteers in an AIDS hospice, doesn't believe that the Bush-Quayles have done enough to combat the epidemic, and plans to continue to talk publicly about AIDS during her reign. The author ended his column with a stirring denunciation of AIDS-phobia and homophobia. It's unclear to me whether Miss America's or the writer's comments would have appeared before the advent—or onslaught?—of the ribbon.

If I've given you the impression that Visual AIDS is largely a sum of its project parts, that's probably not inaccurate. This organizational umbrella-of-a-structure has made it easier to respond to quickly changing AIDS- and media realities. Certainly the one thing we have learned from AIDS-work is that AIDS crises are dynamic. What was needed or useful yesterday is irrelevant or passe today. The *ad hoc* nature of the group has also allowed for a membership where satisfaction derives from working on a project, rather than simply belonging to an organization in which 'membership' is, frankly, a *non-sequitur*. Visual AIDS faces what every AIDS organization faces: Burn out and the illness of many of our most active members. We also face changes in the art world—some of them positive. Over the past few years there's been an attitudinal sea change in the acceptance of tough, AIDS-related content in exhibited artwork. Such works remind us that art's traditional purpose is to teach. And that the anti-didacticism of so much late modernist art is really an anomaly, an exception in Western art's thousand-years'-long history. Effective, socially-engaged art practices can help save lives. But only if large and vocal elements within arts communities work to ensure their broadest possible reach. Silence does equal death.

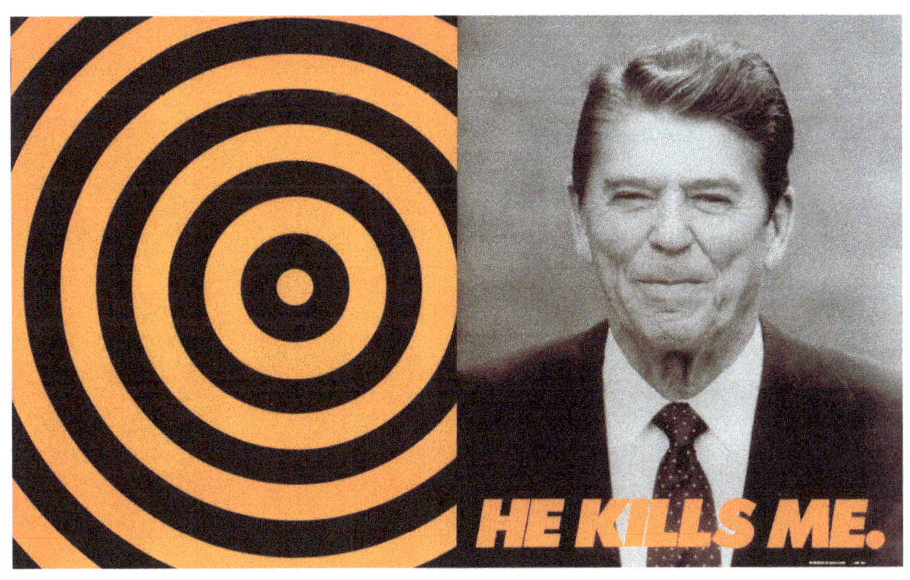

Donald Moffett: AIDS Awareness poster (1986)

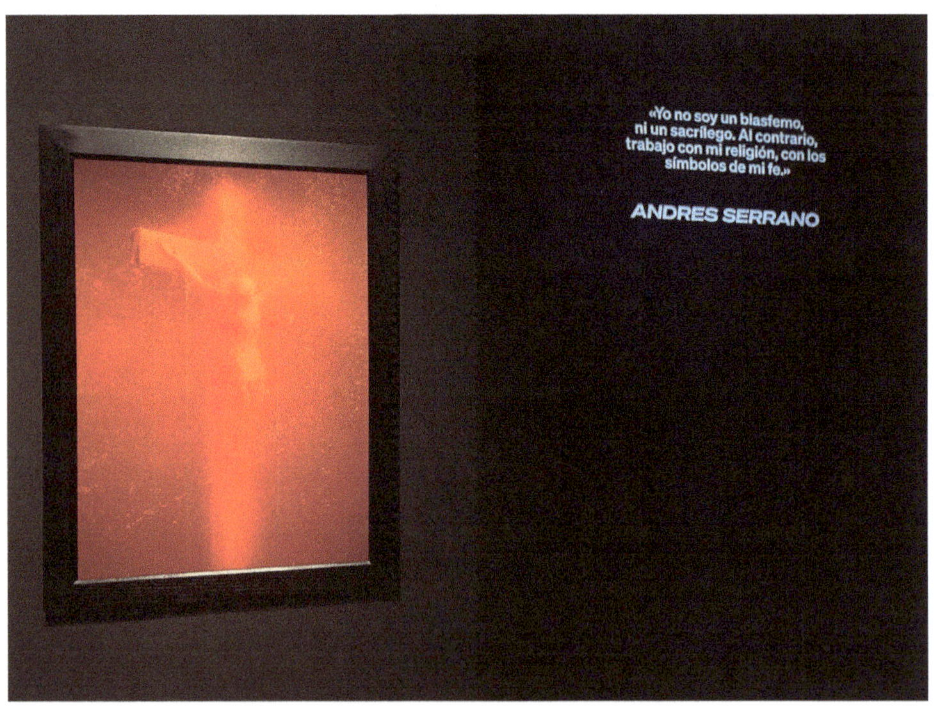

Andres Serrano, Immersion (Piss Christ) (1987)

PART THREE

Making Sense of Censorship

These days too many films require legal defense funds. At a benefit for the BBC documentary Damned in the USA on October 12 [1992], Lou Reed sang a custom version of "Take a Walk on the Wild Side" inspired by the sanctimonious head of the America Family Association. "Take a Walk on the Wildmon" goes like this: "Donald Wildmon was damned in the USA/Tried to get Channel 4 to pay and pay...And the fundamentalists said 'sue, sue, sue"

Robert Atkins, *Village Voice*, November 10, 1992

Introduction to *Censoring Culture: Contemporary Threats to Free Expression*, New Press, NY, 2006
With Svetlana Mintcheva

Censorship in Camouflage

Censorship has always been a dirty word. (It derives from the Latin for "census taker" or "tax collector," designating one of the most reviled citizens of the Roman Empire.) In the legal sense, censorship is the governmental suppression of speech. In a broader sense, it refers to private institutions or individuals doing the same thing, suppressing content they find undesirable. The difference is that the former is prohibited in the U.S. by the First Amendment to the Constitution and the latter is not. Regardless of its legality, however, censorship is unpopular. The classic image of the censor depicts a narrow-minded and prudish bureaucrat blind to the transcendent flights of the imagination we call art, brandishing his red pen or her stamp and inkpad with perverse pleasure. This portrayal renders the censor as the very opposite of the creative artist. But censorship often operates more subtly that that, sometimes disguised as a moral imperative, at other times presented as something structural: an inevitable result of the impartial logic of the free market. No matter how it may be camouflaged, however, the result is the same: the range of what we can say, see, hear, think, and even imagine is narrowed.

Of the many debates about censorship in recent memory, not one has opened with a public official saying, "Let's censor this." On the contrary, the standard initial talking point is "This is not censorship, we do not censor," followed by "We need to be sensitive to community standards"; "We need to protect children who might see this"; "We can't spend taxpayers' money to support work that might offend"; or "We don't consider this censorship at all because you are free to exhibit your art work elsewhere." The censor's current disguises of choice are the moral imperatives of "protecting children" and of exercising "respect for religious and cultural beliefs and sensitivities"—both in themselves, laudable objectives and for this reason, perfect disguises for other, less savory motives.

A discussion of censorship that only takes into account attempts to repress existing works, however, misses all those works that never came to life; perhaps because this novel didn't seem sufficiently commercial, there was no chance of it being published, or perhaps, because that play might have offended somebody, the playwright censored himself at the outset and decided not to write it at all.

Censoring Culture expands the notion of censorship beyond the acts of removing a photograph from an exhibition or canceling a live performance to include a much larger field of social conditions and practices that prevent artists' works of all kinds from reaching audiences or even being produced. The narrow collecting purview of a museum, for instance, might be irremediably problematic for contemporary painters if no museum in their region collects works by living artists. Or, consider the moderately successful, mid-career writer: although her books have earned back her publisher's investments at certain houses, her agents may be ignored given the all-consuming editorial quest for the Big Book. Finally, the temporal extension of intellectual property rights practically prohibits American artists from working with images from the cultural vernacular of their day, such as Barbie and Ken or Batman and Robin. In few of these cases did somebody make a conscious order to frustrate or limit artists' opportunities for expression. Nonetheless, within these situations, we see constraints on creativity and access to needed cultural materials. Such limitations both impoverish our culture and undermine out shared ideal of freedom.

The central goal of *Censoring Culture* is the expansion of the very notion of censorship. The specific disguises, mechanisms, and systemic factors that are discussed within the book—with the exception of the Internet—all predate the culture wars of the 1980s and 1990s. We make no claim to identifying entirely new phenomena. The fact that a phenomenon has been recognized, however, does not mean that it is sufficiently, or well, explored.

The dire effects on free expression of corporate consolidation, especially in the media for example, have been widely noted. The self-defeating extremes of political correctness have been subject to hard criticism. (They are often dismissed as the whining of political "others.") The subtle but powerful force of self-censorship, on the other hand, remains little discussed or understood—although its ubiquity in totalitarian societies, and familiarity to artists and writers in every society, is hardly a secret.

Censoring Culture broadens the debate about culture and free expression by assembling existing contributions into a larger, overarching composition, and by exposing the mechanism that limit free speech today as part of a complex system of economic, political, cultural and/or social arrangements. Although the effects of corporate consolidation are most visible in the communications and publishing industries, they are also present in every other aspect of cultural production. Political correctness, though often ridiculed by the right, is similarly invoked by the right and the left to silence unorthodox speech rather than to engage with it.

We have brought together material in a variety of formats ranging from interviews to round-table discussions and from diary entries to analytical essays. When existing analysis was insufficient, as with self-censorship, we have commissioned essays or conducted interviews with key authorities in the relevant fields. When the views of involved groups as stakeholders were underrepresented, we invited them to speak: a roundtable with teens, for instance, offers an essential reality check for adults who would ban a book from a school library before reading it, much less considering the concerns of the young people they are trying to "protect." Each of the collected pieces touches on one (or more) of a range of sometimes seemingly unrelated issues that affect, directly or indirectly, cultural production and distribution. A number of the writings in this collection do not directly refer to censorship. Nevertheless, within this context they reveal the multiple pressures—social, economic, legal and/or personal—that lead to the shuttering of an exhibition or the decision not to publish potentially controversial material about a particular subject.

Our approach is based on the simple assumption that, to paraphrase the old saw about quacking ducks, if something results in limiting the range of what can be produced, exhibited, printed, imagined, or thought, we are entirely willing to entertain the idea that this condition or phenomenon is censorship. This includes censorship as we know it—a public official making sure that what goes on public exhibition isn't likely to arouse anybody's concerns about "appropriateness," or other subjective criteria for viewing—and censorship outside of our traditional understanding of this concept.

In general, responses to censorship—whether activist or analytical—have come after the fact. By contrast, *Censoring Culture* examines systemic factors, which are poised to bear upon free speech now or at a future moment; that is, it identifies the conditions that present the potential for censorship. This is especially true of new technologies: just as the Internet promised the unfettered exchange of ideas, copyright laws quickly threatened the Net's potential for the uncensored dissemination of ideas. The ability to identify and address systemic factors prior to overt incidents of censorship suggests the possibility of a proactive approach based on dealing directly with the structural conditions that ensure future censorship.

Censorship has generated considerable attention in recent years primarily because of interest in the issues raised by the recent, arts-oriented phase of the American "Culture Wars." Discussions about the controversy surrounding Robert Mapplethorpe's *Perfect Moment* retrospective or Andres Serrano's photograph *Piss Christ* often focused on the divisive question that fueled the Culture Wars: "Why should so-called average taxpayers fund art that offends them?" *Censoring Culture* is an effort to get beyond not only this public-funding tug of war, but also beyond the very notion of a "culture war." The problem with the media-driven concept of a "culture war" is that, rather than simply describing a state of affairs, it helps perpetuate an image of a nation in combat, one divided by radically opposed views. And not insignificantly, it diverts the political conversation from class and race to values, moral codes, and lifestyles.

The concept of a culture war creates the illusion of millions of cultural warriors at the ready, muskets—or at least PCs—in hand. This illusion helps magnify the thousands-strong campaigns organized by special interest groups into actions that seemingly represent the views of millions. Although the issues might change, the strategy of creating controversy in order to mobilize a constituency is standard operating procedure for many activist groups. Once the National Endowment for the Arts (NEA), a focal point of emotion in the 1990s, stopped funding individual artists or controversial projects, right-wing groups returned to another perennially popular call to arms, "decency on the airwaves." As ever, pundits and politicians can be counted on to exploit—and exaggerate—such cultural fissures. To re-enter the realm of reality, the vast majority of Americans do not, in fact, subscribe to the mediagenic, imaginary extremes of the so-called culture wars: they hold judiciously moderate positions. As the texts collected in *Censoring Culture* demonstrate, censorship today is a result of multiple facts, none of them directly related to a cultural rift at the heart of America.

Censoring Culture is divided into five parts that progress from background to foreground, from the systemic and institutional to the personal. The first two parts offer portraits of our era of triumphant corporate capitalism—especially its twenty-first century variant headquartered in Silicon Valley—and their effects on contemporary expression. The next two sections interrogate, analyze, and deconstruct the disguises behind which today's censor often operates: the moral imperative of protecting children from "inappropriate" material, exploitation, or molestation; and the imperative of demonstrating respect and sensitivity toward the beliefs of a diverse population. Together the four parts comprise a multifaceted portrait of the conditions and institutions, attitudes and behaviors that limit expression in the varied precincts of cultural life. *Censoring Culture* concludes with material devoted to what is most likely the most important and least understood topic under consideration—self censorship. This is the point where public and private, economics and psychology, social sensitivities and political repression, intersect. It is also the point where censorship becomes invisible.

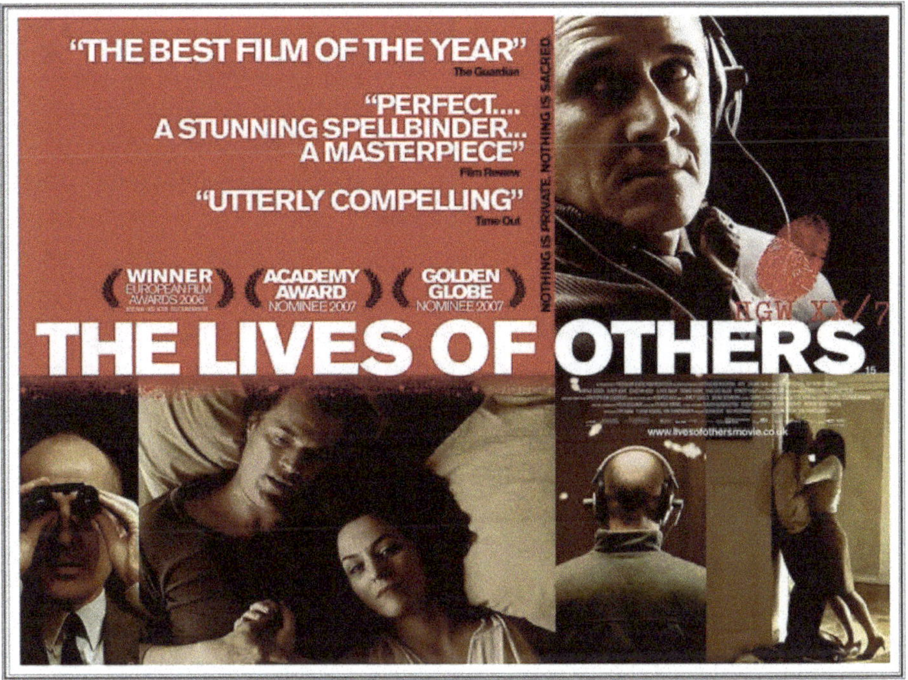

The Lives of Others (2006) the Oscar-winning German film is both a political thriller and an eye opening look at life in the former East Germany. To maintain order, neighbors were encouraged to spy on one another and, in the process, internalize Communist party edicts. The result was the transformation of citizens into (unpaid) Stasi, or secret police deputies and reliable enforcers of the rules,

Contrary to what opponents of public funding in the arts claim, the salvation of free speech is not likely to be found in the marketplace. In fact, possibly the largest threat to free expression comes from the widening influence of corporations. Fewer, larger corporations now wield multinational influence, sharply contrasting with the national reach of previous generations of big business. During the past decade and a half we have seen an unprecedented amount of consolidation within all branches of cultural production. This process of consolidation has frequently resulted in de-facto monopolistic control. Although more books are published than ever, more films are released, and more cable channels seem to go online weekly, quantity should not be confused with diversity, much less quality. Although this anthology focuses on consolidations within the book publishing industry, similar developments affect—and afflict—virtually every other medium.

The pressure corporations exert on expression is also felt in recent, aggressive moves for entertainment and media companies to impose their ownership on material that, by all rights, is of our shared cultural heritage. Congress has supported this power grab by repeatedly extending the duration of the period of copyright invariably at the behest of entertainment industry giants such as the Walt Disney Company. But what is a gift to copyright owners is an impediment to the public-at-large, some segment of which is undoubtedly eager to see Mickey Mouse enter the public domain.

In recent years corporations have sued, or threatened to sue, numerous artists for violating copyright or ignoring trademarks. To cite one typical example, Mattel sued a book publisher, a record company, and a photographer for using image of its Barbie doll without permission. Mattel ultimately lost all three cases, but the mere threat of extraordinarily expensive litigation with an unpredictable outcome is likely to discourage anyone from continuing to use such material in their work or asserting their rights under copyright law's fair use provision. (Chanel, unlike Mattel, has tended to win suits against artists for trademark violation.) Ironically, this trend toward stricter control of copyrighted material flies in the face of contemporary artistic methods. Postmodern approaches such as "sampling" in music or "appropriation" in art both rely on the strategic use of already existing material to comment about contemporary matters.

For a while it appeared that the Internet was the answer to corporate domination of cultural production. It made low-cost publishing available to anyone with a computer and an online connection; it revolutionized access to international news, independently produced music, activist networks, and nonmainstream art works. Best of all, the rhizomatic structure of the Internet made top-down control impossible. However, and somewhat predictably, the Internet's expansion has been paralleled by expanded legal efforts to regulate content.

These efforts are provoked by both economic and moral motives. Economic concerns have arisen from the ease of disseminating copyrighted material online. Endless rounds of litigation over music file-sharing for noncommercial purposes eventually reached the Supreme Court and essentially put home-grown companies like Napster and Grokster out of business. The morality-derived category of issues ostensibly aims to "protect" children from age-inappropriate material or from pornographers lurking in the chat rooms. Instead, these laws have been effective in restricting access by viewers of all ages—especially low-income adults—to constitutionally-protected entertainment and sex sites, as well as sites featuring educational and health information.

Government legislation is not the only problem facing the new medium. The Internet's potentially universal accessibility inevitably clashes with local laws and customs. If a French court could effectively prevent an American Internet Service Provider (Yahoo!) from hosting sites containing hate speech, a Chinese court might well try to suppress information about the Tiananmen Square massacre. It is possible that new and relaxed international regulations will come into play soon, but it is crucial to be aware of the nature of the Internet as contested turf; the conflicts may variously center on the regulation of speech, the ownership of this virtual "real estate," or the possibility of near-monopoly control of bandwidth by large corporations.

Protecting children, one of the rationales for government regulation of the Internet, is also the most convenient disguise under the impulse to control speech operates in general. Children—a king-size blanket term covering the range from toddlers barely able to walk to seventeen-year-olds on the verge of enlisting in the military—are rarely allowed to speak for themselves or, when they are, hardly ever regarded as credible witnesses. Transformed instead into blank slates for the projection of adult fears and prejudices, children provide an effective pretext for banning the display of nudes, installing filters on computers in public libraries, or censoring TV broadcasts. The evocation of an innocent child is so politically potent that the lack of credible evidence to back up the claims that sexually oriented material harms children is almost beside the point.

The moral panic accumulating around childhood sexuality has created collateral damage—perhaps most unjustly affecting those mothers who have innocently taken pictures of their naked kids, only to find themselves criminal suspects. Public officials, including police officers, prosecutors, and judges, are mandated to examine photographs of children with a focus on whether these images might appeal to a pedophile, and whether they might constitute evidence of child abuse. Because federal child pornography law makes no exceptions for writers, scholars, physicians, or journalists researching the traffic in sexually explicit images of children, those undertaking such investigations are themselves subject to prosecution. As a result, the only way to gauge the extent of sexual abuse of children in the production of child pornography is to examine court records, which show little evidence of a rampant problem. This conclusion is seconded by sociologists, who have found that most incidents of child abuse are not sexual. Needless to say, the problems most affecting children—poverty, the state of public education, a lack of health care and, in too many cases, parental neglect—have nothing to do with pedophiles. Hunting for them among middle-class mothers, banning drawn or photographed nudes in public exhibition spaces, or bleeping four-letter words from TV broadcasts is unlikely to solve any of these problems.

Of the disguises worn by censors to mask their generally frowned-upon activities, respect for religious and cultural sensitivities is nearly as popular as the need to protect children. Taking its cue from the left-leaning cultural-diversity movement active in the 1970s and 1980s, the religious right, a decade later, began vociferously to demand sensitivity and respect for its values. The controversies about Martin Scorsese's film *The Last Temptation of Christ*, Terrence McNally's play *Corpus Christi*, and Chris Ofili's painting *The Holy Virgin Mary,* among many examples, focused less on the allegedly blasphemous nature of the works than on the offended feelings of Catholics, who saw in them the "desecration" of their symbols.

Aggrieved sensitivities are not the exclusive property of the right or left; they span the entire political spectrum. Ethnic and sexual minorities, empowered by a growing respect for sensitivity toward cultural difference, also grew more public in their complaints about bias in this museum program or that educational curriculum. African American parents called for the removal of *Huckleberry Finn* from schools because of its (historically accurate) use of the term "nigger," while concentration camp survivors called for the cancellation of an exhibition at The Jewish Museum that contained work by an Israeli artist/peacenik/serviceman who approached the Holocaust in unorthodox, critical fashion.

Whose voice matters more? Who is allowed to speak about the painful history of an ethnic, racial, or sexual minority? Does anybody own identity and history? Some questions are so complex they resist resolution. We acknowledge the complexity of such matters, and—in good faith—insist that not every question is answerable. We also assert that the practice of civility and the cultivation of patient listening can transform shouting matches into discussions, enabling everyone involved to actually hear opposing points of view.

The most difficult sort of censorship to analyze—and even recognize—is self-censorship. Self-censorship is the interiorization (conscious or unconscious) of every mechanism and rationale for censorship: it is present when an artist hesitates about creating a work that might disturb viewers or might infringe on copyrighted material; it is operating when a fiction writer decides to purge sexual explicitness from the language of her characters; and it is apparent when museum curators refuse even to consider exhibiting work by artists with politically contentious points of view; fearing that showing such work might lead to losses of support from audiences, public officials and funders. Typically self-censorship remains unrecognized—even by the person or institution guilty of it.

To be sure, it is often very difficult to draw the line between editing—the discriminations and judgments that are at the heart of the creative process—and the realm of self-censorship. To complicate matters further, there are many motives for self-censorship and some are undeniably legitimate. They range from fear of political retribution or financial fallout, to consideration for one's family or community. Self-censorship is so shaming an activity, though, that those who opt to do it in light of one of the "acceptable" just mentioned rationales—that is choosing to self-censor rather than to disgrace the family or to avoid initiating some unpleasant financial outcomes—tend to deny the nature of their actions. In an informal poll we took, we found that nobody wants to admit he/her ever self-censors. Perhaps the single thing we can all agree on about self-censorship is that a more detailed exploration of this uncharted territory is necessary.

Censoring Culture is an unfinished project, an exercise in connecting the dots. We hope that readers will help continue our work by applying some of the methodological signposts we've outlined to their own lives, to the sometimes-difficult-to-detect-habits of the culture at large, and publicly disseminating their findings for the benefit of the rest of us. We hope that *Censoring Culture* might serve as an antidote, however small, to the appalling and disingenuous lip service frequently paid to championing freedom of speech and the gargantuan volume of hot air expended by those among the powers-that-be who, at the same time, seem neither interested in free expression nor in broadening its reach through promotion or policy.

Happily, the conditions described in this book are not immutable. On the contrary, the mechanisms of censorship also provide openings for possibilities for action, innovation and change. The censor's disguises are not impenetrable, either. *Censoring Culture* may help, we hope, to identify some of those openings and possibilities and to provide encouragement for exposing censorship in all its guises. It is time to state the obvious: it is necessary to restore the value in public life, of reasonableness and respect for others, of truth-telling and plain-speaking, and of the freedoms that have previously been broadened and depended by each generation in succession.

If we are to actually confront the social problems at hand, we must face up to some unpleasant realities as part of the process. If are to ameliorate the condition of children, we must initiate a truth-telling campaign that encompasses the sometimes disingenuous meaning of "protecting" children and the unscrupulous manner in which politicians have used children to impose their views of what is "appropriate." If the Internet is to fulfill its potential as a site for community building and a space for genuinely open, noncommercial communication, we must be alert to initiatives to privatize its infrastructure or to control its content. We should also reassess the balance between stimulating creativity (through copyright protections) and stifling creativity (through copyright over-protections). And finally if we wish for a better world for those victimized by historical injustice, we must do more than purge our vocabularies of a dozen unacceptable epithets and deepen—or initiate—efforts to actually improve our fellow citizens' lives.

In an age when representative governments are on the rise worldwide, societies that seem to understand the nature and operation of censorship are surprisingly rare. Tragically, their understanding is all too often a by-product of their experiences with dictatorships. Despite the ignominy of these pasts, their cultivation of present-day liberties reminds us that the very exercise of freedom of expression is both salutary and life affirming. Free expression resembles nothing so much as art, especially through its provision of pleasure. This makes us hopeful about its future.

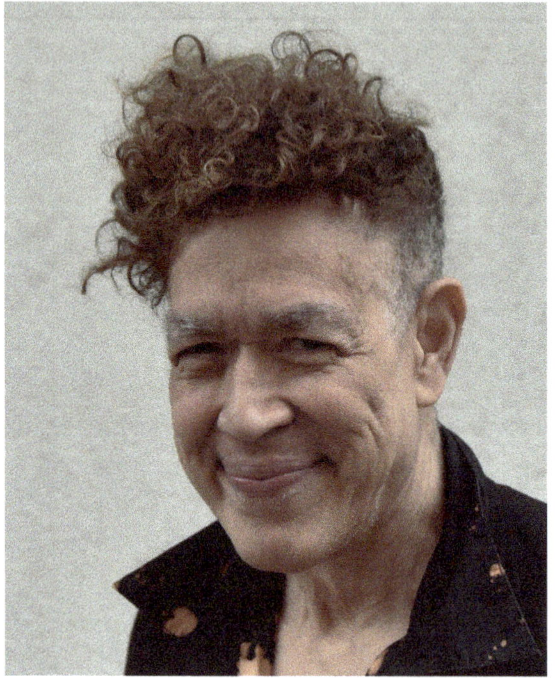

Andres Serrano in 2023

Stream of Conscience: Andres Serrano's 'Piss Christ'

Village Voice, May 30, 1989

"I would never, ever have dreamed that I would live to see such demeaning disrespect and desecration of Christ...Maybe, before the physical persecution of Christians begins, we will gain the courage to stand against such bigotry."

Donald E. Wildmon on Andres Serrano

Donald E. Wildmon is not a beleaguered Christian in first century Rome; he's the executive director of the American Family Association (AFA), the group that organized the boycott of *The Last Temptation of Christ*. The new target of Wildmon's ire is neither the unconventionally reverent biblical blockbuster nor a steamy Madonna video, but *Piss Christ*, a photograph by New York artist Andres Serrano.

Serrano's picture is a 60-by-40-inch cibachrome of a crucifix seen through a swirling haze of bubbly yellow liquid—the artist's own urine. The photograph is one of eight by Serrano in an exhibition called "Awards in the Visual Arts" (a/k/a AVA). The seventh incarnation of a prestigious show sponsored by the Southeastern Center for Contemporary Art, the exhibition was seen at museums in Los Angeles and Pittsburgh last year and ended its tour at the Virginia Museum of Fine Arts in Richmond on January 29. It was in this northernmost outpost of the Bible Belt that the bodily fluids hit the fan.

Sometime after the show closed, AFA (which refused to speak to *The Village Voice* for this article) distributed a statement to its members about Serrano's picture that included the names and some addresses of AVA's sponsors (the Rockefeller Foundation, the Equitable Foundation, the National Endowment for the Arts), and those of the members of the Senate and House of Representatives. By Easter, letters of complaint appeared in the Richmond papers, and arrived at the museum, the sponsoring foundations, and the NEA.

The institutions involved immediately issued statements apologizing for any offense, and all but one—the Equitable Foundation—asserted artists' right to free expression. The most forceful came from Peter Goldmark, president of the Rockefeller Foundation, whose remarks to the Associated Press on April 25 read, in part: "I respect the right of any individual to object to a work of art, and the parallel right of artists to express themselves and of exhibitors to show works that they deem interesting and meritorious artistically." None of the funding institutions has withdrawn support from AVA because of the AFA-fomented brouhaha, although

Equitable will be replaced by BMW as the program's corporate sponsor, as had been announced last year.

The Serrano case is, however, riddled with ironies. The AVA may be the most scrupulously and democratically organized exhibition in the country. Each year 100 art professionals nominate 500 geographically dispersed artists from which 10 are selected by a five-person jury. (AVA 7 was juried by Howard Fox, Donald Kuspit, Howardena Pindell, Ned Rifkin, and Thomas Sokolowski.)

Marcia Tucker, director of the New Museum of Contemporary Art, nominated Serrano. She described him to me as a "terrific artist" and commented that his use of bodily fluids provokes discomfort because it "indicates the extent to which we're unable to deal with our humanity. This is, no doubt, part of the power of Andres's work, to render the sacred secular and vice versa." Tucker's appraisal of the quality of Serrano's work is shared by numerous critics and curators. As Tom Sokolowski, director of NYU's Grey Art Gallery, pointed out, this is "no instance of having to defend third-rate art solely on the basis of the First Amendment."

Even more ironic is the AFA's self-righteous attack on the immorality of Serrano's work. Many of the Tupelo-based, family-run organization's claims about the effectiveness of its actions and boycotts are patently false. Its allegation that Universal lost $10-12 million on *The Last Temptation of Christ* was decisively rebutted in a front page Variety story of November 8, which noted that the picture, in fact, turned a profit. The same article states that "a parallel boycott" of MCA's videocassette release of *E.T.* was accompanied by record-breaking sales. AFA's claims that it persuaded General Mills, Ralston Purina, and Domino's Pizza to drop advertising for *Saturday Night Live* were categorically denied by spokespersons for these companies, as well as by NBC.

Will the Serrano affair be different? It might well have remained just a tempest in a teapot if Congress hadn't gotten involved, which is surely the result of AFA calling attention to the matter. Within the last few weeks, more than 100 members of the House of Representatives have requested information from the NEA about its association with AVA, and Representative Richard

Baker (Republican, Louisiana) inserted a wildly inaccurate and inflammatory statement about the NEA's funding of Serrano's art into the Congressional Record of May 10. An outright assault on the independence of the Endowment itself may be in the making.

In its official response to the Serrano flap, NEA's acting chairman Hugh Southern notes that "the Endowment is expressly forbidden in its authorizing legislation from interfering with the artistic choices made by its grantees." Representative William Dannemeyer (Republican, California) is ready to rewrite that legislation. The archconservative congressman wants "oversight to ensure this doesn't happen again," according to Dannemeyer spokesman Paul Mero. "If it's a choice between leaving the NEA the way it is or not funding it, we'll vote for not funding."

Although it may be too early to forecast the outcome or ramifications of this scandal, it's not too soon to notice the pattern that's emerged. Like the two controversial Chicago artworks of the last year—David Nelson's painting of former mayor Harold Washington in bra and panties, and Dread Scott's mixed media piece that invited viewers to step on the flag—the Serrano situation embodies the current mania for symbol-over-substance epitomized by George Bush flag-pledging himself to electoral victory. Akin to the tepid governmental support Salman Rushdie received for *The Satanic Verses*, no institutionalized support for Serrano has been couched in the relevant language of either "censorship" or the "First Amendment."

Serrano aptly characterized the attacks on his work as "First Amendment double-talk." He wondered how you can "defend my right to make this art, but say that no individual or institution that receives government funds should be allowed to support it...You can't denounce censorship in one breath and demand it in the next."

Not unless you think you have a direct line to god.

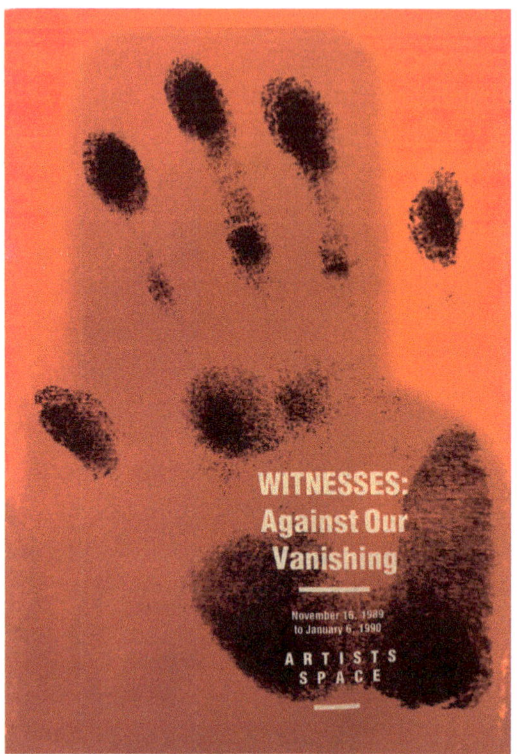

Ultimately the issue behind the NEA-Artists Space conflict over the Witnesses show was reduced to an incendiary catalog essay written by artist, David Wojnarowicz, rather than the exhibition itself.

Black Thursday: Frohnmayer Fiddles, Artists Burn

Village Voice, November 28, 1989 p 31-34

The showdown between the National Endowment for the Arts and the nonprofit Tribeca gallery Artists Space over the exhibition *Witnesses: Against Our Vanishing* ended last Thursday. The suspended NEA grant of $10,000 for the show was restored; funding for the show's catalogue was categorically denied. It was not a victory for the arts community, or for the new NEA chairman John Frohnmayer, or for Senator Jesse Helms, and especially not for David Wojnarowicz, the artist in the eye of the storm.

For eight days, starting with the NEA's November 8 announcement that the grant would be withheld, events have unfolded with the speed and attendant media scrutiny usually reserved for political scandals and Hollywood palimony suits. The Artists Space affair actually began in mid-October, when Artists Space's executive director Susan Wyatt initiated contact with the NEA about the show. Her purpose, she states, was to avoid "embarrassing" the NEA and Artists Space with another Mapplethorpe-like controversy. (Some have characterized this action as self-censorship; others note that until now there's been little reason to regard the NEA as the enemy.) At the outset, she had no intention, she says, of making this exhibition on the theme of AIDS a test of the not-yet-operative "Helms-compromise" amendment outlawing support of "obscenity."

Initially at issue was the text of Wojnarowicz's catalogue essay criticizing Helms, Representative William Dannemeyer, Cardinal O'Connor, and others for their support of policies that ensure the spread of AIDS. Ironically, Wojnarowicz's artworks, which hang in the show, contain similarly pointed texts. Wyatt, sensitive to recent history, says she feared that the catalogue would be misused by the right long after the exhibition had come down.

With the backing of her board of directors, she just said no to Frohnmayer's request to "return" the 1989 grant money, although the contracted check was not yet in the mail. What followed was a series of astonishingly contradictory responses by Frohnmayer (see sidebar, "Quotes From Chairman John"). After calling the show too political, he backed off using what he termed the "P word." Then he found that the exhibition's "artistic focus" had "eroded" and that the catalogue deviated considerably from the one purposed in the grant application. Until November 16, he refused to unlink the catalogue and the exhibition, although Wyatt asserts that NEA program staffer David Bancroft had granted her permission to do so, prior to Frohnmayer's involvement in the matter. Bancroft rebuts this, calling it "Susan's interpretation of our conversation."

Tension peaked at a November 15 press conference at Artists Space. Frohnmayer's hostility toward the catalogue was undiminished and Wyatt's resolve had stiffened. Litigation looked inevitable. But within 24 hours, Frohnmayer's stance shifted. Prior to an early-morning press conference at Artists Space on November 16, a delegation of four local members of the National Council on the Arts (the presidentially appointed, 26-member body that advises the chairman), led by New York State Senator Roy Goodman, toured the exhibition and called Washington to urge Frohnmayer to fund the show. In midafternoon this "good news" was made official.

Like every tempest played out in the media, the entire matter may appear to have died down as quickly as it had sprung up. Many New Yorkers, however, know better—as the obstreperous and sometimes art-negative contingent from Art Positive (an AIDS-oriented, anticensorship collective affiliated with ACT UP) demonstrated outside the mobbed opening at Artists Space on Thursday night. It was becoming clear that the battle with Helms and Company for control of the national cultural agenda has only escalated.

Although Susan Wyatt is well known in New York (and elsewhere) as the sensible and sensitive administrator of a highly regarded artists' organization or "alternative space," John Frohnmayer—with whom the arts communities must deal in the foreseeable future—was a virtually unknown quantity until last week. His behavior showed him to be decent, easily flustered, not overly bright: a player out of his league in the rough-and-tumble arena of national politics.

Frohnmayer was visibly threatened by what numerous participants at a November 15 meeting between the NEA chair and downtown artists and organizations invariably described as a "frank" and "healthy" dialogue. He naively articulated his (understandable) resentment at the press feeding-frenzy. "We can't work this out according to the press's timetable," he lashed out, even blaming the press for its scrutiny in the first place. The most surprising aspects of his consistently inept performance were his unlawyerliness (he was a partner in the Portland firm of Tonkon, Torp, Galen, Marmaduke & Booth) and an apparently genuine discomfort at being labeled a homophobe, a response rarely heard from politicians outside of San Francisco.

Frohnmayer's dithering persona of the past weeks is both

contradicted and contextualized by accounts of his West Coast record. Interviews with more than a dozen Oregonians involved in the arts and media yield a picture of a man who is personally and professionally esteemed. Richard Meeker, the publisher of the alternative newspaper *Willamette Week*, notes that the most damning observation he can make is that "Frohnmayer is more conservative than most people think...But he is a good lawyer and well-respected here."

Frohnmayer also garnered generally positive reviews as a member of the Oregon Arts Commission (1976-80) and as its chairman from 1980 to '84. (According to former commission director Peter Hero and others, Frohnmayer's achievements during those eight financially strapped years include initiating individual artists' grants, fostering state support of folk arts, laying groundwork among legislators for budget increases after he left office, and increasing communication with artist-constituents throughout Oregon.) Bill Foster, director of the Northwest Film and Video Center, states that in Frohnmayer's confirmation hearing, "He cited our [commission-funded] work with school kids making tapes about homelessness and the environment as an example of how art should be [socially] involved." Does Frohnmayer understand contemporary art? "Well, he wouldn't understand a Barbara Kruger."

The NEA chairman's lack of familiarity with recent art contributed to his problems at Artists Space. (A prominent Portland lawyer and art patron quipped, "I think Rauschenberg to him is a new German beer.") Mary Beebe, former director of the defunct Portland Center for the Visual Arts, found Frohnmayer a "very low profile chairman, but there were no major battles either." Christopher Rauschenberg, director of the Blue Sky Gallery—where *Witnesses* curator Nan Goldin's work was shown last year—echoed Beebe's sentiments: "We really don't know much about him."

Charges of Frohnmayer's homophobia seem unfounded based on conversations with several sources in Oregon's gay community. Keeston Lowery, a gay activist and assistant to Portland Commissioner and art maven Mike Lindberg, met with Frohnmayer prior to his Washington confirmation hearings and characterizes his understanding of gay/lesbian and AIDS issues as "in-depth." Lowery also notes that Frohnmayer appeared on a televised mock trial as the attorney opposing Oregon's 1988 Ballot Measure 8, which successfully repealed a gubernatorial directive against gay/lesbian bias in hiring, and that many people confuse John with his brother (and current Oregon Republican gubernatorial candidate) David, "whose record isn't so good on these issues," according to Lowery.

Oregon probably boasts the most consensual politics in the country. When describing Frohnmayer, the term "mediator" came to many lips, as did a picture of a man not prone to acting unilaterally. The former helps explain his discomfort with the public events of the last week; the latter remains a mystery. Was the chairman acting unilaterally (and uncharacteristically) when he suspended the grant? How could an attorney who lists his specialties in *Martindale-Hubbell* (the Bible of lawyers' directories) as "litigation, libel, slander and First Amendment" have so vigorously attacked Wojnarowicz's essay criticizing public figures, i.e., First Amendment-protected speech? And how could anyone so familiar with gay issues have carelessly assaulted an AIDS-related exhibition?

According to council member Wendy Luers, Frohnmayer did not turn to the National Council on the Arts for advice, despite Peter Hero's assertion that the chairman told him "he'd like the national council to be more engaged." Jesse Helms's suspicious remark (see sidebar) suggests input from the far right, rather than from the arts communities. (Neither Helms nor the NEA would comment on the North Carolina senator's advisory role.) Frohnmayer, who lobbied hard for the endowment chair, may have learned that he cannot simultaneously satisfy the right and his arts constituency, the one toward which he seems more temperamentally inclined. Meanwhile, the rest of us have learned that he has no comprehension of the fact that today's ideological battles are being waged on the bodies of gays and women. The massive and largely celebratory prochoice rally in Washington took place four days after the Artists Space grant was withheld; unfortunately, none of the speakers at the rally made the connection.

The Artists Space controversy hits the NEA at the most vulnerable point in its 24-year history. Washington observers cite serious morale problems at the endowment. The troubled agency is riddled with vacancies: five of its 13 arts program directorships are vacant. Stephen Goodwin, director of the literature program, announced last week that he will not renew his expiring contract and claimed no connection between his resignation and current events, although sources close to Goodwin assert that he has been "deeply disturbed" by recent NEA events. Against this backdrop, Congressman Pat Williams is pursuing a wily strategy that proposes mandatory legislative reauthorization of the NEA, which would extricate the endowment from the 1990 election-year politics.

Normally, the NEA would be reauthorized for five years in 1990. Endowment supporter Williams says that he will seek to reauthorize the status quo (including the Helms-compromise amendment) for a single year and then go ahead with normal reauthorization in 1991. How will the shift in the duration of reauthorization come about? "We'll have eyeball-to-eyeball discussions between the NEA's active supporters, and we'll see [in January] if there are serious objections." What about Helms? "The Senate hasn't scheduled reauthorization hearings yet," Williams says.

Helms was the biggest loser in last week's fracas in Tribeca. Credit for this goes to the non-establishment art world forces that mobilized so quickly. Wyatt worked closely and publicly throughout the week with the National Association of Artist Organizations (NAAO) president Inverna Lockpez and Washington-based NAAO director Charlotte Murphy. Members of Art Positive spoke frequently at press conferences and tried to make sure that the issues of homophobia and censorship remained linked, although their statements invariably ended up on cutting room floors and in editorial office trash bins. Along with curator Goldin and artist Wojnarowicz, Art Positive members repeatedly called for Frohnmayer's resignation, once to his face at the November 15 meeting of downtown artists and organization representatives at Artists Space.

Ad hoc support came from many sources: Visual AIDS (the organizers of the upcoming December 1 *Day Without Art* to which the scheduling of *Witnesses* was pegged); PEN; Leonard Bernstein, whose refusal of the National Medal of Arts riveted public attention; New York City's Department of Cultural Affairs; the Coalition Opposed to Censorship in the Arts; and the Art Dealers' Association, which donated $10,000 to Artists Space. (At a board

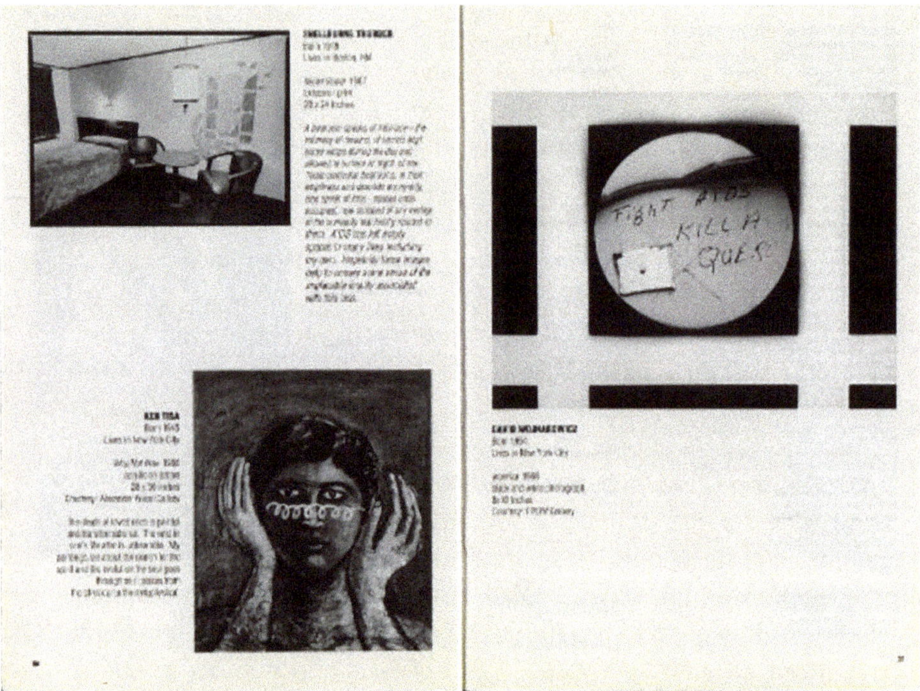

*A double page spread from the catalog for **Witnesses: Against Our Vanishing** (1989) organized by Nan Goldin at Artists Space, NYC*

meeting on November 17, Artists Space committed net proceeds from donations it had received to an as yet undetermined artist-advocacy project.) David Dinkins sent a chiding letter to Frohnmayer, copied to Wyatt, New York State Council on the Arts chair Kitty Carlisle Hart, and DCA commissioner Mary Schmidt Campbell, but he, as well as the vast majority of elected officials, were not vocal. Notably absent was support from NYSCA (is having no public relations director really an explanation?), the U.S. branch of the International Association of Art Critics, and the entire museum community. The silence of the museums was a disquieting reminder of the existence of *several* "art worlds."

Artists organizations fought this battle, and it seems that they, too, are capable of making artists feel disenfranchised; institutions and individuals inevitably have different needs. Having signed a waiver holding the gallery harmless for any legal costs arising from the publication of his catalogue text, artist David Wojnarowicz feels that Artists Space should have rejected the reinstatement of the NEA grant.

Wojnarowicz believes that the division of the fundable show and the un-fundable catalogue sends the message "to every space in the country that they should never touch work of this kind or the work that I do. I'd call it legalized murder," he continued. "The NEA's action legislates the silence of gays and lesbians, the silencing of PWAs [persons with AIDS], and the denial of safe sex information for people to protect themselves."

As the events at Artists Space unfolded last week, the powerlessness of artists to control the uses and abuses to which their work is subjected seemed strikingly analogous to the powerlessness of PWA's to control the medical treatment on which their lives depend. Plenty of people have speculated that Wojnarowicz's new and unwelcome notoriety will lead to increased sales of his art. But how so you compensate for the Post likening your work to a glorification of Hitler, or the *Washington Post* characterizing it as "the rambling death bed curse" of a person dying with AIDS?

QUOTES FROM CHAIRMAN JOHN

"I believe that the use of Endowment funds to exhibit or publish this work is in violation of the spirit of the Congressional directive."

—NEA chairman John E. Frohnmayer in a letter
to the director of Artists Space, Nov. 3

"A large portion of the content is political rather than artistic in nature."

—The New York Times, Nov. 9

"We all live in the real world here and we have been through an exceptionally difficult time, and I think the last thing we need is for public funds to be used to try to rub it in the face of the critics."

—The Washington Post, Nov. 9

"Any show that is primarily intended to make a political commentary must be privately funded," Frohnmayer told me. But isn't any exhibit about AIDS political? "No, it's a question of tone."

—The Village Voice, No. 47

"Obviously, there are lots of great works of art that are political. Picasso's Guernica and the plays of Bertold Brecht are strongly political."

—The New York Times, Nov. 10

"I think it has sounded like I was saying you look at the political content and you decide whether or not you like it. What I meant to say was you look at the artistic quality and you decide on that..."

—The Washington Post, Nov. 11

"The word political, I'm coming to see, means something different in Portland, Oregon, than it does in Washington, D.C."

—The Washington Post, Nov. 11

"In looking at the application...there was a substantial shift and, in my view, an erosion of the artistic focus."

—The New York Times, Nov. 14

After viewing a controversial art show on AIDS, the chairman of the National Endowment for the Arts yesterday said the Tribeca show is "without artistic merit."

—New York Daily News, Nov. 16

"I visited Artists Space in New York City yesterday and saw the exhibition 'Witnesses: Against Our Vanishing.' Prior to this time I had seen only the catalogue...I have agreed to approve the request of Artists Space..."

—The New York Times, Nov. 17

"I can understand the frustration and the huge sense of loss and abandonment that the people with AIDS feel, but I don't think the appropriate place of the national endowment is to fund political statements."

—Los Angeles Times, Nov. 10

Frohnmayer said yesterday that he did not want the NEA's withdrawal from the Artists Space show to suggest that the agency was not "invested in the AIDS epidemic."

—The Washington Post, Nov. 11

"I described that [the erosion of the artistic focus] with the P word, and it was taken by the arts community as a suggestion that I had been influenced by political pressure..."

—The New York Times, Nov. 14

Senator Jesse Helms: "I do hope that Mr. Frohnmayer is not retreating from his voluntary commitment to me..."

—The New York Times, Nov. 17

Continuing Coverage: N.E.A. 1989-92

June 7, 1989

Writing about the Moral Majoritarian savaging of **Andres Serrano**'s *Piss Christ* a few weeks ago I suggested that "an outright assault on the independence of the **NEA [National Endowment for the Arts]** may be in the making." Talk about understatement! Certain members of Congress have latched onto the Serrano flap like pit bulls in heat.

The action seems to have shifted from the House to the Senate. A few excerpts from **Senator Slade Gorton**'s (Republican, Washington) breathless remarks of May 31 entitled "On the Official Funding of Religious Bigotry": "Given that one of the most generously reviewed exhibitions of recent times was the artist **Judy Chicago**'s mixed-media depictions of female genitalia arranged on dinner plates, and that one of the masterpieces of Conceptual Art was minted as the artist himself was thrown out of a window into a tremendous pile of horse manure, am I supposed to..? [What, follow him?]...Where is the consensus for *Piss Christ*?...Is there anyone who will declare that this is not religious bigotry? What will the NEA pay for next? A mockery of the Holocaust? A parody of slave ships?... [Serrano's argument] is a religious argument, and the Government of the **United States** should not take sides in religious arguments. Here by subsidizing one of the parties, it has done so."

How to rectify such crimes against Christendom and humanity? Senator Gorton proposes depriving the **Southeastern Center for Contemporary Art**, which organized the exhibition containing Serrano's work, of federal funding for "say five years." According to Gorton's press secretary, **Sharon Kanareff**, the senator "wants to give the NEA a chance to rectify the situation before introducing legislation." (Our own **Senator Alfonse D'Amato** is also "outraged" by Serrano's photo. He circulated a letter of protest on the floor of the Senate which was signed by 25 senators, including **Jesse Helms**.)

NEA's acting chairman **Hugh Southern** will be meeting with Gorton this month, according to spokesman **Joe Slye**. But Southern is beginning to look like part of the problem, rather than the solution. His June 6 response to congressional inquiries contains the promise to "review our process" and the remarkably inappropriate admission that he "personally found it [*Piss Christ*] offensive." This was balanced by no art professional's interpretation or appraisal of Serrano's work. In fact, the kitschy, plastic crucifix submerged in urine is read by many viewers as an indictment of the commercialization of **Christ**, rather than a blaspheming of His image.

Why isn't Congress worried about the "debasement" of Christian symbols at the hands of demonstrably corrupt tax-exempt televangelists? Why haven't the NEA and its supporters demonstrated even a modicum of political will in this matter? What will happen when the **Robert Mapplethorpe** retrospective opens at the **Corcoran Gallery of Art** on July 1?

Press time news flash: The **Corcoran** has indeed declined to take *Perfect Moment*, the Mapplethorpe retrospective, caving in to anticipated pressures and giving real meaning to the term "self-censorship." Director **Christina Orr-Cahall** observed that she doesn't want her institution "politicized." She apparently thinks that the last-minute cancellation of an exhibition containing sexualized, homoerotic imagery sends no political signal? An outraged **Jock Reynolds**, director of the **Washington Project for the Arts** (WPA), may save the day by picking up the show. Stay tuned.

Art Chain Gang *March 20, 1990*

What's become standard operating procedure for AIDS activists and eco hell-raisers has finally hit the art world. I'm talking about civil disobedience. A March 1 "art chain-gang march" in Los Angeles culminated in the arrest of 27 "art convicts" dressed in black and white stripes and carrying likenesses of censored artists such as **Colette** and **Pasolini**. Sponsored by the **National Coalition for Freedom of Expression** and **ACT UP/L.A.**, the eight-hour agitprop extravaganza was designed to focus attention on the impending reauthorization hearing of the **National Endowment for the Arts** that took place on March 5 at the **J. Paul Getty Museum** in Malibu. Its official message to the agency was to protest restrictions on the content of publicly funded art as well as to end homophobic and racist assaults on art, and to promote increased federal arts funding.

Following a 7 a.m. kickoff at the **Los Angeles County Museum of Art**, the chain gang wended its way up Wilshire toward the downtown Federal Building. Linked by a cardboard chain and kept in line by "art police," more than 200 art supporters marched, according to participant **Brad Thompson**. Art cops and criminals chanted new versions of "Working on the Chain Gang" and made pit-stop press conferences at several locations. At the **Macondo Espacio Cultural**, Central American-born artist-speakers likened censorship here to repression in their homelands.

When the group reached the Federal Building on Los Angeles Street at 1 p.m., those prepared to be arrested (for real, this time) linked arms and blocked access to the modern office building. Selections from censored literary works were read, and as each participant was arrested, the crowd shouted its support: "**Frida Kahlo** was arrested." "**James Joyce** was arrested." The **Ellay 27** were cited for disorderly conduct and blocking entrance to a federal building and fined $25 apiece.

Was the action a success? "It was a beginning," responded march organizer **Joy Silverman**. "We reached thousands of people and demonstrated that there are other viewpoints than the far right's. We need a variety of approaches—doing civil disobedience one day and getting the endorsement of major institutions the next. We just wanted to show that art isn't a crime."

May 29, 1990

By the time you read this, the NEA reauthorization bill is likely to be out of committee and headed to the floor of the House, encrusted with crippling amendments that include the elimination of grants for individual artists. Many unprincipled arts administrators have prematurely thrown in the towel and begun to help plan for the dismemberment of the NEA. Although National Assembly of State Arts Agencies' executive director **Jonathan Katz** has taken the heat for a plan to disperse 60 per cent-rather than the present 20 per cent-of NEA funds to state arts agencies, the actual sender of the May 10 memorandum outlining the plan to siphon off arts funding from the NEA, was NYSCA executive director and NASAA chair **Mary Hays**. Some will interpret her actions as realism, others as appeasement. I'm in favor of the latter view.

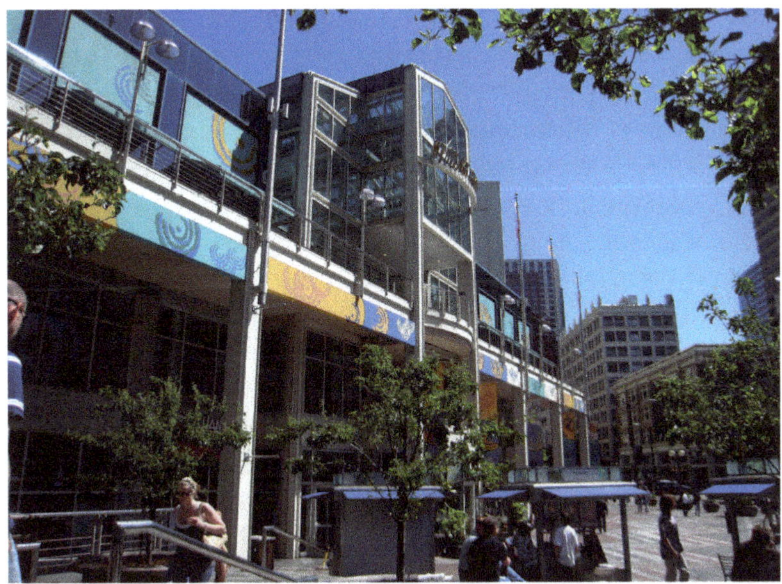

Westlake Center, Seattle, one of several malls slated to receive funds from the NEA to present Wagner's Ring Cycle to Emerald City shoppers

NEA Malls Itself *June 25, 1990*

In an astonishing year of "firsts" for the **National Endowment for the Arts**, the federal agency has racked up yet another: its first direct financial support for a corporate art program. Last month the NEA (quietly) announced that the **Rouse Company** has been awarded $50,000 to fund art projects in its shopping malls. Although NEA chairman **John Frohnmayer** was unavailable for comment, he observed in a statement that Rouse's aptly named **Art in the Marketplace** program "helps to bring American families that much closer to the cultural riches our nation's artists have created. The shopping center of today reflects the fairs and marketplaces of Renaissance times." Rouse, the Columbia, Maryland-based real estate developer, will match the award with $100,000 to sponsor programs in 10 malls from Seattle to Staten Island.

Seattle's **Westlake Center** will work with the **Seattle Opera** to present Wagner's Ring cycle through performances and costume displays, while the **Staten Island Mall** will team up with the **Staten Island Children's Museum** to offer an interactive exhibition called "Food for Thought." Other NEA-funded projects include "Senior Arts Week" at **Harundale Mall** in Glen Burnie, Maryland, and "City Visions," a showcase for local artists at Baltimore's **Harborplace**. While the concept of reaching new audiences in accessible locations is appealing, this unprecedented award to the Rouse Company establishes a dangerous precedent. It also raises disturbing ethical questions, including the specter of censorship and the matter why a highly profitable corporation shouldn't fund such programming from its marketing budget?

The noncompetitive award to Rouse is called a cooperative agreement-rather than a grant, because the NEA can make grants only to nonprofit groups eligible to receive tax-deductible contributions. Cooperative agreements are nothing new to the NEA. Spokesperson **Joshua Dare** told me that the NEA has a history of such agreements, usually to supply sites for Endowment-supported activities. What is new about this one is that it authorizes the company to act as a conduit for the distribution of NEA funds to artists and groups, a function exclusively delegated-until now-to financially disinterested groups such as the **New York Foundation for the Arts (NYSCA)**. In the Republican vernacular, the privatization of such activities is touted as "public-private partnerships" although most of the NEA's public-private initiatives have involved foundations rather than corporations.

The potential for conflict of interest in the Rouse Company award is built-in. The publicly funded presence of arts audiences in the 10 shopping centers will, of course, draw thousands of potential customers to businesses leasing their spaces from Rouse. **Lenwood Sloan**, director of the NEA's Interarts Program, which funded the award to Rouse, dismisses concerns about conflict of interest by noting that "in a partnership, the partners have equally important agendas. We can't deny that they want to draw visitors to their properties. We see this as a way to advance accessibility of the arts."

Although Sloan calls the award a "project-in-study," he also evoked a future expansion of the program observing that "we could extend [this sort of award] to **Olympia & York**, who do such a brilliant arts program at Battery Park City." Is it possible that two of the biggest real estate developers in North America really need NEA funding? Especially troubling is an element of the Harundale Mall's "**Senior Arts Week**" festival. Three artists in residence there will produce a mural "for permanent display in the mall"; put another way, publicly funded art will be produced for a privately owned space. Rouse Company vice-president and director of corporate public affairs **Cathy A. Lickteig** remarked that concerns about impropriety in relation to the mural "are not an issue for any of us. The space is a mall, a place to have a lot of different experiences. It's not like other kinds of businesses."

What she (and Sloan and Frohnmayer) evoke is the changing sociological landscape. The malls may indeed be the new American Main Street, but that analogy should not be pushed too far. Unlike Main Street and the Renaissance marketplace, shopping centers are neither public property nor public arenas for the exercise of First Amendment rights. As arts attorney **Barbara Hoffman** noted, "The tendency of the Supreme Court has been to reject consideration of shopping centers as traditional public forums for the exercise of First Amendment rights" If you've ever tried to set up a table in a mall to advocate abortion rights you know what Hoffman means.

Perhaps the most distasteful aspect of this award is the signal it sends to struggling arts organizations that must fundraise in an increasingly competitive and unresponsive climate. "It's shameful to give money to a huge corporation when there are arts organizations that not only deserve it more, but need it more," said **Holly Block**, executive director of **Art in General**. Or as one arts lobbyist told me, "When there are limited funds, highly profitable corporations should not be subsidized. And the bottom line is that's what this is—a subsidy."

Crit Beat *March 5, 1991*

Switch-hitting **National Endowment for the Arts** chairman **John Frohnmayer** recently reversed himself on yet another grant. St. Paul's **Center for Arts Criticism** will get the $25,000 award to import art writers and editors to the Twin Cities that Frohnmayer rejected last fall. Changing his mind is nothing new for the NEA chair: one of his latest reversals was the approval of a $10,000 grant to environmental artist **Mel Chin** that the wishy-washy agency head vetoed late last year.

What makes the CAC flip-flop significant is that it may signal a shift in the NEA's long-established hostility toward art criticism. Despite the agency's stated mission to help foster art understanding, a vocal minority on the National Council—the chairman's presidentially appointed advisory group—spent much of the '80s lobbying against "anything that smell[ed] of criticism," as NEA fellow **Ann McQueen** put it in her 1990 report obtained by the Voice.

The council's neo-con cabal—comprising **Joseph Epstein, Jacob Neusner,** *New Criterion* publisher **Samuel Lipman,** and painter **Helen** (nary-a-good-review-since-'62) **Frankenthaler**—killed what it regarded as the left-leaning-critic's fellowships in 1983. (Some have suggested that the council's assault on critics was a dress rehearsal for the contemplated dismantling of the entire NEA.) By the late '80s, the National Council's antipathy to criticism had grown so virulent that a rejection of a 1988 grant to the Center for Arts Criticism was actually overridden by **Reagan**-appointed chairman **Frank Hodsoll.** Are things looking up? Frohnmayer's favorable response to the CAC's appeal is a positive sign, although agency spokesperson **Joshua Dare** could find no evidence of any public statement about art criticism by the chairman. (Frohnmayer was traveling and unavailable for comment.) But based on private conversations, visual art program director **Susan Lubowsky** believes that Frohnmayer is pro-"discourse... Education and outreach are two of his priorities," she said, "and criticism is part of them."

More important, the intransigent anti-criticism minority on the National Council is nearly history: Lipman's tenure ended in 1988;

Neusner's, Epstein's, and Frankenthaler's terms were up in 1990, although the last two continue to serve pending replacement. While report-writer McQueen feels optimistic that criticism will be more broadly funded by the NEA of the '90s, she also observed that "I don't think they'll ever go back to individual grants for critics."

Abort Supreme Court *June 11, 1991*

The **National Campaign for Freedom of Expression**'s new executive director, **David Mendoza**, didn't officially assume the leadership of the feisty artist advocacy group until last week. But that didn't stop the savvy director of Seattle's **Artist Trust** and former assistant to NYSCA chair **Kitty Carlisle Hart** from crisscrossing the country in late May to advise a convocation of foundation honchos about censorship and to help devise a strategy enabling a certain off-the-record artist to exhibit his safer-sex images without censorship. Now Mendoza's worried about the **Supreme Court**'s noxious ruling upholding the ban on abortion counseling—that is conveying relevant medical information to patients—at federally funded clinics.

"The minute I heard about the decision, I wondered about the affect on our suit charging that the **NEA Four—Finley, Fleck, Miller** and **Hughes**—were denied funding for the politics of their art," Mendoza told me. He wasn't anxious for no reason. A day later prudish, anti-Clinton solicitor general **Kenneth W. Starr** publicly applauded the Supreme Court's gutting of the First Amendment: "The government is able to take sides; it is able to have viewpoints when it is funding. It can choose to fund **Shakespeare** and decline to fund **Moliere**." Starr wouldn't respond to Washington reporters' questions about restrictions on federal arts funding. Could his choice of an arts-related example of government control have been mere coincidence? "Extremely unlikely," responded NCFE's legal counsel, **Ellen Yaroshevsky**.

Movement Research *October 15, 1991*

The **NEA** version of the current **Movement Research** flap would have us believe that the downtown dance/performance organization violated the terms of the federal agency's grant with its recent **Performance Journal No. 3**. The offensive material? The publication's gender-issues theme (that "does not appear to speak to the dance community on issues specific to dance or performance art," according to a September 9 letter to MR from Endowment staffer **Laurence Baden**), as well as a prochoice artwork complete with female genitalia in close-up. (It was charged with "intending to influence the public and to lobby members of Congress with regard to pending legislation."). The NEA demand? Return $1400 of the $4400 grant. Let's not consider how many tax dollars it took to send an NEA auditor to New York to examine MR's books, much less the cost of the likely lawsuit ahead.

Progressive advocacy groups' interpretations of the NEA's assault on the small organization differ markedly from the federal agency's. **David Mendoza**, of the **National Campaign for Freedom of Expression**, characterizes the endowment's demand as "completely ridiculous, yet another instance of the chilling effect." In a September 26 letter to NEA chair **John Frohnmayer**, **ACLU** executive director **Ira Glasser** terms the endowment's motives "essentially political" and observes that, "As a practical matter, this strategy is doomed to fail...But the principle is more important. We fear the NEA has abandoned a grantee—and, by inference, artists more broadly—as part of its appeasing." Glasser has not-as of this writing-received a reply to his letter.

February 4, 1992

The **ACLU** free-expression project also recently joined ranks with the **National Campaign for Freedom of Expression** and the **Center for Constitutional Rights** in the long simmering "NEA 4" lawsuit. (That's the case brought by artists **Karen Finley, John Fleck, Holly Hughes**, and **Tim Miller** charging that in 1990 the four were denied grants on political grounds.) Oral arguments will finally be heard in Los Angeles Federal District Court on February 3 and the importance of the suit is burgeoning.

What's at stake now? The NEA 4's legal team is attacking not just the allegedly illegal rationale for the grant rejections, but the constitutionality of the "decency language" contained in recent NEA funding bills. NCFE attorney **Mary Dorman** told me that Justice Department memoranda reveal that the government will attempt to apply *Rust v. Sullivan* content restrictions—the gag rule that prevents doctors at federally funded clinics from mentioning the A-word—to encompass arts funding, making virtually any of Jesse Helms's censorious mandates legal. "They're formidable adversaries with deep pockets," Dorman commented. "But if we're going to lose our rights, it ought to happen in public." Dorman predicts that **Judge A. Wallace Tashima** will take a month or two to reach a decision about whether to either dismiss the case, to find against the NEA in summary judgment, or to proceed to a trial.

Bushanan's NEA *May 12, 1992*

Anybody who thinks that **George Bush**'s firing of NEA chief **John Frohnmayer** was an isolated incident should think again. Pandering to the Bushanan crowd [George Bush + extreme conservative Pat Buchanan = Bushanan] is virtual policy under the agency's new acting head **Anne-Imelda Radice**.

Some current targets include New York's **Creative Time** and three California organizations: **Frameline** (in San Francisco), **Installation Gallery** (San Diego), and **LACE** (Los Angeles). Although each instance is different, together they are a trio of variations on a theme. LACE and Installation Gallery were asked by the NEA to remove credits for the agency's support from outreach and fund-raising materials. LACE has long mentioned the agency (among 76 other funders) on its bi-monthly calendar. Calendars also promote such naughty (unfunded) events as the annual "**Valentine's 'Erotica' Bash**" and the "**Tribute to Tom of Finland**." (Perhaps the NEA will present a tribute to **Joseph McCarthy**.)

Other strategies for covering the endowment's right flank are calculated to prevent funds from getting into troublemaking hands in the first place. Creative Time's and Frameline's grant applications have been tied up since January. That was two weeks after the Manhattan-based organization faced a firestorm of controversy in the right-wing press for sponsoring pro-choice and AIDS-prevention videotapes. Frameline director **Tom Di Maria** says that he was told by NEA staffers in January that funding for the **San Francisco International Lesbian and Gay Film Festival** was in jeopardy due to its potential "impact on the future of the NEA." Given such illegal NEA capitulations to political pressures, Frameline had to choose between self-censorship and a potentially expensive lawsuit. This is how censorship works.

If the agency can't keep funds from pesky artists before hand, they can always complain about their activities after the fact. Recently, the federal arts agency scolded Installation Gallery artists—and UC San Diego art department faculty **Louis Hock**, **Scott Kessler**, **Carla Kirkwood**, **Elizabeth Sisco**, and **Deborah Small**—for supposedly deviating from its grant proposal plan for the exhibition "**NHI**." The acronym is police jargon for "no humans involved," referring to the show's subject of the barely-investigated murders of 45 San Diego women tagged as prostitutes and/or drug users since 1985. Hock asserts that former NEA Inter-Arts program head Loris Bradley was updated as the project evolved. (She could not be reached for comment by press time) Hock believes that modified plans were not the point of the agency's actions. "The NEA will do anything to distance itself from this work," the artist said. "If they're so concerned, why haven't they sued to recover the money?" (NEA spokesperson **Joshua Dare** refused to comment on any of this, citing agency policy precluding discussion of grant applicants.)

NEA Update *June 9, 1992*

Despite the mainstream media's lackadaisical coverage of recent **NEA** events, the troubled agency is rapidly imploding. Following the May 15 walkout by the Visual Arts Program's sculpture panel to protest acting chair **Anne-Imelda Radice**'s veto of grants to MIT and Virginia Commonwealth University for show's about the body, other panels have responded in kind: the, special exhibitions panel whose recommendations Radice overrode, delivered a vehement letter of protest to the agency on May 19, as did the Museum Program's normally conservative overview panel two days later. On May 20, the solo theater artists panel refused even to consider grant applications in the current, poisonous atmosphere.

As of this writing, there's uplifting news, too. Boston's **Beacon Press** and Washington's **Artist Trust** (along with three Seattle artists) have rejected grants totaling $56,000 to protest Radice's vetoes. Pulitzer Prize-winning novelist **Wallace Stegner** has declined his National Medal of Arts on the heels of Broadway composer-lyricist **Stephen Sondheim**'s earlier rejection, making it two down and 10 to go for the dozen NMA medalists who will be honored in July. The rock group **Aerosmith** gave $10,000 to MIT on May 20 to fund the university's body-art show, establishing a Broadway-to-CBGB sensibility range of support that mirrors the broad backing for an independent NEA in a recent Harris poll.

In the near future, count on more controversy. Flash points include already approved and likely to be problematic grants awaiting Radice's assent or veto. Recipients in this category: include **Visual AIDS** (for the *Electric Blanket* show of AIDS images), **Frameline** (for the presentation and distribution of queer films), **Highways** (for the commissioning and production of multicultural and queer performances), and **Creative Time** (for programs, including Art in the Anchorage). Also expect fragmentary, soothing reports from our local press. *The New York Times*'s minimal coverage suggests that it has already adopted the elite "save the NEA at any cost" position. Sondheim's barely noticed statement and Stegner's unmentioned rejection of the NMA contrast sharply with the headlines accorded **Leonard Bernstein**'s rejection of the same award in 1989. *New York Newsday* remains a better bet—for spotty wire-service briefs, at least.

The weirdest aspect of current NEA reporting is the on-again, off-again coverage of lesbian Radice's outing. Most of the "problematic" grants mentioned above involve the sort of queer visibility with which the **Helms** and now Radice crowd continue to bludgeon the NEA. On May 15, **Queer Nation** held a press conference outing the acting chair, which was covered by such mainstream non-New York papers as the **Philadelphia Inquirer** and *The Oregonian*. *The Advocate* issued a release titled "NEA Chief Not Even Worth an Outing," noting that Radice is not a closeted lesbian, although it seems that she returned to the closet after her latest appointment. The **National Campaign for Freedom of Expression** issued a release observing that "it is too late to try to keep a finger in the dyke at the NEA."

According to NEA and Washington insiders, Radice is already out to the White House. It's been reported that she's contacted the PR honchos at **Hill and Knowlton** for spin control, which suggests why she will not be appointed NEA chair. Perhaps it will also prevent her from nabbing the European ambassadorship that the same sources say has been promised her after she's "straightened out" the NEA. (The White House did not return calls for comment.) Either way, Radice has already earned a place in history alongside **Lynne Cheney**, who eviscerated the **National Endowment for the Humanities** during the '80s.

NEA to LA: Drop Dead *July 21, 1992*

While it will take at least $500 million to physically rebuild riot-torn areas of Los Angeles, the **NEA** has allocated the first installment of an eventual $150,000 to help "heal" South Central L.A. But even that pitiful figure is misleading: $50,000 previously approved for the **L.A. Cultural Affairs Department** has simply been transferred to the L.A. agency's **Arts Recovery Fund**. A munificent $30,000 is destined for artists' residencies and after-school programs at a Crenshaw district art center. But the kicker is a $70,000 grant to **Urban Innovations**, the nonprofit branch of **UCLA's School of Architecture and Urban Design**, for redesigning a portion of the decimated ghetto in conjunction with community-based planners. When the NEA convened five urban-design experts to evaluate the

UCLA proposal, the group unanimously rejected it as ill-conceived. (Architect **M. David Lee** termed the proposal process "public relations.") Reflecting the NEA's indifference to panel input—and the administration's desperation to appear to be doing something about urban malaise—the federal arts agency simply repackaged the proposal and submitted it to a largely non expert panel of state arts administrators. The cooperative panelists approved it, as did acting chair **Anne-Imelda Radice** on June 24.

NEA Chairs Remember

Excerpted from reviews of John Frohnmayer's Leaving Town Alive: Confessions of an Arts Warrior. Houghton Mifflin. (Village Voice, 1995); & Jane Alexander's Command Performance: An Actress in the Theater of Politics, Da Capo Press.

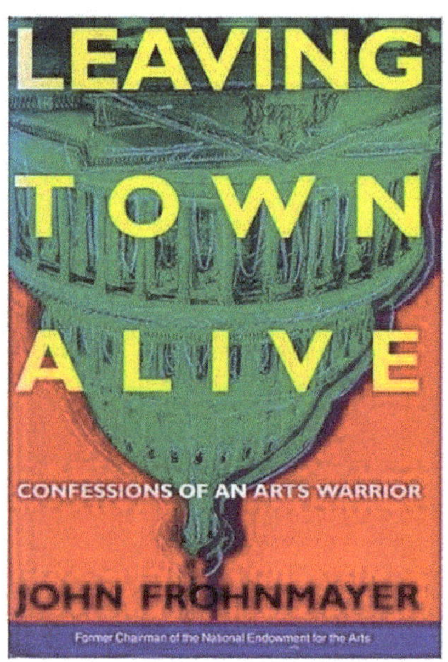

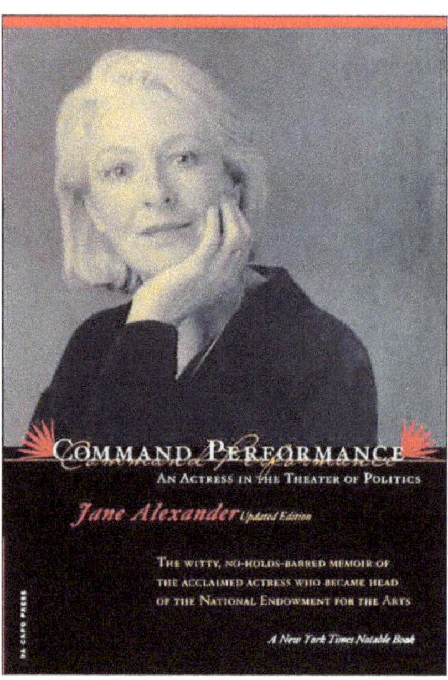

"Who (NEArly) Killed the NEA?" *Art in America, July, 2001*

Readers of John Frohnmayer's *Leaving Town Alive: Confessions of an Arts Warrior* may suspect something's amiss when the former National Endowment for the Arts chair revealed that he "expected to be Washington's darling." He's recounting a worrying moment—in September 1989—just five months post-*Piss Christ*, two months after the Mapplethorpe debacle at the Corcoran, and two months before his self-ignited trial by fire at Artists Space. At this point in his tenure as agency chief you want to give Frohnmayer the benefit of the doubt simply for his intention of coming clean about his embarrassing naïveté. But Frohnmayer's recollection also signals his attempts to position himself as a country lawyer cast adrift in a sea of snarky politicos.

This "innocent abroad"-style motif is one of a pair of familiar tropes around which he's organized this dishy sounding but surprising juiceless memoir. (The title even evokes Julia Phillips's Hollywood tell-all, *You'll Never Eat Lunch in This Town Again.*) The other is the attempt to cast *Leaving Town Alive* as a *bildungsroman*, a heroic coming of age.

The book's cover copy explains that Frohnmayer "entered the fray a First Amendment moderate [and] emerged a free-speech radical." As if...

Both tropes are designed to transform a bureaucrat who vainly tried to please both the right and the left into an "art warrior" whose values jibe with the more liberal ethos of the Clinton era. He will instead, be remembered as the wishy-washy federal-arts-agency counterpart to his often hapless boss in the White House. (He reviles Bush for not standing up to Jesse Helms and other extremists on his behalf.) Yet he shared Bush's propensity for flip-flopping on issues of principle such as the President's "flexibility" about abortion, which parallels Frohnmayer's changing views on artists' First Amendment rights as mandated in the Constitution. Regarding the conflict about the AIDS exhibition at Artists Space, *Witnesses: Against Our Vanishing*, he told the Voice that "any show that is primarily intended to make political commentary must be privately funded." Yet he mouthed the opposing view the next day as published in *The New York Times*: "There are lots of great works of art that are political."

As First Amendment warrior Charlotte Murphy, the former head of the National Association of Artists' Organizations, characterized Frohnmayer's defense of artists: "It was simply too little, too late."

Command Performance begins with Jane Alexander's childhood and ends with her departure from the NEA in 1997, considerably older and wiser, following her four year stint as chair of the agency for four years.

Like *Leaving Town Alive*, by her predecessor John Frohnmayer,

Alexander's memoir is a *bildungsroman*, a coming of age saga in which an idealistic agency head loses her innocence in the snake pit of corruption and ambition that is our nation's capital. While Frohnmayer attempted to whitewash his hapless record; Alexander is more self critical. She blames herself for dissing performance artist Annie Sprinkle in a letter to Jesse Helms's staff, for instance, and for excess honesty in characterizing the NEA as on "life support" after the midterm elections in 1986.

Such memoirs constitute a genre like Presidential Libraries, predictably heavy on self promotion and excuses, and lacking a clearly identifiable audience apart from "posterity." Alexander's most valuable inclusions are never-before-published letters between the NEA and senatorial staffers, especially those of Jesse Helms, that underline the siege mentality that prevailed at the NEA after the election of Newt Gingrich's Contract-With-America classes of 1992 and '94.

Advice on how to be an effective chair came to Alexander from many quarters. Roger Stevens, the revered, former NEA head, counseled her to speak directly to the President, yet it took nearly two years for Clinton to squeeze an Oval Office meeting with her into his schedule. For her patience, Alexander was rewarded only with the warning she'd already heard everywhere: The public is simply not going to stand for funding controversial art. She (pop) psychologizes that Bill Clinton is such a "people person" that art's inherent "interiority" doesn't interest him. Surprisingly, she never articulates her views on art and artistic quality. She does however drop hints, concluding that current art is "tame" and we lack a "Shakespeare."

Perhaps this is why she proudly waxes about educational collaborations with the Health and Human Services Department and cultural tourism initiatives with the Department of Commerce, while glossing over the loss of fellowships for individual artists in just a few sentences.

Initially, such awards were the heart of the NEA and its support for democratically-selected experimental art was among the agency's premier accomplishments during the 1970s and '80s.

The awarding of grants by rotating peer panels, a revolutionary process, was pioneered at the NEA. Artist Newton Harrison, who, as chair of visual arts policy sat in on many peer panels expressed the task's virtual impossibility in so fraught a climate. "The charge to the panels, sometimes unspoken, sometimes spoken, was to choose the best work but be careful how you define best," Harrison told critic Michael Brenson. "Look for the greatest creativity. Don't be afraid to fund something that's crude, that feels very creative against something that's very refined."

Thanks for your service, panelists!

Continuing Coverage
Censorship & Freedom of Expression 1990-94

Global Censorphilia: From Washington, LA & NY, to France & the Soviet Union *Le Boycott, June 26, 1990*

When three Jewish members of Nice's city council quit to protest Mayor **Jacques Medecin**'s alliance with the racist right, the mayor responded by observing that "I don't know any Jew who will refuse a gift offered to him, even if he doesn't like the gift." The French section of the International Art Critics' Association and a group of artists retaliated with a boycott of all Nice art institutions, including the new Museum of Modern and Contemporary Art slated to open on June 21. **Arman** courageously pulled the retrospective of his art that was to have inaugurated the museum in his hometown. Solidarity comes from these U.S. comrades-in-art who've joined *le boycott*—**Roy Lichtenstein**, **Robert Rauschenberg**, **Julian Schnabel**, **George Segal**, and **Frank Stella**.

SCENE & HEARD *September 25, 1990*

Art-world determination seems to be stiffening in the face of the censorphilia that dominated last season. This month's most provocative show may be "**Censored/Censured**" at the new Baltimore alternative space, **BAUhouse**. It examines 10 years of mid-Atlantic-region censorship/censureship, and what's surprising is that so many of the exhibited works offended their censors for non-sexual, non-religious, usually unfathomable grounds. Plastic guns, images of dead babies, and a painted list of actual jailhouse dos and don'ts (it was deemed "depressing") were a few of the reasons artists in this show were (re)moved. The show's criteria for inclusion? Works ejected from exhibitions, works moved within shows for political reasons, or works altered by those who disapproved. And what's executive Director **Pat Creswell**'s rationale for doing the show? "We're too new; we haven't had the opportunity to turn down grants yet."

One of the 28 artists in the "Censored/Censured" is **New York**

State Council on the Arts visual arts director **Carlos Gutierrez-Solana**. You may recall that his elegiac AIDS installation at 1708 East Main gallery in Richmond last spring prompted a "cover-up" by city officials of his on-window drawing of a figure with an erect cock. What's gone unreported in the New York press is that Gutierrez-Solana and the gallery (represented by the **ACLU**) took the case to federal court in June. The co-plaintiffs won a restraining order from prosecution and a declaratory judgement that the work is not obscene. The installation was uncovered and the run of the show extended into mid-July.

Wojnarowicz Redux *January 12, 1991*

The latest round of the ongoing **David Wojnarowicz-Donald Wildmon** grudge match recently ended in a draw. **American Family Association** head Wildmon had his wrists slapped in a New York district court ruling of September 19 for distributing the same pamphlet violating Wojnarowicz's rights that he'd been ordered to stop circulating over a year ago. The artist/activist got a letter of apology from Wildmon, but his motion to hold Wildmon in civil contempt was denied. Nor was Wojnarowicz awarded court costs and attorney's fees for (pro bono) co-counsels **Kathryn Barrett** and **Jonathan Olsoff**. In case you've forgotten, back in 1990 the Bible thumpin' Wildmon "appropriated" fragmentary porno stills that were tiny parts of Wojnarowicz 's "Sex Series" prints. Re-contextualized in ADA's anti-**NEA** pamphlet, they made the artist look like a pornographer. Wildmon was found to have violated the **New York Artists Authorship Rights Act** in June 1990, and two months later was enjoined from distributing the pamphlet and ordered to send a "corrective mailing" to each of its recipients. Wojnarowicz was later awarded $1 in token damages (!), but despite the 1990 ruling, the AFA admits to having since sent out two copies of the pamphlet that brought them to court.

In his decision, **Judge William C. Conner,** found no "willfulness" on the AFA's part and concludes that the "mailings were mistakes from which no malevolence may be presumed" (!!). Wildmon's letter of apology assures Wojnarowicz that "this will never happen again." Wojnarowicz concurs: "He's onto other people now and I'm sure he'll make lots of money."

Some Print, Others Won't *February 19, 1991*

The printer who refused to print the **Heresies** collective's nudity-filled "Sex Issue" of 1981 was ahead of his time. During the 80's, printers have become the new censors—and formidable obstacles to the publication of controversial art images. ***Afterimage*** coeditor **Grant Kester**, who informally surveys the problem, reports that "every month or two we hear from an editor who can't get a publication printed or an artist having trouble with an exhibition announcement."

Kester is an ex-staffer at ***New Art Examiner***, which regularly publishes pictures of censored art. The Chicago-based monthly has paid dearly for its policy of allowing readers to make up their own minds about artworks in the news. To find printers lacking **Jesse Helms**'s censorious instincts, it has twice conducted expensive searches since 1988—each time with only partial success.

The **Johnson Press** promised to "print anything," according to *NAE* managing editor **Allison Gamble**, then balked at a reproduction of **Lynda Benglis**'s infamous ***Artforum*** ad-with-dildo from the mid-'70s. The same company later rejected photographer **Joe Ziolkowski**'s image of two embracing men with shadowy erections, as well as **Robert Mapplethorpe**'s *Honey*, the photo of the little girl with lifted skirt that occupied center-stage at the Cincinnati trial.

What's a publication to do? "Once a printer has your boards," Gamble observed, "there's rarely time to switch." A blank spot appeared on the page where the Benglis image—or *NAE*'s typeset statement suggested by Benglis that the printer objected to the printing of the image—should have been. (Johnson Press did not return the *Voice*'s call for comment.) Last year, *NAE* switched to the **Ovid Bell Press**. But the Fulton, Missouri, printer caved in when confronted with photos of a **Gran Fury** installation that included a picture of an erection. Press owner Bell told me that decisions about printing images are made by "two or three of us who get together and pitch pennies at it… We consider the concept as art. Nudity doesn't bother us, an erection might, and we draw the line at perversion." What is perversion? "You caught me in the middle of a column of figures. It's hard to focus on that now."

More War *March 19, 1991*

The six antiwar protesters in the Assyrian galleries of the **Metropolitan Museum** on March 2 solemnly began to read. Snippets of Iraqi poetry—ancient and contemporary—alternated with discomfiting facts about a war already laid to rest in American consciousness. The reminder that there was "1 bombing run every minute of every day against the people of Iraq" segued into a 4000-year-old lamentation for the city of Ur: "In all the streets and roadways bodies lay. In open fields that used to fill with dancers, the people lay in heaps, bodies dissolved-like butter left in the sun." After eight minutes, the performers were hustled out of the museum by nervous security honchos fingering handguns.

The readers belong to **Artists and Writers Out Loud** (AWOL)—a direct-action group that was joined at the Met by a contingent from the like-minded **Poets Against the War**. (Members of both read on the sidewalk after being ejected from the museum.) None of the protesters believe that the Gulf War is actually over, at least not in the Gulf. "We want people to start thinking about the effects of the war," PAW organizer **Hal Sirowitz** told me. "Thousands of kids will be dying in Baghdad because no hospitals or sewage systems remain. We're concerned about a long-term occupation, too."

For ongoing reminders that life is cheap, but masterpieces in museum galleries dear, AWOL is translating their concerns into projects such as "Out Loud: Artists Engulfed Against War," an open, non-juried exhibition at **Art in General** gallery, April 13 to May 11. PAW is staging antiwar readings at the **Knitting Factory** on Thursday nights in March, and at **Wetlands** on April 17. (For information about the AWOL show and the group's weekly meetings call **Lisa Maya Knauer** at 533-3032; for PAW info call 274-1324.)

Bad Nudes *February 4, 1992*

Now that eroticism and pornography have been conflated, what's the puritans' next gambit? Attack any image of the naked human body. Whether reading *Playboy* in a Berkeley diner or gazing at **Francisco Goya**'s *Naked Maja* in a Penn State classroom, art and nudity buffs, beware: no nudes is good nudes.

Prof. **Nancy Stumhofer**'s Goya bashing—her university-supported contention that teaching in front of a *Maja*-repro constitutes sexual harassment—has drawn sharper comment from the British press than from its American counterpart. ***The Independent*** polled art mavens about the tempest-in-a-classroom. Former **Victoria and Albert Museum** director **Roy Strong** called it "a bizarre manifestation of feminism," while novelist **Anita Brookner** tartly observed that "this woman must be cracked." ***The Art Newspaper***'s highly critical report led with the neocon opinion that "the Nineties sees the U.S. dominated by a craven fear of offending against 'Political correctness.'" A preemptive strike to ensure that our p.c. paradise doesn't get exported?

A poster for Franklin Furnace's latest enterprise—A January 23-24 performance/symposium called ***Explicit Sex: Art or Phallacy?***—drew fire from **Michael Miller**, Associate Dean of **NYU's Tisch School of Arts**, whose Performance Studies Department cosponsored the event. What was the problem with the image-free flyer? According to FF director **Martha Wilson**, Miller demanded that it be displayed only in "reputable institutions" and was fearful that the title would attract "**42nd Street** types." Miller told me that he didn't want to extend an open invitation for the public event following the City College tragedy. "This is for people with a serious interest in performance," he sniffed. (FF made no attempts to assess the seriousness of those making reservations.)

Censorship Redux *June 23, 1992*

Not many arts administrators (or non-arts administrators) seem to have paid much attention to the past three years of art bashing. Some of the former continue their arrogant "I know what's offensive" ways; many of the latter rely on Republican-style, slash-and-burn techniques to act out their powerlessness at artists' expense. The censorship drums never stop beating.

Some current imbroglios: "***Seeing Red White or Blue-Censored in the USA***," a thoughtfully conceived exhibition of 55 artists' work ranging from **Phillip Pearlstein**'s clinically observed nudes to **Alice Sims**'s bear-rug-style photos of her kids, raised quite a ruckus during its just-finished run at **Anchorage's Visual Arts Center of Alaska**. **Robert Mapplethorpe**'s image of his handiwork with a bullwhip predictably annoyed the local **American Family Association**, while **Dread Scott**'s *What is the Proper Way to Display a U.S. Flag?*—the apparent artistic equivalent of screaming "fire" in a crowded theater—even more predictably infuriated Alaska's **Veterans of Foreign Wars**.

VFW state commander **George A. Pikus** pulled off the first of several thefts of Scott's flag, each of which was followed by the donation of another flag to the center by a Scott supporter. According to Alaska district attorney **Edward McNally**, it is now up to the state to decide whether or not to prosecute. Don't bet on even the misdemeanor charge under consideration: McNally told me that Alaska statute defines theft as "permanently depriving an owner of property" and VFW members left cash deposits and written promises to return the flags. McNally also noted that "the First Amendment cuts both ways," implying that theft might be constitutionally protected in such a case! Bear in mind that this non-NEA-funded exhibition came complete with communications mechanisms including a questionnaire and an NEH-funded program of speakers keynoted by born-again First Amendment advocate **John Frohnmayer**.

Censorama *November 10, 1992*

Censorship can also slip in through the back door of your property-oriented legal system, suggests attorney **John Koegel**. He's been representing artist **Jeff Koons** in his losing court battle with photographer **Art Rogers** over Koons's unauthorized use of a photograph by Rogers. *Rogers v. Koons* is essentially over—the Supreme Court recently refused to hear an appeal, and a trial date to determine monetary damages will be set on November 20—but Koegel believes that this "ground-breaking" case may impact on Dennis Oppenheim's conflict with **The Walt Disney Company** over the artist's use of **Mickey Mouse** in his recent sculpture *Virus*.

Koegel disparages Disney's tough-guy zeal deterring any non-licensed use of the cartoon characters: "Of course it's legitimate to go after products that unfairly compete, but an artwork is discussion and commentary. Disney's gone after three day-care centers that had drawings of its characters on the walls. If Mickey Mouse isn't part of the American cultural dialogue, then how do you account for Disney promoting itself through a new **Hyperion Press** book of **Claes Oldenburg**'s—and other artists'—works called *The Art of Mickey Mouse*?"

Museums: In & Out *December 22, 1992*

It continues to take a lot of pushing and shoving to make room for lesbians and gay men under New York museums' multicultural umbrella. Congratulations to **Brooklyn Museum** curator **Elizabeth Easton** for positively responding to a postopening complaint [author's 2001 note: by me] by rewriting a wall label in her intriguing **Frederic Bazille** exhibition. The original text discussed a painting of eight male bathers that's absolutely queer—without raising the biographical issue of the artist's sexuality, which informs the work. In the show's catalogue, Bazille scholar **Dianne Pitman** quotes art historian **Kermit Champa**'s observation that "the bathers' comportment reveals the artist's homosexual tendencies," and a *New York Times* review observed that "there's a sensuality to... [Bazille's] images of the male form entirely unlike his renditions of women." Now the wall labels make sense.

Porn Flakery *March 30, 1993*

Anybody who thinks that the passage of laws outlawing "pornography" will help curb violence against women—rather than against free speech—might look North. Canada's first year of **MacKinnon-Dworkin** style prohibitions against erotica that "degrades" or "dehumanizes" has led mainly to the suppression of queer mags and videotapes, according to censorship specialist and University of Manitoba law professor **Karen Busby**. When Winnipeg architecture student **Joanne Crozier** ordered performance artist **Annie Sprinkle** and videomaker **Maria Beatty**'s *Sluts and Goddesses*, how could she have imagined that Canadian Customs would confiscate the tape? Crozier had, after all, heard about this engaging primer of pleasure and purification in a Sprinkle interview on the government-operated Canadian Broadcasting Company.

The Canadian Supreme Court's so-called *Butler* decision established new obscenity criteria last year: Sex with violence and sex that degrades is out; explicit sex—as long as it doesn't involve children—is in. Sounds good in theory, doesn't it? But within a week of the ruling, Toronto police had seized the lesbian s & m mag *Bad Attitude* from Glad Day bookstore and last month successfully prosecuted the queer emporium for carrying it. (Busby characterized the prosecution as "an almost calculated move to split feminists.") Post-Butler, the government also prosecuted Glad Day for a large shipment of gay male erotica seized by customs in 1991. The presiding Ontario judge ruled that the magazines were "degrading" and "dehumanizing" simply because they depicted sex between men.

Crozier, who has appealed the customs ruling, vows that if her case fails (as, she assured me, "99 per cent do"), she'll appeal again. She doesn't have the money to go to court, but she does have the moral support, at least, of artists' rights advocate Busby, who sits on the boards of the artists' organizations **Video Pool** and **MAWA (Mentoring Artists for Women's Art.)** But Busby is also a legal committee member of **LEAF (the Women's Legal Education and Action Fund)**, which pushed for the MacKinnon-esque language in Butler. After a year of prosecutions against women and gays, Busby says she still supports legal limits on pornography. "I'm devastated by the way that the law's been used," she said. "But I'm not ready to give up on it."

Ceremonies and Censors *May 25, 1993*

One way to silence a roomful of arts-organization and foundation honchos is to talk about fist fucking. That's what **Laurie Anderson** did on May 5 at the **Museum of Modern Art**. The program at which she spoke was called "On Freedom of Expression," but I'd characterize it as a behind-the-scenes skirmish in the culture wars.

Sponsored by five assets-heavy foundations, the invitational event honored 16 individuals who "made unusual contributions to upholding the principle of freedom of expression." From former **Cincinnati Contemporary Art Center** director **Denis Barrie** to **Franklin Furnace** founder/director **Martha Wilson**, virtually everyone denied grants during the **Frohnmayer** regime at the **NEA** was recognized. Other honorees included a censored art team, theater impresarios whose advertising was banned from buses, and the besieged director of Michigan's Monroe County library system, **Gordon Conable**. His presence was a reminder that school librarians and film programmers—not to mention pro-bono attorneys and freedom of expression groups—are the foot soldiers in the First Amendment struggle.

As the schmoozy high-mindedness at MoMA reached its zenith, I wondered whether Organizing 101 rules would apply: the purpose of political pep rallies is to get those attending to commit to your cause. Appropriately enough, that task was assigned to the charismatic artists near the end of the bill. Anderson slyly invoked fist fucking in her discussion of censorship and social control, while choreographer **Bill T. Jones** extended the theme with this challenge to the audience: "Can you stick your neck out? Can you speak out in defense of something talking about fist fucking?" Anderson also asked an equally pressing question, "Where were you [cultural leaders] three years ago?"

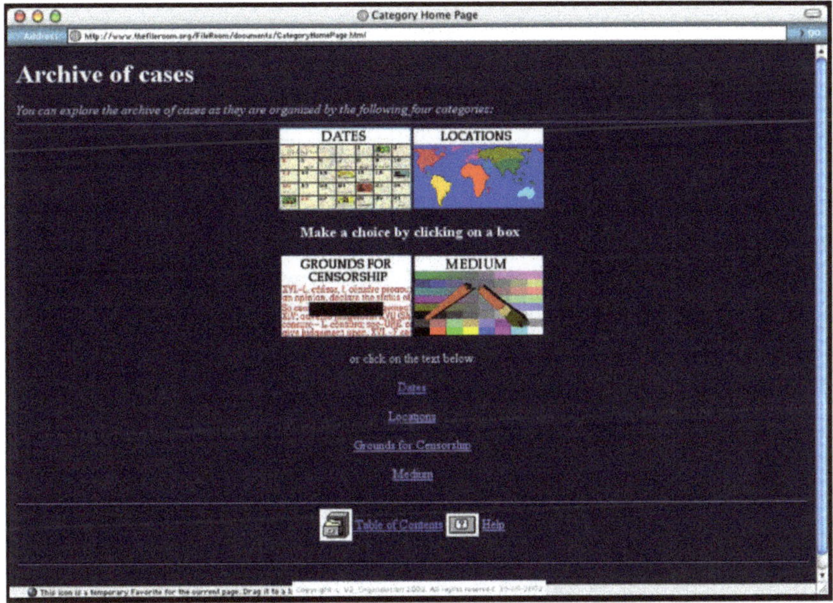

The File Room (1994), artist Antoni Muntadas's online, interactive archive of censorship throughout the ages, debuted in installation format at the Chicago Cultural Center

Censor Sensibility *June 12, 1993*

What's censorship and who's a censor? For some of us, moving a controversial artwork from a prominent to an obscure place in an exhibition fits the bill. But what about a juried show in a mall that excludes nudes? Or an art institution that never shows the work of artists of color? And let's not even mention self-censorship. **Antonio Muntadas**'s *The File Room* may be the first artwork-cum-exhibition to grapple systematically with such matters, while documenting 500 years of art censorship and human rights violations. (Included topics range from Inquisition-era book-burnings to Persian Gulf media censorship.) An interactive database, the Room will allow both on-site and remote access. The temporary installation of metal file-cabinet walls punctured by computer terminals will eventually assume the dematerialized form of an electronic archive. Its **Randolph Street Gallery** producers plan to send the *Room* on tour after its Chicago debut next May and find a permanent home for it. Although some exhibition logistics are in flux, now is the time to send accounts of your experiences with censors to Muntadas c/o Randolph Street Gallery, 756 North Milwaukee Avenue, Chicago IL 60622. . . .

Megabytes should be reserved in The File Room's database for **Canadian Customs**' recent transgressions. My March column about the agency's confiscation of **Anne Sprinkle** and **Maria Beatty**'s *Sluts and Goddesses* videotape generated voluminous mail—most of it from Canada. Ever since the Canadian Supreme Court's **MacKinnon**-esque *Butler* decision last year outlawed depictions of violent and degrading sex (but left their definitions dangerously open to interpretation), the customs jackboot has stomped down hardest on feminist and queer material. **bell hooks**'s *Black Looks: Race and Representation* was recently detained but released, while *Black Men/White Men* (which includes writing by **Langston Hughes**) and *Lovers* (non-porn fiction by **Tee Corinne**) have been seized—that is, banned. One reader sent me *Blueboy*'s safe-sex guide in which terms including (presumably) "anal" and "fucking" were meticulously blacked-out, demonstrating all too literally that censorship can kill.

October 23, 1993

More censorship: **Barbara Alper** shoots her photographs on the street, off the TV set (a recent series examined Gulf War media coverage), and sometimes at sex clubs. She's done the circuit from Chippendale's and Hellfire, to Bangkok and private boudoirs Appreciators of her sex-images include the **New York Public Library** (it owns 20 prints), Paris's *Bibliotheque Nationale*, and London's **Akehurst Gallery**, which wanted to represent her. But the gallery lost interest in repressenting Alper when 40 slides and a valuable exhibition print were seized by British customs on September 1. According to her American counsel, **Ira Lowe**, British law is quite similar to ours, and the images (some of s & m, but none of penetration) have obvious artistic value. When it comes to artists exploring sexuality, harassment remains the m.o. of customs in the English-speaking world. Not many can afford to fight back, but Alper is undaunted. She told me that she's retained **Mark Stephens** as her virtuoso London counsel. "He got Mapplethorpe images into U.K., and his firm is named—get this—**Stephens Innocent**.

SCENE & HEARD *March 8, 1994*

Vandalism took its toll on a show of erotic art presented by the **National Museum and Archives of Lesbian and Gay History** at the **Lesbian and Gay Community Services Center** in the West Village. The vandals were presumably queer gallery visitors and/or Center tenants. The show, called *"OUThouses,"* was mounted to celebrate the center's newly revamped first-floor bathrooms. Art collective **fierce pussy**'s makeover of the woman's room was delayed by construction beyond the February 13 opening, while **Big Dicks Make Me Sweat Productions**' series of 30 erotic photo-and-text works occupied the men's room. Twenty-five of them were, however, removed "immediately" by a member of **Sexual Compulsives Anonymous**, according to a press release from the show's volunteer curator **Seth Gurvitz**.

Sexual Compulsives Anonymous is one of the many 12-step groups that rent meeting space from the center. The center's deputy director **Robert Woodworth** refuses to point the finger at SCA. Nor has he (or anyone else at the center) apologized to the artists or taken any steps to educate this community about legal ways of expressing strongly held opinions. (The centers powers-that-be forbid the curator from speaking to the press.) "Artists know that we are not responsible for their work since we don't have an actual gallery space here," Woodworth noted. Despite this technicality, neither the word ethical nor responsibility crossed his lips. Big Dicks's **Joe E. Jeffreys** told me that he and his partner **John Burger** will reinstall their show, and that the center had posted a new sign posted outside the bathroom announcing sexually explicit images inside and urging the potentially offended to use the second floor men's room. "But that," Jeffreys laughed, "is the bathroom with the **Keith Haring** mural of men sucking and fucking."

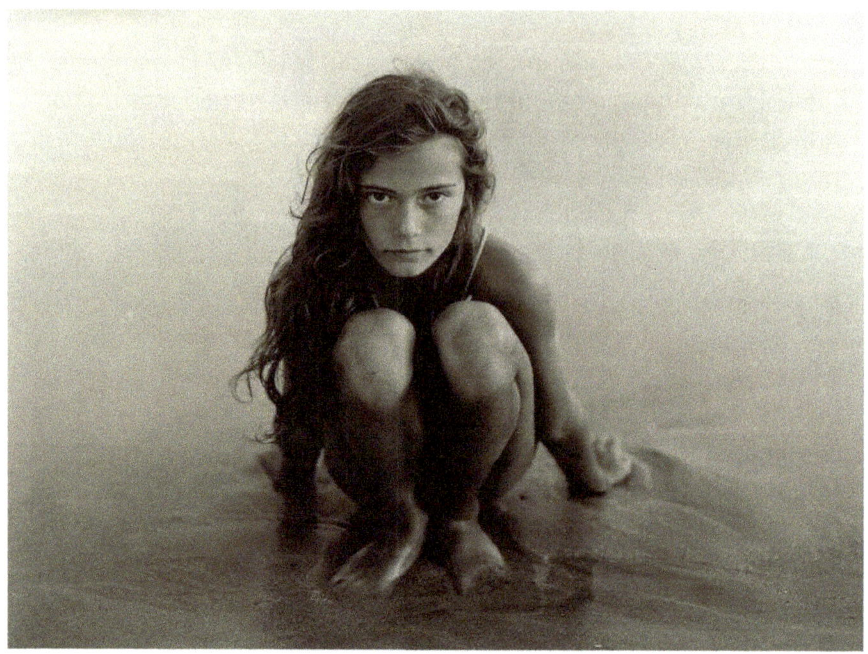

After being reported by a photo booth operator, then harassed by the FBI and law enforcement, San Francisco photographer Jock Sturges pleaded guilty to a charge of sexual misconduct, but a grand jury refused to indict him.

Art Police Strike in S.F.

Village Voice, June 12, 1990, p. 75-76,

Photographer Jock Sturges felt "on top of the world" as he bicycled home to his Richmond district apartment in San Francisco on April 25. He'd been swimming at the University of San Francisco pool and was pleasurably anticipating the opening of his exhibition at the prestigious Roger Ramsay gallery in Chicago the following week. As he got off his bike he was confronted by a phalanx of FBI agents and San Francisco Police Department officers. They believed Jock Sturges was a child pornographer, and they'd come to put him out of business.

One of their first questions that afternoon was. "Do you know Joe Semien?" Sturges, who normally makes black-and-white, large-format nudes, had given a batch of color slides to custom-color printer Semien (to make inter-negatives) so that Sturges might make C prints. The images were outtakes intended as gifts for Sturges's subjects and characterized by the photographer as "portraits, nudes on beaches, and images of fathers and daughter, most of them old friends."

Semien had exposed the film and sent it on to Newell Colour lab for processing. Lab customer-service manager Robert Couse-Baker notified the authorities. He felt obligated to do so, he told me, under California's "very specific reporting laws, which [proscribe] photos of children under 14 either engaged in sex acts or graphic displays of genitalia." (The affidavit for the warrant to search Sturges's apartment also showed that Couse-Baker informed the SFPD that the professional quality of the prints suggested that they "could be used in a magazine or other such publication.")

During the predawn hours of April 25, the FBI-SPFD raided Semien's apartment and jailed the black, 26-year-old small-businessman. Under state law, he was charged with two felony counts of producing child pornography and 10 misdemeanor counts of possessing it. A former honor student and art-school scholarship recipient, Semien was finally released the night of April 26 on his own recognizance (after failing to post $81,000 bail, later determined unnecessary.) Shortly thereafter, the public defender assigned to him urged Semien to plead guilty and plea bargain. Sturges and his lawyer, Michael Metzger, put Semien in touch with attorney Howard Specter, who is mounting a defense.

Photos and negatives by Semien confiscated in the raid on his apartment have been returned, suggesting the possibility that charges might be dismissed. (This will be determined at a pretrial conference slated for late June.) "My client committed no crime," Semien's attorney told me. "They're simply using him in an attempt to get Jock Sturges."

Sturges, however, has not yet been charged with a single crime. After meeting the FBI-SPFD squad in front of his apartment building, he climbed the stairs to his second-floor flat. An official foot was stuck in his door, so Sturges asked for a search warrant. He was informed that a search warrant is not necessary to occupy premises where suspects may destroy evidence. "We'll go easy," Sturges says they assured him, "if you cooperate." According to the artist, he refused to let them search his apartment; they entered anyway.

Sturges described that afternoon as a "nightmare." He frantically sought legal assistance as the agents and policemen entered every room of his apartment. Within an hour, Ephraim Margolin, a $350-per-hour lawyer, arrived. (Sturges later replaced Margolin with Metzger.) To escape eavesdroppers, the two retreated to the bathroom to converse in Russian! Sturges and Margolin left around four, as did the FBI-SFPD, and when Sturges and Margolin returned around five, so did the law enforcers. This time they brought a search warrant and a van.

Two hours later, Sturges's apartment—and life—was turned upside down. According to Sturges, the FBI-SFPD confiscated thousands of valuable prints and negatives, damaging some of the prints. They took his cameras, a computer, his business records, books (including *Lolita* and a children's primer in Japanese), an issue of *Mothering* magazine (for which Sturges is a contributing photographer), and slickly erotic photographs by the French photographer Jacques Bourboulon—possession of which may lead to prosecution, according to Metzger. They also removed items with no apparent evidentiary potential, including a photographic enlarger, computer printer, and darkroom light fixture.

Lawyer Metzger met with Assistant U.S. Attorney Rodolfo Orjales on May 25 to discuss the case. Nothing conclusive came of their meeting, Metzger reported, save for an agreement to schedule another confab if charges are going to be pressed. (The FBI, the SFPD, and the U.S. attorney's office did not return repeated calls for comment.) But even if the investigation is dropped and Sturges is allowed to pick up his own possessions, he's already lost $15,000 to $20,000 in legal fees, thousands of dollars worth of prints, thousands of income dollars, his equanimity (he began seeing a psychiatrist for the first time last month), and very possibly his good name. The day an article about the raid on his apartment appeared in the *San Francisco Chronicle*, he lost a seven-year-long job photographing students and members of the Marin Ballet.

Are Sturges's pictures pornographic? Not according to Peter Galassi, Museum of Modern Art photography curator, who describes Sturges's work as "a serious artistic endeavor. This work is not pornography. Sturges photographs public scenes that existed before he came along." (MoMA owns one of Sturges's photographs, as do the Metropolitan Museum and the *Bibliotheque Nationale* in Paris.) In Sturges's pictures, subjects are never engaged in sexual acts and, if under-age, are always photographed in the presence of parents or guardians. Any possible undercurrent of eroticism is both what you'd expect from male and female pubescent subjects and precisely what makes the work effective.

Until recently the legal distinction between art and pornography was crystal clear. *Miller v. California*, a 1973 Supreme Court case, stated that a work could not be found obscene unless it met three criteria, one being that "the work, taken as a whole, lacks serious literary, artistic, political, or scientific value." (Our legal system has never equated nudity and pornography.) But now, under the pretense of concern for child abuse, a full-fledged moral panic about child pornography has been fomented by the Reagan-Bush administrations. The Cincinnati-Mapplethorpe case is the best-known recent example; another involved Alice Sims, the Virginia artist whose two children were temporarily taken from her in 1988 because of the buff snapshots of them she uses in her work.

Metzger believes that despite the state charges against Semien, it is far more likely that any prosecution against Sturges will be federal. (He suspects that no California prosecutor would waste the time and money to try to get such a conviction in San Francisco, although other attorneys disagree.) In any legal venue, the relevant matter will not be the *Miller* standards of obscenity, but the prohibition against sexually explicit (i.e., pornographic) representations of minors, which makes it unnecessary to establish obscenity. Explicitness is usually statutorily defined as "sexual intercourse...bestiality...masturbation...sadistic or masochistic abuse...and *lascivious* exhibitions of the genitals" [italics added]. Lasciviousness is determined by highly subjective "tests" of whether there is a focus on the genitals, whether the setting and circumstances are sexual, and the like. In other words, lasciviousness is in the eye of the beholder.

I call the hullabaloo surrounding child pornography a *moral panic* (defined by Nina Eliasoph, author of *The Missing Children Myth*, as a situation "in which a minor social problem expresses and preempts a deeper related one") because no epidemic of child pornography exists and no child abuse-child pornography link has ever been scientifically established. At its height, prior to Anita Bryant's "Save Our Children" crusade of 1977, the total number of children involved in kiddie porn *worldwide* during the 1960s and '70s (most of which was produced abroad) did not exceed 5,000 to 7,000. What little child pornography did exist was halted by the Protection of Children From Sexual Exploitation Act of 1977. (According to the Illinois Legislative Investigating Committee report, commercially distributed child pornography had disappeared by 1980.) By the mid-1980s the U.S. Customs and Postal Service were virtually alone in "mass-marketing" child pornography in this country, according to researchers including attorney and obscenity expert Lawrence Stanley. The government's purpose, ACLU legislate counsel Barry Lynn believes, has been "a kind of entrapment."

This may help explain why the number of child pornography-related federal indictments has increased from 61 in fiscal year 1984 to 244 in 1987 and continues to balloon, according to First Amendment attorney Martin Garbus. The figures are also an index of the vast resources thrown at this "problem" by the Justice Department. Garbus cited the "spectacular funding" of the JD's Meese-founded National Obscenity Enforcement Unit (*The New York Times*, April 28), which gives money to enterprises like the Bay Area-wide task force on child pornography-headed by none other than Assistant U.S. Attorney Orjales.

When it comes to measuring this pepped-up law enforcement activity—which is typically and circularly invoked to justify increased funding—the harassment of artists such as Sims and Sturges must be taken into account. Given the amount of SFPD research entailed in compiling the affidavit on which Sturges's search warrant was based, it seems remarkable that Sturges's status as an award-winning artist who shows in San Francisco was either undiscovered or considered irrelevant to the investigation.

The FBI's long-standing interest in the regulation of sexuality hardly ended with J. Edgar Hoover's death. According to Sturges, several subjects of his photos have been unnerved by recent calls from FBI agents. One Californian I spoke with—all the members of his family have been regularly photographed by Sturges for more than a decade—clammed up in fear when I asked him about what he termed the "invasive, frightening, and upsetting call" the FBI made to his preteen daughter. He'd earlier described Sturges's extended series of photographs as "a priceless spiritual record… proudly displayed in our home."

It is ironic that this "nightmare" should be happening to Sturges, a photographer so determined to avoid embarrassing his subjects that he told me he uses onetime, instead of blanket, model releases for exhibition or publication so subjects may change their minds at any time. The Navy veteran and Rhode Island-born blue blood also reported that he recently rejected the maquette for a book of his pictures to be published by French publisher *Contrejour* because he found the selection of images a bit too "sexually oriented."

After concluding one of many conversations with Sturges, I tuned into the final episode of stylishly reactionary *Twin Peaks*, where evil lurks everywhere and must be exorcised. I arrived just in time for yet another reference to the photo-appearance of teenage coke head Laura Palmer in *Flesh World*, the series' porn periodical. What is the real meaning of the pervasive fetishization of the untouched and untouchable child (or young adult)? As Lawrence Stanley observed, "So-called child pornography—which tends to be loosely defined—is another expanding category of constitutionally unprotected speech." Photographers such as Sturges are the scapegoats for the right-wing agenda of criminalizing any representation of sexuality. In conjunction with the crusade against "obscenity," protecting the rights of crime victims becomes one more rationale for gutting the First Amendment. Jock Sturges and Joe Semien are simply pawns in this despicable game.

Thanks to Daniel Tsang for research assistance.

Follow-up: SCENE & HEARD *September 17, 1991*

From the West Coast comes the bracing news that a San Francisco federal grand jury refused to indict photographer Jock Sturges on child pornography charges, despite a wasteful, 15-month federal probe conducted in the US and France.

Continuing Coverage: Kiddie Porn 1991-94
From the *Village Voice* column *SCENE & HEARD*

Art-Porn Redux *July 19, 1991*

Congress' latest blurring of the distinction between child pornographers and artists is the "**Child Protection Restoration and Penalties Enhancement Act of 1990**." Passed in the final moments of the 101st Congress last October, the law requires anyone involved in the production or distribution of "visual depictions of actual sexually explicit conduct" to maintain detailed records of the ages and whereabouts of the models depicted and to affix to each work a statement of where those records are kept. (Anyone includes photo-finishers, book distributors, librarians, and art dealers.) Failure to do so is a felony, whether or not the work might be deemed legally obscene!

The law is currently on ice for at least 60 days, thanks to a suit filed by trade organizations including the **American Booksellers Association**, the **American Society of Magazine Photographers**, and the art world's **National Association of Artists Organizations** and **National Campaign for Freedom of Expression**. On February 26, district court judge **Stanley Sporkin** of Washington D.C. issued a restraining order preventing the justice department from enforcing the law until it issues record-keeping regulations mandated in the bill. Once regulations are issued though, it's back to the courts again.

Sponsored by senators **Strom Thurmond** and **Dennis De Concini**, this version of their unconstitutional 1988 law was passed by a gutless Congress on the eve of the 1990 elections. It is, of course, another assault on artists dealing with sexuality—and perhaps the least principled yet. Although the law's ostensible objective is the elimination of the kiddie-porn production, it will have no such effect. "The rationales advanced on behalf of this law are nonsensical," observed **David Ogden**, an attorney for the **American Library Association**. "Although proponents say it will get child pornographers convicted, offenders can't be convicted of child pornography, only of not keeping records."

How will it affect artists? It will transform some of them into felons by creating a body of work exempted from the protection of the First Amendment. Ogden noted that if the law had been in effect last year, several Mapplethorpe photos might have been targeted for lack of required labeling, even though a Cincinnati jury found that they did not violate Ohio's extremely tough obscenity and child pornography laws.

Charlotte Murphy, executive director of the National Association of Artists' Organizations, finds the language of the bill so vague that it could be "used against" artists ranging from **Nan Goldin** and **David Wojnarowicz** to **Sally Mann** and (even) **Eric Fischl**. "How do we know how some sheriff is going to interpret the nudity in Sally Mann's photos?" Murphy asked warily. "And what about when **Allen Frame**'s picture was gay-bashed in the East Village last year? Should his name and address have been affixed?"

Barbara Pollack—an artist, ex-attorney, and mother—filed an affidavit in the case expressing her concerns about the new law. She makes what she calls "viewer-interactive peep show" assemblages focused on images culled from straight (adult) porno mags. How she'll meet the new law's reporting requirements is a worry itself. "My art is about the forbidden. How can it operate with a government stamp of approval? What we'll have," she sighed, "is the sex regulation bureau."

Artists who think they might be affected by the law should contact the National Association of Artists Organizations (at 202-347-6350) or the National Campaign for Freedom of Expression (at 202-393-2787) to submit statements for the next round in court.

February 4, 1992

The **ACLU's Arts Censorship Project** recently initiated its campaign for the abolition of the Justice Department's Child Exploitation and Obscenity Section. Given that commercially distributed kiddie porn disappeared during the late 70's—according to an Illinois Legislative Investigating Committee report—the oddly named outfit now works to eliminate adult videos and other First Amendment-protected forms of expression. Last month's kick-off press conference in Washington featured photographer **Jock Sturges**, playwright **David Henry Hwang**, and novelist **Susan Isaacs**. "How come," Isaacs asked, "we've become a nation of weenies, unable to see or hear anything that offends us?"

Lolita Syndrome *April 14, 1992*

Despite a decade of evidence that kiddie-porn trafficking in the U.S. is virtually nonexistent, the feds keep harassing artists who've photographed nude children: including **Alice Sims**, **Jock Sturges**, and **Robert Mapplethorpe** (or his estate). Add British artist **Graham Ovenden** and his Manhattan publisher, **Lawrence Stanley**, to the list. The former is well known in the U.K. for his moody paintings and photographs of nude girls—imagine **Balthus** by way of **Alex Katz**—and the latter just happens to be an attorney and author of an award-winning *Playboy* expose documenting the government's current role as the perhaps exclusive commercial distributor of pornography depicting minors.

The allegedly lascivious goods in question were seized by **U.S. Customs** last October. They include photographs and the final page proofs of **States of Grace**, the book of Ovenden's nudes that Stanley is publishing. At a March 20 hearing in Eastern District Federal Court, Assistant U.S. Attorney **Brigid Rohde** finally announced that civil forfeiture proceedings would be brought against the entire packet of materials, valued by Stanley at $4,500. The reason? One page proof shows 10-year-old subject **Maud Hewes** sitting nude with one leg propped on a ledge, the other dangling down over the ledge.

Since obscenity does not have to be established where minors are concerned—obviating the artistic-value criterion of the so-called three-prong *Miller v. California* obscenity test—Hewes's parted legs are the prosecutorial key to determining lasciviousness. The kicker is that it's not the government that has to prove lasciviousness here, but Stanley who must essentially demonstrate its absence. Once again, the laws of the last decade paying lip service to protecting children are being used to fetishize their supposedly untouchable bodies. (The prevalence of incest and child abuse tells the real story about too many children being touched.) Ovenden's model Hewes, now 18 years old, explained to me, "When I modeled for Graham, I'd make up the poses and he'd shoot them. He never asked me to be sexy and I never tried to... he's been a family friend since I was four years old."

Censorama *November 10, 1992*

It's the courts, of course, that define pornography, and an October 15 ruling by the **Third U.S. Circuit Court of Appeals** expanded that definition. The Philadelphia court ruled, for the first time, that clothed depictions of children may be pornography, if "lascivious" displays of the genitalia (actually the clothing covering the genitalia) are the focus. This focus—much less the image-maker's intent—is often difficult to pinpoint, as the **Mapplethrope** trial demonstrated. **Lawrence Stanley**, an attorney for Pennsylvania defendant **Stephen Knox**, noted that "Congress clearly meant nudity when it wrote the law." Although the depictions at issue were not artworks, Stanley observed that the implications of the ruling are potentially broad: "Anyone who photographs the kids around the pool—8parents, artists like **Gerard Malanga**, better watch out." On-the-beach music videos with under-18 models are also at risk.

Ironically, today's most vociferous defender of the **First Amendment** is **John Frohnmayer.** I heard the ex-NEA chair speak at the New York State arts conference on October 15, and he was the scheduled main event at a two-day "community dialogue on censorship" in Minneapolis at the end of October. The public official who made a career of caving into **Jesse Helms**'s fundamentalist cabal is now preaching that "freedom of expression is not a compromisable position." The attempt to rehabilitate his reputation isn't merely **Nixon**ian, it also seems to be working. The weirdest part of Frohnmayer's 9 a.m. performance was his vocalization of a parody he sang (!) to the tune of "We Are Marching To Pretoria": "We are marching to oblivion/Don't give in, not to sin…"

Art Molesters *February 15, 1994*

Roseanne Arnold's view of **Michael Jackson**—"the perfect picture of a child molester"—apparently jibes with many prosecutors' image of photographers who take pictures of their unclothed children. Late last year, police seized the work of two photographer-mothers, **Marilyn Zimmerman** and **Robyn Stoutenburg**. The good news is that no charges were filed against Zimmerman, and that those filed against Stoutenburg have been dropped. The bad news is that both were forced to obtain costly legal representation and to face the horrific prospect of losing custody of their children.

When it comes to imagery of children-in-the-buff, federal law encourages citizen surveillance of other citizens. Zimmerman, a tenured **Wayne State (Michigan) University** art prof, was brought to the attention of campus police by a janitor who retrieved (filched?) from the trash a contact sheet depicting Zimmerman's three-year-old daughter bathing and sometimes touching her crotch. After questioning Zimmerman, 12 police officers made a shambles of her home and office as they confiscated eight boxes of pictures, negatives, and exhibited artworks.

Tuscon, Arizona, police learned about Stoutenburg from a school principal who was concerned that her students could see the photographer's prints of nudes and foods by looking through the window of **Gallery Six & 13**, where they were hanging. (No, the principal didn't bother to call the gallery.) A dozen pictures—including images of a partly nude woman with an egg on her stomach and Stoutenburg's four-year-old son holding a plucked chicken in front of his genitals—were seized. Tucson mayor **George Miller** sensibly asserted that the seizure of pictures without art-expert input "smacks of censorship," while deputy Pima County attorney **Kathleen Mayer** believes that the chicken picture implies felonious sexual contact.

Although Zimmerman and Stoutenburg's travails seem depressingly contemporary, such artist abuse hardly began post-**Ed Meese**. Consider an incident in which the *Voice* was involved (long before I worked here) in 1979. Photographer **Jacqueline Livingston** produced a series of multi-image posters of male nudes during the late '70s, including one with shots of her six-year-old son playing with himself. Two days after the *Voice* printed an illustrated article about Livingston, she received a letter notifying her that she was the subject of a report of suspected child abuse.

Four months later, **New York Child Protection Services** declared the report "unfounded." In 1979, the existence of child sexuality (and presumed innocence) seems to have been at least tacitly acknowledged; today Livingston, who lost her **Cornell University** teaching job because of the widely publicized incident, might be doing time.

More: At the urging of anticensorship groups, the House recently deleted language from the **Violence Against Women Act** implying a causal link between porn and violence. Let senators **Moynihan** and **D'Amato** know you want this offensive linkage removed from the Senate's version of the bill....An **ACLU** survey on censorship in Minnesota libraries found that 73 per cent of respondents felt pressured to censor themselves. One noted that "in 19 years of being a school librarian my biggest problem has been elementary teachers worrying about their students' minds being corrupted by witches or sex in books."

O, Canada *January 18, 1994*

Canada's precipitous slide into a free-expression-free zone continues unabated. The **Canadian Supreme Court**'s adoption of the so-called *Butler* decision, a **MacKinnon**-esque outlawing of imagery that "degrades" women, has led yahoo customs officials repeatedly to ban feminist and queer materials from entering

Canada. (**Annie Sprinkle** and **Maria Beatty**'s self-help tape, *Sluts and Goddesses*, recently banned on appeal, is both.) Last June, under election-time pressure, the conservative government hastily passed an anti-kiddie-porn bill that bans the depiction of (undefined) "sexually explicit activity" involving people under 18 or those depicted as being under 18. In other words, Canadians over age 14 can legally engage in consensual sex, but nobody can depict it.

It was only a matter of time before an artist was charged under this draconian law; 26 year-old **Eli Langer** now faces up to 10 years in jail for allegedly violating it. At a December 22 press conference, the Toronto painter defended his Old Masters-y paintings of masturbation, and sex between adults and children, as an "effort to address both personal and social issues." Artist **Elaine Carol** characterized them for the Toronto Sun as "beautiful paintings that bravely explore the patriarchal abuse handed down from grandfather to youth."

I haven't seen images about these works about child abuse (nor will you), because Langer's lawyer, **Frank Addario**, can't send photos of them to the *Voice* without exposing himself to charges of possessing and distributing child pornography!

Why did Langer have to explain his intentions at a feeding frenzy of a press conference? Astonishingly, according to Addario, it is unclear whether the burden of proof of artistic merit rests with the artist or the government. Think this couldn't happen here? Thank 104-mostly Republican-members of Congress for their December 27, friend of the court brief to head off the **Clinton** administration's more-morally-macho-than-**Pat Robertson** attempt to widen our child pornography laws to include depictions of clothed children not acting lasciviously.

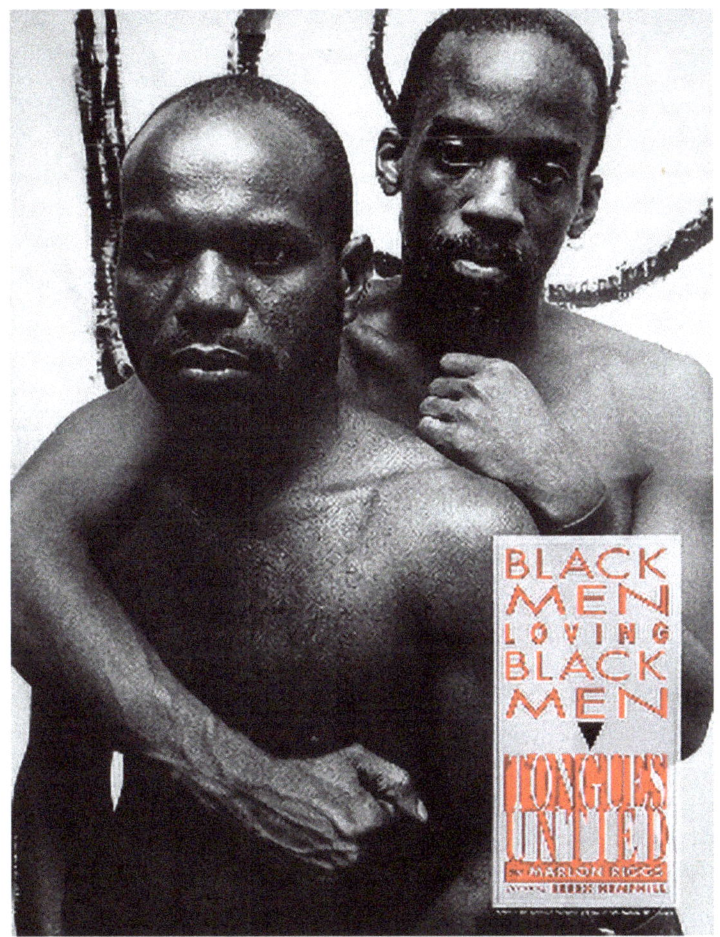

Tongues Tied

Village Voice, July 2, 1991

The censorship drums are beating again. Their tattoo is *Tongues Untied*, a lyrical meditation on black gay identity by filmmaker Marlon Riggs. Scheduled for nationwide distribution on July 16 as part of PBS's *P.O.V.* series the film will not be aired by at least 17 of 50 PBS station in the largest U.S. television markets. Another 11 stations have rescheduled it for late-night viewing after the usual 10 p.m. national "feed."

Tongues is one of the most honored films of the past decade.

Since 1989, it's garnered the best documentary award at the Berlin International Film Festival and the Los Angeles Film Critics' designation as Best Independent/Experimental Work. Not incidentally, *Tongues* was broadcast last year without any problems on public television stations here in New York, as well as in Los Angeles and San Francisco. It's difficult to imagine a more apt contribution to a series of personal documentaries like *P.O.V.*

But not for everybody. The five objecting PBS program managers and spokespersons I talked to blandly cited audience sensibilities about language (the F-word is spoken in the film) and "community values," but—no fools, they—each insisted that homosexuality *per se* was not an issue. None of them—from places as disparate as Portland and Wichita—described the film as "reprehensible," a comment that was attributed to an anonymous programmer by Paul Lomartire, the *Palm Beach Post* TV critic who made this fuss public a few weeks ago.

As with Andres Serrano's infamous *Piss Christ* photo, a word can be worth a thousand pictures. To describe *Tongues* in Lomartire's words, as "contain[ing] sexual street language rarely heard on television, as well as full frontal nudity and drawings of male genitals" is akin to describing *Mona Lisa* as a bosomy gal with a goody smile. Not exactly inaccurate, but not quite the whole story, either.

In fact, *Tongues* is remarkably poetic. It is also sensuous and frank. Evocations of homosex and racially charged material cohabit; shadowy images of men kissing follow hard on defiant accounts of racial prejudice. The film's refrain "Let's end the silence" allusively echoes ACT UP's Silence=Death dictum. *Tongues Untied* is not merely Riggs's title, but his aim as an artist and an activist.

It's an apt metaphor; silence is precisely the issue in this censorious climate. Since both *P.O.V.* and *Tongues Untied* are NEA-funded, it's no surprise that Donald Wildmon of the American Family Association has leapt at the opportunity to play on both homophobia and racism. (Wildmon, who told me he hasn't seen the film, is, interestingly enough, encouraging public television to air it because "this is the first time average viewers will be able to see how the NEA spends their tax money.") Whether such a smear campaign will succeed or blow over like the recent *scandale* about Todd Hayne's *Poison* remains to be seen.

Marc Weiss, *P.O.V.*'s executive producer, describes Tongues Untied as "extraordinary and powerful...it transforms consciousness with its humor and passion and intellect." Will the controversy make it harder for *P.O.V.* to deal with gay/lesbian and racial issues in the future? "That's part of our mandate," Weiss said matter-of-factly. "If we aren't open to provocative work, then we should put ourselves out of business."

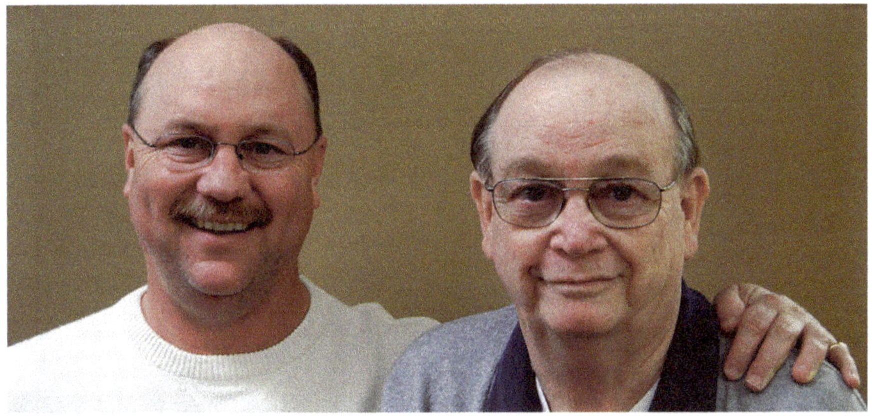

Tim Wildmon (Left) & his Dad Donald (Right)

Damned Undammed

Village Voice, Sept 22, 1992, Nov 10, 1992

Only the merest chance remains that a September 8 decision releasing Reverend Donald Wildmon's hold on the American distribution of *Damned in the U.S.A.*, an Emmy Award-winning documentary about arts censorship, might be reversed. That's good news for the British producers of the film.

The ruling by federal district court judge Glenn Davidson caps an August 11-12 trial in Abeerdeen, Mississippi, and rejects Wildmon's assertion that he has a contractual agreement granting him virtual control of the British film's distribution in the U.S. in exchange for his filmed interview. Davidson instead sided with the filmmakers, who were supported in a countersuit against the anti-porn crusader by a lengthy roster of film and civil rights groups.

On September 10, Benjamin Bull, aptly named counsel for Wildmon's American Family' Association, filed a motion with Davidson to stay the enforcement of the judges decision while the 5th Circuit Court of Appeals reviews the case. But Russell Smith, an attorney for the documentary's producers, Paul Yule and Jonathan Stack, isn't worried: He terms the motion "pure harassment". Smith also predicts that any stay granted by Davidson will be vacated immediately by the appellate court because the lower court found "every issue of fact in our favor and the legal questions are relatively straightforward."

Perhaps more reassuring, the distributors who balked at picking up the documentary until legal matters were resolved have now booked it. Bull—described in *TV Guide*'s September 5 issue as a crony of convicted S&L looter Charles Keating, Jr.—did not return calls for comment.

The case's symbolism is more important than its potential to set progressive legal precedent. So too is the irony especially rich. Despite the participation of heavy-hitting, free expression co-plaintiffs such as the ACLU's Arts Censorship Project and People for the American Way, the decision was reached on the basis of contract, rather than First Amendment, law. Sidestepping most philosophical concerns, Judge Davidson succinctly noted in his ruling that "both parties focus their attention on a single [disputed] paragraph of contract." But he also acknowledged that public interest was in favor of open viewership and debate.

Surely the most loathsome aspect of the trial was Wildmon's hypocrisy in bringing the suit. The latter-day Comstock said in a written statement that his motive was to avoid being seen alongside "pornographic and anti-Christian imagery" by the likes of artists Robert Mapplethrope, Andres Serrano, and David Wojnarowicz. Put another way, he damned *Damned in the U.S.A.* for presenting dirty pictures.

Bear in mind that Wildmon's AFA issued a press release on June 20, 1991, urging Americans to watch the PBS presentation of *Tongues Untied*, Marlin Rigg's film about queer African Americans, in order to see for themselves how NEA funds were spent. Or consider the fact the late David Wojnarowicz successfully sued Wildmon in 1990 for using, without his permission, a porno-photo fragment from the artist's "Sex Series" prints on an AFA fund-raising newsletter. (He had to take the anti-porn crusader back to court on contempt charges a year later for continuing to distribute the same publication. Smith told me that both of these items were introduced as evidence.) I remember a conversation with Wojnarowicz after he prevailed on the art-mutilation charges, but received just $1 in damages. "I'm sure the Rev's making plenty of money," he chuckled. Amen.

Follow Up SCENE & HEARD *November 10, 1992*

Fresh from its courtroom vindication, I saw *Damned in the USA*, Paul Yule's artful documentary about the censorship wars at a benefit for the film's Legal defense fund on October 12. The BBC's Channel 4 production puts ploddingly "balanced" American documentaries to shame. The benefit also featured Lou Reed singing a new version of "Take a Walk on the Wild Side" called "Take a Walk on the Wildmon," The new lyrics?."Donald Wildmon was damned in the USA/Tried to get Channel 4 to pay and pay.../ And the fundamentalists said 'sue, sue, sue.'..."

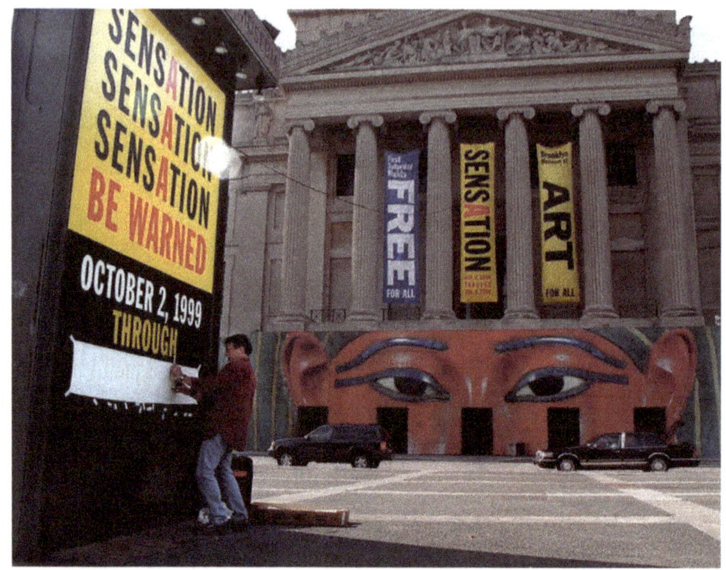

Sensation! *gave new meaning to the notion of conflict of interest at contemporary museums. Shown at the city's Brooklyn Museum, the exhibition showcased works by the so-called Young British Artists, all owned by Charles Saatchi, an advertising exec instrumental to the success of Margaret Thatcher's campaigns for Prime Minister*

New *Sensation!* Old Question

Media Channel website, 2000

When did the media start hating artists? Was it in 1948, after Jackson Pollock hit his loose-limbed stride? Or 1848, when Gustave Courbet first exhibited his revolutionary socialist screeds in paint? Whatever date you choose, one thing is certain: The current Culture-War brouhaha over a supposedly blasphemous painting in the Brooklyn Museum's Sensation! show is simply another step in the victory of the symbolic over the real, the morphing of the modern art world into the postmodern media realm. President Theodore Roosevelt dissed Marcel Duchamp's *Nude Descending A Staircase* by likening it to a Navajo rug during its presentation in the Armory Show of 1913. But unlike mayor Rudolph Giuliani's recent attack on Chris Ofiili's lyrical canvas *Holy Virgin Mary* (1996) and the Brooklyn Museum for exhibiting it, he wasn't bashing the painting as a campaign strategy. And Roosevelt—at least—had not only seen the object of his amused disaffection but written a review of the epochal show.

Duchamp helped bring to the US both avant-garde art and the idea of ongoing cultural controversy, the *succes de scandale* that often accompanies it. American art with some notable exceptions hadn't been taken seriously enough to raise hackles until the post-World War II "triumph of American art" thrust it into the international limelight. A sort of cultural schizophrenia began to develop with Jackson Pollock. During the quarter-century after the war, artists tended to be regarded not only as innocents—that is tortured souls and saintly fools a la van Gogh—but simultaneously as duplicitous tailors of the emperor's new clothes. In pop cultural terms, this is the distance between movies with traditional attitudes about artists like *Lust for Life* (1956) and other, newer ones like *Blow Up* (1966) that preach a more up-to-date art-gospel: Artists could now be young and sexy; art could be fun and even profitable. (Good-bye existential angst, hello recognizable imagery!)

Perhaps it was the money that turned the tide of a feckless media against artists. By the mid-eighties, the burgeoning American art market did for artists what Watergate had done for politicians: It revealed the industry behind the idealistic rhetoric. Pop-culture-*meisters* were shocked (*shocked!*) and made an abrupt about face in their treatment of artists. They turned on them with a vengeance. Beginning in the mid-eighties, art in films became a joke (*After Hours*), an accessory for the status conscious (*Wall Street* and *The Moderns*), a commodity subject to unscrupulous manipulation (*Legal Eagles*) and an aphrodisiac (*9 1/2 Weeks*.) Artists were similarly trivialized as narcissists in Martin Scorsese's *Life Lessons* segment of *New York Stories*, Merchant/Ivory's *Slaves of New York*, and the TNT biopic *Margaret Bourke-White*.

But Hollywood's art bashing seemed almost subtle compared to television's. Morley Safer's emblematic "Yes—But Is It Art?" segment of *60 Minutes* on September 22, 1993 plumbed positively pre-modern depths. It coupled fifties-style my-kid-could-have-painted-that insults with preposterous assaults on artists like Cy

Twombly (whom Safer dubbed the creator of "scrawls done with the wrong end of a brush.") The segment's vilification of artists smacked of the Blacklisting of the fifties, the last time the credibility of artists *en masse* was attacked. Safer's targets included Robert Ryman, whose retrospective was due to open that month at the Museum of Modern Art (MoMA). Journalistic ethics obliged that Safer seek a comment from the show's curator, Rob Storr, but apparently ethics can be damned when it comes to art. The "Yes-But Is It Art?" segment proffered so venomous a view that MoMA director Glenn Lowery refused to let Safer's camera crew inside the museum to cover its Pollock retrospective in 1998, calling Safer's art reports "drive-by shootings."

This is also an accurate description of the media's unconscionably superficial approach to the arts in general. If you don't believe in the power of sound bytes, just ask Karen Finley, one of the so-called NEA 4. For a work in which the debased condition of women was vividly inscribed on her body, the performance artist was branded "the chocolate-smeared woman." Most of the contemporary artists under attack have seen their complex works reduced to a politician's inane one-liner. Artistic intention is either ignored or passed over in favor of a focus on controversial acts or even a provocative title: Consider Andres Serrano's *Piss Christ*, or *The Holy Virgin Mary*, the work by Ofili deemed blasphemous by Mayor Giuliani for the Anglo-Nigerian-Roman Catholic artist's signature incorporation on his work of elaborately wrapped, shellacked, and jeweled packets of elephant dung, a conventional practice within a Nigerian cultural context.

Is art so complex we can't expect media makers to understand it? Indeed contemporary art requires some specialized knowledge to be understood, but so do Serbian politics and leveraged buyouts. The biggest part of the problem may be the ghettoization of arts coverage at the back of the back. Whether news or reviews, the arts tend to be treated (badly) by critics sometimes lacking the training of journalists. And vice versa: the *Times*' two front-page stories by non-arts reporters about the Brooklyn Museum's financing of *Sensation!* were embarrassingly ill-informed. They cited such alleged ethical irregularities in the exhibition's corporate sponsor (Christie's) and in the museum's showing of a private collection, apparently unaware of how common such practices are at American museums. Given the huge size of the art industries, the demand for more sophisticated coverage would seem to be a no-brainer.

Still, the *Times* worked hard on the hometown *Sensation!* story, producing far more extensive reporting about it than any previous Culture War subject. (An editor friend remarked to me "they're crusading for a Pulitzer on this one.") A slew of reporters covered infighting among museum directors (some of whom are dependent on city funding) and the attempts of Metropolitan Museum director Philippe de Montebello and MoMA director Glenn Lowry to obscure their failures to protest the mayor's action in a timely way. The paper has also covered the case of the Cuban Museum in Miami, which was shuttered for political reasons. But only the *Daily News* noted the political fallout for the New York Mayor by reporting the happy results of a poll from *Crain's New York Business* that had respondents "support[ing] the Brooklyn Museum in its current confrontation with the mayor" by a majority of 95% to 5%.

Nor was the print media attuned to community support for the Brooklyn Museum, including a large New York Civil Liberties Union-organized event on the steps of the museum the night before the show opened. It featured thousands of demonstrators and more than four dozen speakers including former NEA chair Jane Alexander, actress Susan Sarandon, politicians, artists and writers, including myself. (You can watch my speech on RealVideo.). And no media outlet I'm aware of set this controversy within the context of expansion-minded and cash-strapped museums operating in a climate of reduced public funding. To offset these losses, museums increasingly turn to corporations single-mindedly intent on communicating their public-minded support for museums, which comes at (literal) prices far cheaper—and more savory—than the equivalent advertising.

But the real story for New Yorkers that should have appeared on front pages—rather than relegated to editorial and op-ed sections—is the Mayor's long and demagogic history of First Amendment assaults. When Federal Judge Nina Gershon ruled against the city on November 1 on clear-cut constitutional grounds, Giuliani promptly promised a taxpayer-funded appeal. Unfortunately, the city has won only two of more than twenty such suits it has already filed and the chances of winning this one are thin.

Stranger still, around Thanksgiving, a crime our garrulous, law-and-order mayor chose not to deplore was a physical attack by Dennis Heiner, a retired teacher, on Ofili's work. Echoing the Mayor, he termed Ofili's work "blasphemous." The story received only the scantest attention from the dailies. Perhaps they'd already moved on to other stories. Or perhaps they were simply falling back on their conventional attitudes about contemporary art. If they ever manage to get over this hostility, they would be able to perform a much-needed public service: connecting the dots coupling freedom of the press and freedom of expression.

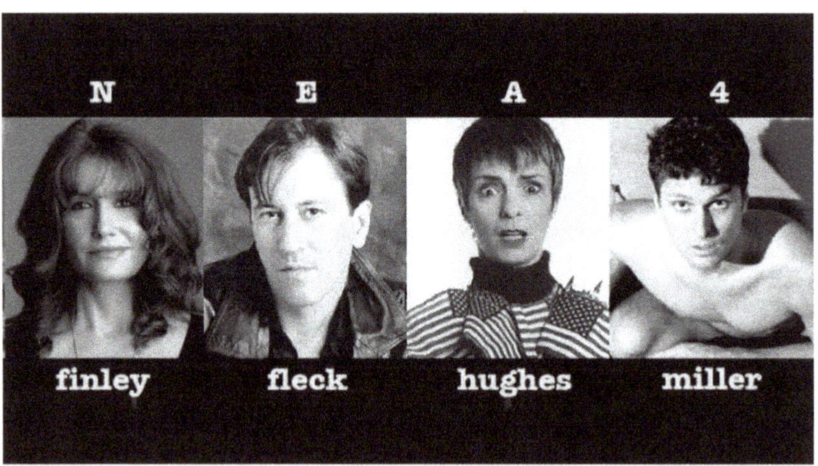

The N.E.A. Four (all right, 2 of them) Re-Unite

From Artery: The AIDS-Arts Forum online, spring 2000 issue, "In Motion" MS pp

Tim Miller and Holly Hughes write and perform text-based works about being queer in America. In 1990 they became notorious as two of the so-called NEA 4 performance artists who sued the National Endowment for the Arts for rescinding their grants based on content, that is the illegal application of political criteria in evaluating their work.

Both arrived in New York in the late seventies. Hughes began working with a group of women at WOW Café and developed her early plays such as *The Well of Horniness* in these collaborations. A collection of her plays has been published under the title *Clit Notes: A Sapphic Sampler* and a piece she is currently writing, *Preaching to the Perverted,* is partly an account of the lawsuit the "NEA Four" filed against the federal government.

Miller, soon after arriving in New York, co-founded with Charles Moulton and Charles Dennis Performance Space 122 (PS 122), the prominent East Village performance venue. In 1986, Miller returned to Los Angeles and soon co-founded Highways Performance Space. Since then, he has produced numerous works including *My Queer Body* (1992), *Fruit Cocktail* (1996), and *Shirts and Skin* (1997), based on his autobiographical novel of the same name. His latest work, *Glory Box*, is based on the INS problems he and his Australian lover have faced in connection with the latter's move to the U.S.

Robert Atkins (RA): Refresh readers' memories about the NEA 4 trial. What were the central issues and what happened?

Tim Miller (TM): In 1990, I, a wandering queer performance artist, had been awarded a National Endowment for the Arts' Solo Performer Fellowship, which was promptly overturned under political pressure from the Bush White House. No doubt because of the lush, wall-to-wall homo themes of my creative work. We so-called "NEA 4" (me, Karen Finley, John Fleck and Holly Hughes) then successfully sued the federal government with the help of the ACLU—if you're not a card-carrying member, become one!—for violation of our First Amendment rights. We won a settlement where the government paid us the amount of the defunded grants and all court costs.

Holly Hughes (HH): For the record my grant was also an individual performer's fellowship. Of course, the defunding happened at the height—or perhaps we should say the depths—of the panic about federally funded queer art. Think Robert Mapplethorpe and

Andres Serrano.

TM: The last little driblet of this case was the "decency" clause, which Congress had added to the NEA appropriation at the cattle prodding of Jesse Helms. Judge Wallace Tashima of the Ninth Federal Circuit Court had sagely declared this "decency" clause unconstitutional and thrown it out. This might have had a happy ending, except for our supposed friend Bill Clinton, who allowed the Justice Department to appeal this decision to the highest court.

HH: Some friend! As if Jane and John Doe rose up off their couch and demanded this. It was another calculated move by the religious right to raise money and raise their profile. The Christian Coalition was a fringe group before the attacks on the NEA began. Whoever encouraged the NEA to dump the four of us was either very smart or very lucky. We are four artists whose art often aims to be provocative or controversial, working in a marginal field that is poorly understood. Few people have seen performance art and the phrase is often used as shorthand for "bad theater".

RA: Most people think that this litigation ended in the early nineties. But that's not true.

TM: Oh, no. If you read your newspaper in 1998, not so long ago, you'll know that the Supremes decided that it was okay not to fund "indecent art" in their NEA 4 decision. The law "neither inherently interferes with First Amendment rights nor violates constitutional vagueness principles," Justice Sandra Day O'Connor wrote in her majority opinion. In a disappointing 8-1 decision the high court hitched up with Helms and his ilk and said the National Endowment for the Arts can consider "decency" in deciding who gets public money for the arts. I was grateful that at least Justice David H. Souter showed that he understood the assault on artists that has been taking place in this country for the past ten years. He was the lone dissenter, saying the law should be struck down as unconstitutional because it was "substantially overbroad and carries with it a significant power to chill artistic production and display."

HH: The decision is typical of the kind of "justice" stigmatized groups receive when they seek redress through the legal system. You think you have proof of some wrongdoing, in our case, a paper trail clearly demonstrating that the defunding was based on our sexual identities, rather than our work. Not to mention ten years' of other defundings, other exhibits closed, etc. But the Supremes ignored all this. In fact I'd bet that only Souter and Scalia read the briefs. They claimed that discrimination against "minority" viewpoints would be wrong, had it ever happened. Hello? Do they read the papers?

RA: Let me give you an opportunity to dispel the notion that this litigation made you rich and famous. What was it really like?

TM: A colonoscopy! I felt my work was trivialized and misrepresented all over the place. Whole swaths of the country that I used to perform and teach in became off-limits. I lost so many jobs. Here's an example of how this goes on and on and on. Last year, [years after the case had taken place] I was performing in Chattanooga. As the audience arrives at the theater so do the protesters. They are a motley bunch of seven or eight men who have stashed their wives and children at the corner and set up shop across the street, The audience members were forced to walk by the protesters across the street who by now are waving their confederate flags. (The black cops we had hired for security don't seem too thrilled.) The protesters shouted the usual charming greetings: "Faggots! God made Adam and Eve, Not Adam and Steve! Sodomites Burn in Hell," etc. The children down the street join in these cries, which seem to demonstrate this particular denomination's version of family values: Not! There is unsated blood lust in the air. The barkers lend the air of a carnival as well as public hanging. The situation is simultaneously absurd and terrifying.

HH: The belief that there is no such thing as bad publicity is so widespread and so deeply rooted that it's stronger than any evidence of harm I could offer. Ultimately, that was what was most painful for me; even most of my friends were jealous. I felt incredibly isolated.

But here is an answer: Even if it was personally the greatest thing that ever happened, if I'd made piles of money and bought a few tropical islands and the like, it was a terrible thing for this country. It legitimized the religious right, it eviscerated the NEA so that there is no more funding for individual artists, and, most important, it established a precedent for more attacks on free expression in any publicly funded domain.

RA: Can you talk about a direct affect on your work?

HH: Sure...I really like working under the threat of a Justice Department investigation of me as a child pornographer! And I can't be the only artist in the country who is actually inspired by bad reviews. Every day the press was going on about what a rotten artist I was, was a day I was able to churn out more operas, more books, and more paintings. I loved it! I just wish every artist could have the advantages I've had!

TM: Actually, the NEA struggles didn't influence my work nearly as much as the reality of HIV-AIDS had in the early nineties or my struggles with the INS these last five years. I do have a major case of NEA fatigue, but I know that it is something important to keep looking at, even if it's something I don't think about much these days.

The culture wars seem all squishy and homey compared to the real-life war the US government continually wages on my relationship with my Australian partner Alistair through its denial of the immigration rights that every straight person is afforded by marriage. This other "culture" war will almost certainly force us from the US next year into exile to a civilized country like Australia or the UK. These battles are connected, of course.

RA: How do you deal with the possibility of self-censorship? Do you actually see it going on in others—that is, in the culture? Or intuit it happening?

TM: There is no question that the "chilling effect" is as real as the [melting] polar ice cap! I hear this from artists and students all over the country. It's so embarrassing that the Supreme Court made this decision that undermined the First Amendment. I will look forward to the time—in the not too distant future, I hope—when a teacher will step before a community college class exploring late twentieth century social movements and say, "Now, students, I know it is shocking to believe this, but there was once a time as recent as the late 1990's when lesbian and gay men were actually denied certain civil rights within our democratic society. The Supreme Court even upheld a series of laws that made discriminations against them constitutional!"

HH: You look at what is happening in theaters and performance spaces it's easy to see—at least to me—that there is not much of an edge these days. I think there is more edgy subversive stuff happening in other media. Can a presenter make money by presenting controversial work? Undoubtedly. But it's short term gain. The box office bump is not going to cover increased scrutiny by funders. Unfortunately, the only way the dominant culture pays attention to art is if there is some scandal.

RA: Tim, you spoke of being picketed by fringe right-wingers. Do people in their twenties know anything about the history of the Culture War and censorship struggles?

TM: Certainly people study the thrills and chills of the (on-going) culture war in college and universities. I get several emails a day from people writing their theses and dissertations about my penis and such.

HH: I think people know about it in a general way, but many of the young people were just kids in 1990. And the media coverage was—and remains—so problematic and sensationalistic when any controversy arises. You get a few villains, a few victims, no cause and effect, no context or connections. But I think there is interest, definitely.

RA: Many American artists working in hybrid and avant-garde live-art forms have found more support for their work in Europe than the US over the past two decades. Is there an interest in your queer or AIDS work outside the US? In identity-politics-related work by anybody?

TM: Europe has always been more receptive to formalist, interdisciplinary work. The more politicized, identity-based performance work around sexuality, AIDS and race is seen as a peculiarly American discourse. Some of this is on account of language issues, of course. Much of this work is very text-based and presumes fluency in English.

HH: I agree with Tim. The type of work I do does not translate to Europe as easily as more abstract, multimedia works. Not only is my work very text-based, but I think that identity-based performance work is a particularly American idiom. There is a long tradition of representing history in the first person here that has been part of social change movements like the civil rights movement, second wave feminism, and post-stonewall gay liberation. But it's also rooted in the tradition of romantic individualism that is so American.

RA: Do you see a difference between homophobia and AIDS-phobia? If so what?

TM: Homophobia is a deep-rooted theme of American life, like racism. AIDS-phobia is a pernicious variation on that theme. I think we can't overstate how poisoned our country is by homophobia in all its variations. Anti-gay bigotry is really the lingua franca, the gold standard, the cream in the coffee of the radical religious right's final gasp at controlling our country. The jury is still out on whether they are going to be successful in this. As I've mentioned, this toxic bigotry reaches into every corner of my life here and determines whether I will even be able to remain in my country with Alistair or leave.

HH: Tim is perhaps more knowledgeable about this than I am, but I think that AIDS-phobia is not so much a variation of homophobia so much as part of a collection of phobias that revolve around the body, sexuality and race. They are two points of light in the same constellation or maybe two black holes in the same astronomical cul-de-sac. Americans have always imagined their sexual anxieties as fear of a contagion. Couple this with a sexually transmitted disease that first affected the most stigmatized communities and some people imagine that they've found "proof" that these deeply-rooted prejudices are based on something rational.

RA: It's exhausting but maybe there's nothing to do but keep making a fuss or at least continuing to talk about it.

TM: Thanks for the opportunity.

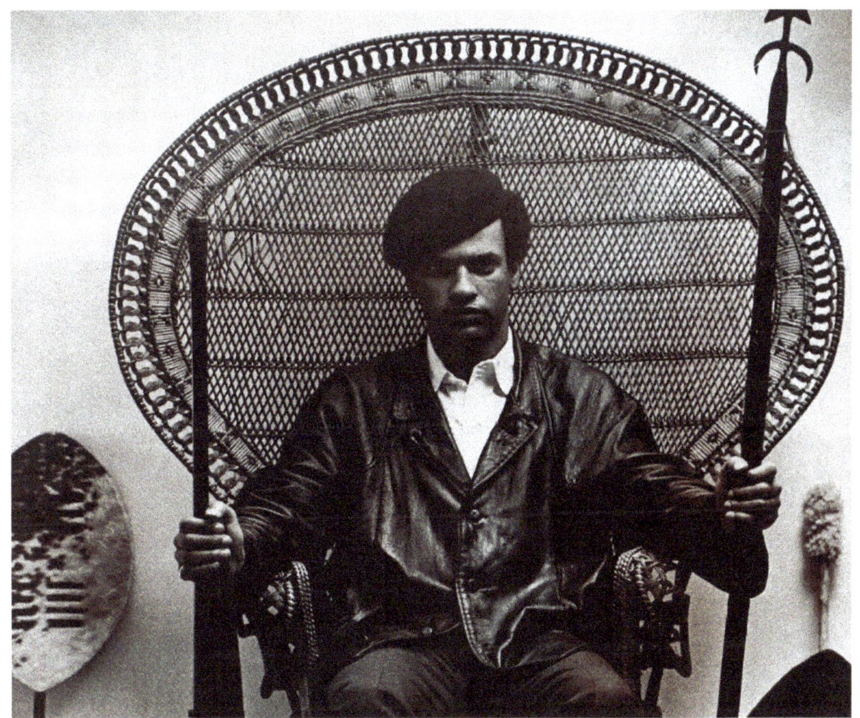

Take a selfie as Huey Newton in a replica of the iconic chair that is part of the Oakland Museum's fascinating exhibition

The Black Panthers at 50: Art on Ice

Square-Cylinder.com website January 12, 2017

All Power to the People: The Black Panthers at 50 is an unorthodox—and fascinating—exhibition. Employing multiple materials, media and curatorial methods, it is simultaneously a respectful montage and a mash-up of history, art, and politics. The Oakland Museum, which organized the show, is located just blocks from the sites of many of the exhibition's historic events, Time seems far more distant than space though. Even those who lived through this tumultuous era may not recall just how different are past and present: Welcome to a time when Republicans dominated Sacramento and railed against the Panthers' insistence on their right to own guns and Black Panther Party members who survived the police campaign to eradicate them and moved from prison cell to candidates' debate, some *en route* to holding elected political office in Oakland.

An abbreviated list of the boundary blurring show's contents provides a sense of its scope. Among the showcased art and historical materials include a treasure trove of interviews with Party members produced by radio station KPFA, information on the walls in the form of labels or texts (statements ranging from the Panthers' manifesto-like *What We Want Now!* to the curatorial note that two-thirds of Party members were women by the early 1970s), architectural artifacts from West Oakland, largely recent artworks both documentary and fictional, installations featuring pop music or a hushed, funereal soundtrack, books that influenced the Panthers (in physical form as well as available on a reading list), contemporary performances on-screen, and the Black Panther Party-produced weekly newspaper with its gorgeous cover illustrations by Gayle Dickson.

Entering the exhibition the first thing you see is the show's most artful vignette: the iconic image of Huey Newton in black leather jacket and beret, holding rifle and spear, sitting in a regal peacock chair, which is adjacent to a bronze facsimile of the wicker chair by Sam Durant, his ironic *Proposal for a Monument to Huey Newton at the Alameda County Courthouse*. The theatrical photo is among the most resonant of the late sixties, what Black Panther Party co-founder Bobby Seale, called "a centralized symbol of the leadership of the black people in the community." Bear in mind Durant's reference to the notorious Alameda County Courthouse, a symbol of unequal justice and police brutality near the Oakland Museum, which you will encounter later in the show as backdrop for Keith Dennison's news photo of a group of Panthers seen from behind. Be sure to take a seat in Durant's peacock throne—and a selfie. This makes you an imaginative part of the vibrant culture exploding into being following the Black Panther Party's founding in 1966 by Newton and Seale, who met at Merritt (now Laney) College, like the Alameda County Courthouse, just a few blocks from the Oakland Museum.

*   *   *

There's plenty of history inside the exhibition, too. The Black Panther Party existed for only sixteen years, until 1982. Its immediate influence came quickly after its inception and is illustrated by its meteoric growth: By the end of 1968 the Party had grown to more than 5000 members, in 38 chapters throughout the US. By the early 1970s, the FBI's COINTELPRO (short for Counterintelligence Program)—which had been initiated in 1967 by J. Edgar Hoover to infiltrate and undermine Black nationalist groups—had already taken a deadly toll on the Black Panthers. Kathleen Cleaver, a lawyer, former Panther and widow of Eldridge Cleaver, author of *Soul on Ice*, succinctly observed that: "The Black Panther Party appeared like a comet and it reverberates still."

If there's as much history in the exhibition as most viewers can absorb, the history it presents—perhaps appropriately—is basic. Every exhibition is a narrative and this one focuses on the story of Black Panther achievement—the positive accomplishments and peaceful aims of the Party in the face of the distorted historical record promulgated by the powers that be, including the Right-wing Hearst empire which dominated Bay Area media at the time. (Unfortunately, the museum's apparent lack of money for a catalog means the omission of contextualizing information locating the Party within a web of resistance movements including the feminist, LGBT and anti-war movements, as well as the influence on the Black Panthers of earlier US movements for racial equality.)

To get its point across, the show's curator Rene de Guzman (assisted by an unnamed team of "award winning advisors") placed special emphasis on the Panthers' manifesto-like ten-point program *What We Want Now!* (1967). Intended to publicize the lack of services and civil rights accorded African-Americans in Oakland, it appeared first in the Panther's weekly newspaper and married a few radical demands "We want all black men to be exempt from military demands" (remember that this was the Vietnam War era when African-Americans were drafted and killed out of all proportion to their numbers) with demands for full employment, "decent housing fit for shelter of human beings" and, in summary, for "...land, bread, housing, education, clothing, justice and peace." Such calls for constitutionally mandated civil rights and tax-funded services are hardly the stuff of revolution; they are far closer to the rhetoric of Bernie Sanders than Nat Turner. That the Panthers would act on these demands and provide some of the services they called for—including health clinics and children's breakfast programs—was one source of the Party's popularity.

But there's a problem in the exhibition attributable to the gigantic presentation of What We Want and other texts, no matter their historical importance. In an environment of striking, mostly small images and non-standard-looking text-works, the over-scaled wall-works—in the case of the ten point plan repeating rather than interpreting the text housed in a nearby vitrine—are disorienting. They level the distinctions between art and text, newspaper illustration and documentary photojournalism. The artwork's function is sometimes reduced to illustrating the exhibition narrative, as with the handsome, documentary photo-portraits of living Panthers.

In the postmodern realm of multiple identities and simultaneous functions is this a problem? Not necessarily. Black Lives Matter, for instance, originated in Oakland as the expression of the political and aesthetic, personal and public impulses of Alicia Garza, Opal Tometi and Patrisse Cullors, its queer founders. But in this instance, I was bothered not only by the billboard-scaled text, but by installation difficulties imposed by the museum's awkward, multi-purpose space and the display of architectural artifacts oversimplifying the physical destruction of West Oakland. Between them, I was unable to recall much about the work of any artist with whom I was not already familiar.

Only Carrie Mae Weems's stunning installation, *Constructing History: A Requiem to Mark the Moment* (2008), rises above the leveling effects of the exhibition. Its church pew seating provides a place to meditate on Weems's related still and moving images. The very large, remarkable photograph, *The Assassinations of Medgar, Malcom and Martin*, shows us two black men and a black woman in a hijab bending over a third man laid out on a spot lit, altar-of-a table, linking the slain Civil Rights leaders' deaths to that of Christ. Rendered in shadowy, black and white chiaroscuro, the effect is dramatic, evoking both Rembrandt and the crisply painted contrasts of Van Eyck and early Flemish painters. The installation's video embodies the work's funerary aura and through words, the moment—Barack Obama's election—being commemorated. Weems has said of the work that she was also "dealing with the issue of appropriation. I didn't want to have to appropriate anybody's material; I just wanted to revisit this history." The result is an abstracted coupling of past and present, of recollection and regret, presented in indelible images.

*　　　*　　　*

Questions about new ways images, artworks and other materials are employed in exhibitions are always timely. I have a theory: The hybrid exhibition utilizing both historical- and art materials is a product of the need for multiple forms of knowledge to comprehend the most incomprehensible or intractably inhumane conditions.

Following World War II—the cataclysmic global conflict that ended with the dawning of the atomic age—two exhibitions of non-art materials at two prestigious museums in New York attracted huge audiences. Both were devoted to photography at a time when it was a decidedly not-yet-art form and both were eventually regarded as retrograde embarrassments. The earlier show, *The Family of Man* (1955) at the Museum of Modern Art, featured 503 pictures of smiling athletes, newborns and the dignified poor, *en masse* telegraphing the idealistic message "We are all one," in the face of existential anxiety about the very future of humanity. The later, *Harlem on My Mind: Cultural Capital of Black America, 1900-1968* (1968) at the Metropolitan Museum, was a photo-record of Harlem focused on the epochal Harlem Renaissance of the arts, as seen by both little- and (later) well-known photographers including Carl Van Vechten and James van der Zee. Despite its subject, it featured not a single artwork, inspiring artists including Benny Andrews and Romare Bearden to form the Black Emergency Cultural Coalition in protest. The group picketed the Met and other New York museums for their inequitable racial representation. Metropolitan Museum director Thomas Hoving pulled the catalog—for an anti-Semitic essay written by a 17-year old—and soon publicly apologized for the exhibition.

Photo exhibitions such as *The Family of Man* and *Harlem on My Mind* are not only milestones in the elevation of photography into a medium of art, but also, as non-art offerings of a medium predicated on its "realism", provided arenas for engaging ideological issues connected with the representation of reality. While the naively propagandistic *The Family of Man* failed to acknowledge the existence of racism, the *Harlem on My Mind* show embodied it through its ethnographic approach and racist treatment of African-American artists vis-à-vis their White counterparts. All Power to the People: The Black Panthers at 50 is equally revealing: Its hybrid presentation of art and historical materials helps make it a breakthrough effort, assisting in the exhibition's judicious, lively and fact-based approach to the still-contested ideological turf the Black Panthers inhabit.

*   *   *

If there's a theoretical line extending to *All Power to the People: The Black Panthers at 50* it runs through the opening, in 1993, of the United States Holocaust Memorial Museum in Washington, DC. Devoted to one of the most horrific episodes of the twentieth century, it is the rare museum as cautionary tale, especially in its high-profile location on the Washington Mall. Equally revolutionary were the commissions of artworks by world-class artists. The use of art in such circumstances reflected profound changes in contemporary art practice and artists' engagement with history. The hybrid m.o. functions perfectly at the museum—the display of one sort of material validates and gives meaning to the other: the fact-based reality of the artifacts makes history literally tangible and counters absurd claims by Holocaust deniers, while the subjectivity of art offers intellectual interpretation and spiritual sustenance.

On a recent visit to the Metropolitan Museum's new contemporary art branch, the Met Breuer, I was struck by the progressive language—the use of "Watts Rebellion" rather than "Watts Riot" for instance—on the wall labels of *Kerry James Marshall: Mastry*, a retrospective exhibition devoted to work by the African-American artist. When flexibility about what constitutes truth, or even fact, is rampant, any exhibition's plain speaking is, of course, welcome. The task of Oakland Museum staffers, however, was far more complex than celebrating a universally admired artist. The museum's decision to mount a show dealing with so incendiary a subject is in itself highly laudable. One can only speculate about why no other institution is taking the exhibition: It makes their audiences poorer and the Oakland Museum responsible for the entire cost of *All Power to the People: The Black Panthers at 50*. Apparently the price of progressive programming is high—and rising.

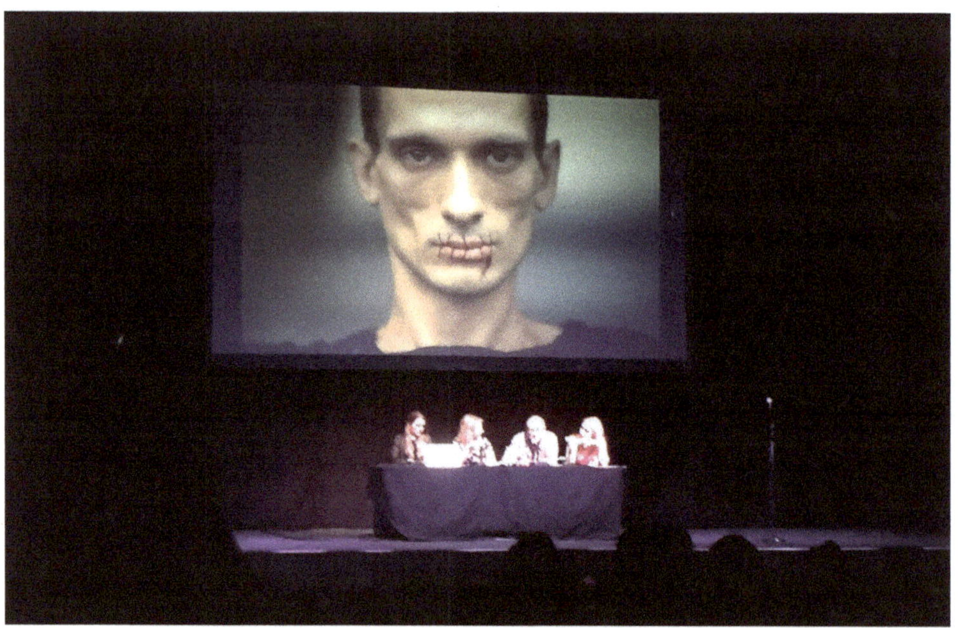

Since its founders were released from prison in 2016, the band has become a fixture on the punk music circuit outside of Russia. It recently toured the U.S. to benefit Planned Parenthood.

Pussy Riot's Teach In

From the blog, Public Eye: Art, Politics & Culture, March 2016

We're going Pussy-Rioting" shouted a couple of gender-ambiguous millennials entering San Francisco's Warfield Theater on February 10th. The dissident Russian performance troupe and punk band's appearance there barely resembled the Warfield's usual fare. There was plenty of shouting and drinking, but not any music, since Pussy Riot never charges for concerts. To justify the $45 orchestra seats, my friends and I adopted the view that this was a tribute, a fund-raiser and perhaps a once-in-a-lifetime experience.

An hour-long "pre-show" opened with a wonky performance piece featuring some comradely joking around between a *faux* Donald Trump and a *faux* Vladimir Putin. It was followed by a 45-minute rough cut" for a documentary about the Russian group and offered close-up views of actions by about a dozen women most off them previously affiliated with the feminist street-art performance troupe Voinal formed in 2011. Their "stages" included the platform of a cavernous subway station and the roof of a trolley car, where a burly female conductor assaulted the women, anonymous in their balaclavas. But it was the group's seizure of the altar of the new Cathedral of Christ the Saviour for its performance of *Punk Prayer* (2012)—a brief entreaty to the Virgin Mary to remove Putin from power—that raised the hackles of both Church and state officials.

(A queer architectural aside re the cathedral: Stalin had the nineteenth century "old" Cathedral of Christ the Saviour on the banks of the Moscow River demolished to make way for the Palace of the Soviets. Foundations for it were laid, but little else was completed. During the fifties, Kruschev had the flooded foundations converted into the world's largest swimming pool, creating one of Moscow's premier gay cruising spots. With the opening of the reconstructed cathedral in 1995, this function was eliminated, but figuratively evoked in *Punk Prayer*.)

Punk Prayer shared the spirit—if not the massive numbers—of ACT UP's controversial *Stop the Church* (1989) demonstration in St. Patrick's Cathedral in New York. Both protested the collusion of Catholicism and the state in constitutionally secular societies. Although *Punk Prayer* gained Pussy Riot the moral high ground—at least abroad—its insolence apparently could not be tolerated by officialdom. It resulted in two-year jail terms for the three performers who had been arrested; while two others fled the country.

Pussy Riot's prominence surely saved them from worse treatment and more hard time. As with other incarcerated revolutionaries like Angela Davis, their prison sentences became the impetus for a more sober approach to struggles for liberation. If less exhilarating than their mediagenic, Putin-baiting performances, their more conventional human-rights activities may ultimately prove even more dangerous: "The difference between being a human rights worker in Russia and the US," said Masha Alyokhina later in the evening. "Is that in the US it's like being a middle manager. In Moscow it's Molotov cocktails and beatings and [being] branded a foreign agent."

Pussy Riot's San Francisco appearance was the last stop of a fund-raising trip that included Seattle and Portland. Their efforts are a reminder that political art practices ought to be evaluated by both their message and by the audiences they reach. Being "about" an issue is rarely enough. (Ai Weiwei's recent reenactment—impersonation?–of a disturbing photo of the drowned Syrian three-year-old Alan Kurdi, for instance, falls into this category of narcissistic, art tourism.) Some may question whether Pussy Riot's advocacy and fundraising activities can even be discussed within an art context. They can if you ascribe to artist-theorist Hans Haacke's belief that art is another branch of the "consciousness industry" (linking it to advertising and propaganda). There's little doubt that Pussy Riot's punk performance antics reached—and altered the consciousness of—millions worldwide. Given Russia's saddening slide into oligarchy and authoritarianism, any taxonomic concerns—that rarely interesting "But is it art? question–seems less relevant than Malcolm X's injunction to seek (revolutionary) change "by any means necessary".

There's also a relevant Russian tradition of moral fervor in art that the West abandoned in the mid-nineteenth century for modern formal experimentation. Just as Nikolai Chernyshevsky's now unreadable novel *What is to Be Done?* (1863) supplied the emotional back story for the Russian revolution(s) of the early twentieth century, it also pointed to future works of conscience, such as Alexander Solzhenitsyn's *Gulag Archipelago*, written precisely a century later. Solzhenitsyn's historical and essayistic account of Stalin's death camps earned its author a Nobel Prize in 1970 and the attendant publicity made it impossible for authorities to "disappear" him.

In their program, Pussy Riot provided a fascinating slide show about the work of some contemporary visual artists and kindred spirits. The most interesting of them is Pyotr Pavlensky. Reminiscent of many US body- and AIDS-artists of the past 30 years—David Wojnarowicz especially—he's tortured himself by nailing his ball (sac) to the pavement of Red Square and by sewing his mouth shut in zig-zag stitches to protest Pussy Riot's arrest. At a recent trial Pavlensky's designation as an artist—rather than a hooligan–was deemed a victory. But like many Soviet artists before him, Pavlensky was silenced in January by the authorities who had him committed (again) to a psychiatric center for "evaluation." The differences between incarceration in prison and in a psychiatric hospital are barely discernable. Putin's campaign of repression sadly contrasts with the relative freedom artists enjoyed in the 1990s with representation by Western galleries and the attendant bank accounts. Will they even be able to return to their roles of domestic gadfly, goad and/or prankster? Writing between the lines (or mashing up music, art and politics) remains the current—and perhaps only—strategy of choice. For those who know their work, Pussy Riot is at least an inspiring forebear.

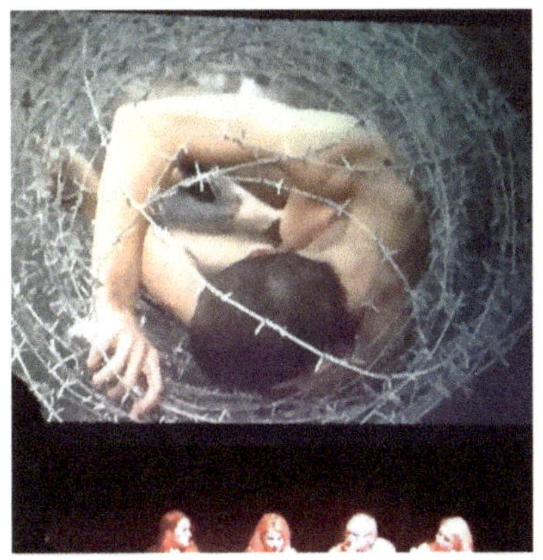 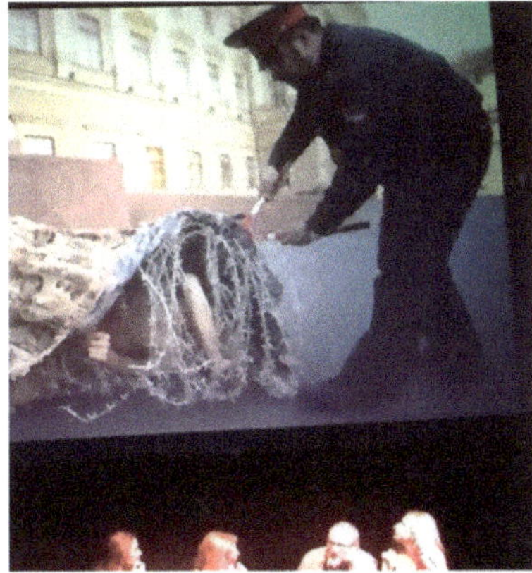

Pussy Riot's art history lesson

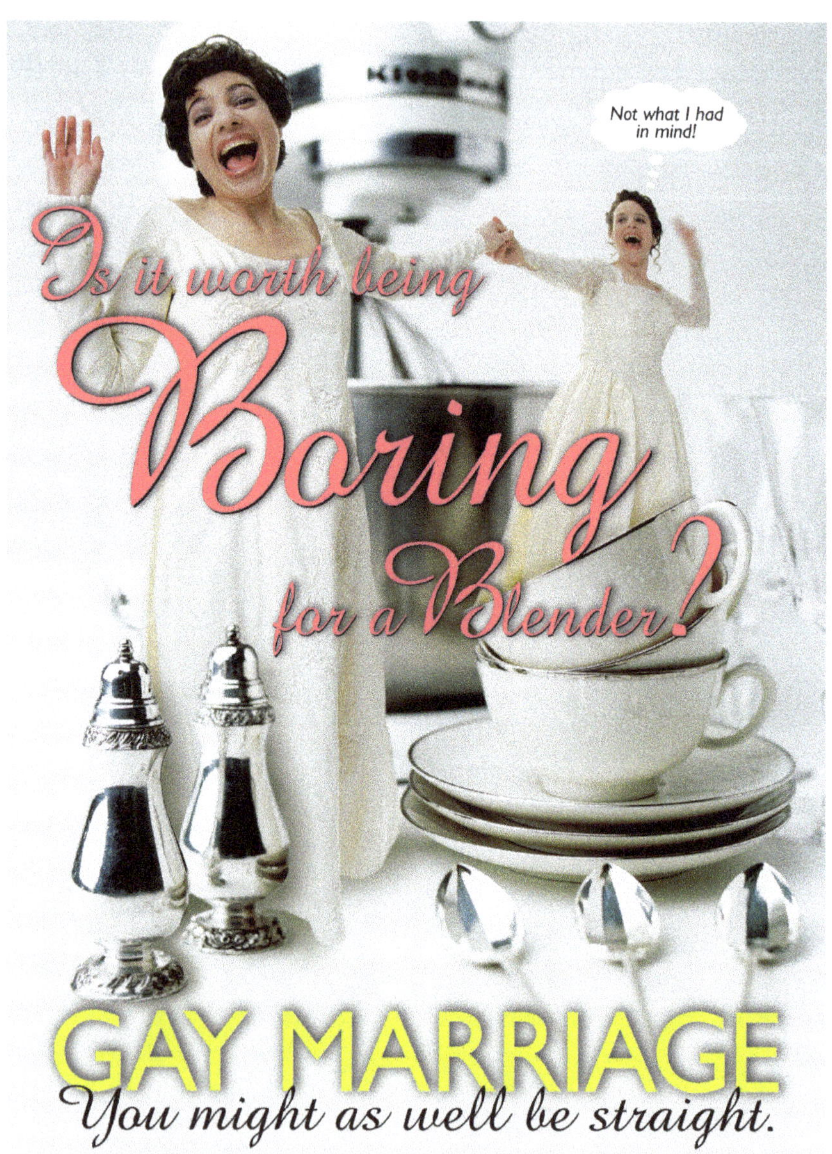

Dyke Action Machine (1997) from the Gays Against Gay Marriage series

PART FOUR

Queer Expressions and Icons

Civil rights and later liberation struggles are a reminder that no one gives us permission to be free. We take it. Few career-minded gay and lesbian artists came out during the '70s; it was not until the mid-80s that AIDS began to empty the art-world closet.

Robert Atkins "Queer for You," *Village Voice*, 1994

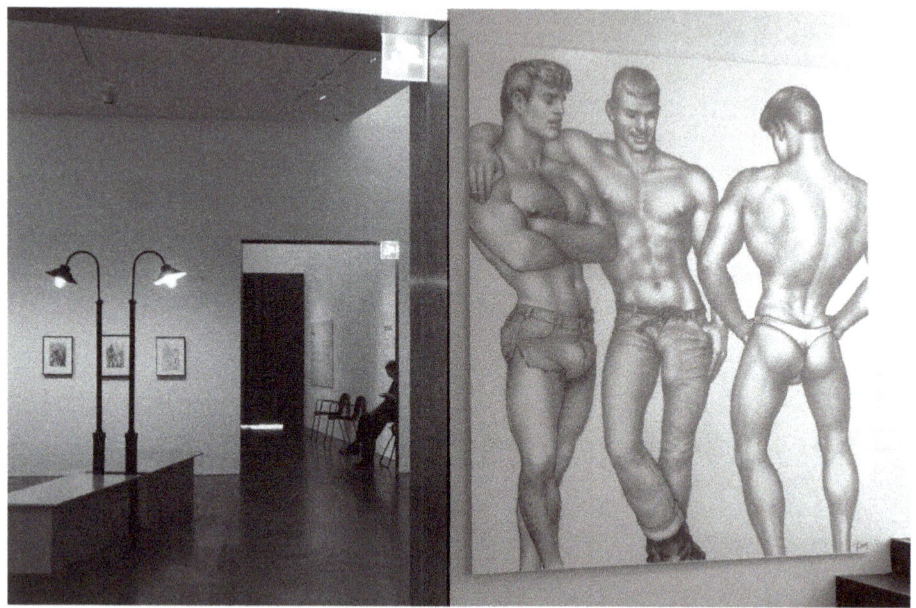

Tom of Finland exhibition at the Kiasma Museum in Helsinki

Hudson In New York: Feature Gallery's Gay Gaze

Village Voice, December 27, 1988

It was no ordinary art opening. Feature's main gallery was packed with men in leather biker jackets, boots and the coded signifiers of desire—keys and chains dangling from garments and announcing specific erotic interests. Their dress seemed an elaborate homage to Tom of Finland's homoerotic drawings hanging on gallery walls but normally known through reproduction in porn magazines. Art seemed to imitate a pre-AIDS life inspired by art like this. This gathering of thirty- and forty- somethings was a poignant reminder of a now distant heyday of a Saint-ed past: As one friend remarked about the opening "You'd think there'd at least have been some sexual tension..."

In Feature's rear gallery, a group show called *HoHoHoMo* offered decidedly more "mainstream" artworks by five gay artists who usually show in East Village or Soho galleries: Arnold Fern, Richard Hawkins, Kevin Larmon, Johnny Pixchure, and Kevin

Wolff. If the juxtaposition of their "high art" and Tom of Finland's pop cultural "artifacts" is rare, the regular exhibition of gay art in a mixed, mainstream context is even more unusual. Hudson, the pioneering integrationist behind Feature, is beginning to garner a national reputation for this blend. Just a few months ago, he moved his four-year-old gallery from Chicago to its present location on Broome Street in Soho.

Hudson's integrationist approach flies in the face of the art world status quo, a scene not especially homo friendly despite its ballyhooed liberalism and financial response to AIDS. The number of lesbian and gay artists who populate it is, of course, legion, while those who make gay or lesbian art are fewer and their exhibition opportunities even slimmer. Plenty of dealers feel comfortable showing conceptually oriented artworks by gay artists such as Kevin Larmon whose paintings mine the divide between figuration and abstraction but do not immediately read as gay-made. Very few dealers, on the other hand, show tenderly drawn images of homosex lovemaking. Or worse, engage essential conversations about gay art. In the case of Tom of Finland, Hudson believes his homages to machismo paradoxically reinforce art world homophobia: "If you want to discuss Tom's work in terms of simulation or codification you can," he said. "It's the [gay] content that's being discriminated against."

Ghettoization has been the typical modus operandi of galleries showing work by gay and lesbian artists on both coasts, whether they exclusively exhibit homoerotic art or less sexualized "high art" production. In New York, Gay galleries have come and gone, the ambitious Robert Samuels Gallery being the most notable of late. Feature is charting a different direction. The current pair of shows is not typical Feature fare, Hudson told me. Only 20 percent of artists he shows make gay art, he says, but the ratio seems natural to him. "Of course, I want to see gay representations, but that's not all I want to see. Who doesn't like diversity?"

Whatever one thinks or thinks about, there's no getting away from the commercial obligations of operating a gallery today. Much of Hudson's reputation derives from his knack for spotting original and assured artists of any sexual persuasion. He opened his Chicago gallery in 1984, with a Richard Prince show, followed by exhibitions of then emerging artists work over the next year and a half including Haim Steinbach, Sherrie Levine, and Jeff Koons. No longer drawn to the Koons/Steinbach brand of commodification-oriented art, Hudson is currently attracted to what he terms "Softer-edged, less slick art with a poetic criticality about it." This difficult-to-imagine characterization makes sense in connection with upcoming shows of Peter Huttinger's ambiguous abstractions of festering surfaces, and Jeanne Dunning's photographic gender-plays on women with facial hair and hard-to-identify orifices.

Hudson's taste for aggressively edgy art continues to apply to his own work as a performance artist, as well. The 38-year-old MFA-painter with the shaved head danced professionally with Contemporary Dance Theater and the Judy Gregg Dance Company from 1974 to 1980. By 1979 his choreographic gestures and theatricalization of everyday activities led to solo performance works. The five-minute climax of one performance is intriguing: While walking between two rows of chairs to the accompaniment of a punk-ish rendition of *Strawberry Fields Forever*, he carried signs citing the consequences of AIDS and recited Tennyson's *Charge of the Light Brigade* ("Into the valley of death rode the six hundred"). This year's single performance piece, *The Back Way*, will debut in January as part of Los Angeles Contemporary Exhibition's *Against Nature* exhibition. He makes paintings and constructions, too. The varied activities required to present and produce art all seem to be constituent parts of Hudson's routine. "We've got to have art," he grinned. "It's an unacknowledged bodily function."

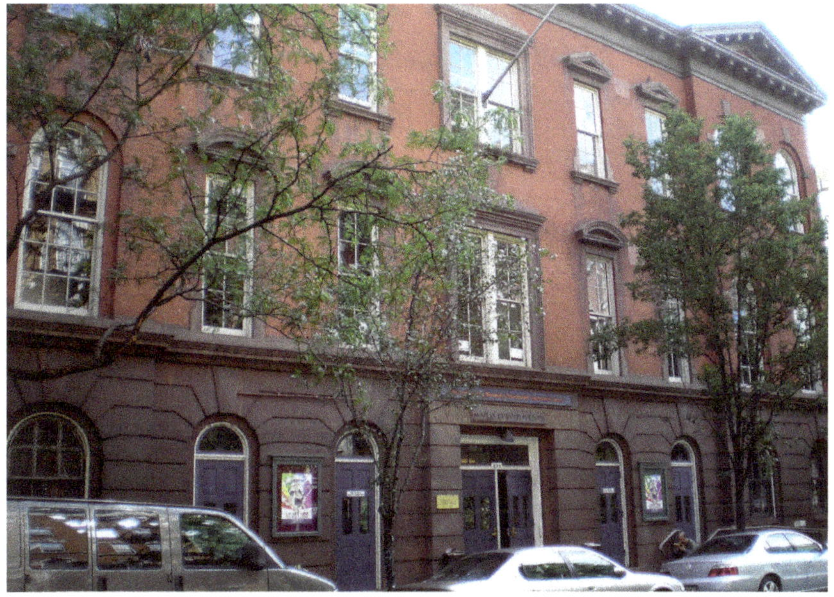

Founded in 1983, the Lesbian and Gay Community
Services Center, formerly schoolhouse on
W. 13th St, is the largest such facility on the East Coast.

Art on Stone Walls

Village Voice, June 13, 1989

Spend a day at the Lesbian and Gay Community Services Center and you'll get an earful: the raucous politicking at ACT UP meetings, the tasty harmonizing of the Salsa Soul Sisters' rehearsals, the murmur of medical consultation being offered by the Community Health Project, and the presumably angry invective of the Mad Dykes Support Group—to name just a few of the 150 nonprofit groups that use this resource. Until last week, the warren of classrooms and assembly halls in which they meet vividly recalled the Center's former life as the Food and Maritime Trades High School, a drab and dingy red-brick pile-of-a-building built in 1841. But *The Center Show* has changed all that. Virtually every room, stairwell, and closet has been transformed by this ambitious exhibition into a celebration of the twentieth anniversary of the Stonewall rebellion that helped spark gay liberation.

For the 51 artists and collectives involved, what the center sounds and looks like is crucial. They were invited by co-organizers Rick Barnett and Barbara Sahlman to create *site-specific* artworks, potentially permanent murals or sculptural installations designed for places within the center and its garden. Here "site" means far more than just physical place. It also embraces the social context of the center, the political basis of the show, and the diverse audiences likely to view the exhibition.

Conditions at the center couldn't have been more unlike those of the professional art world: gay artists got the opportunity to come out in their work; non-gay artists (about a quarter of the total, according to Barnett) got to work within a gay environment; and gay artists accustomed to exhibiting in pristine galleries had to adjust to the funky, cluttered spaces. Above all, professionals who ordinarily operate in the exclusionary culture of the cutthroat art world found themselves in the inclusionary culture of a community center. This exhibition could have been subtitled "When Worlds Collide."

Art naturally looks different in these circumstances and this sort of space. That's why similar mega-shows such as P.S. 1's *Rooms* of 1976, which occupied a former schoolhouse in Long Island City, and Colab's 1980 *Times Square Show*, in a former massage parlor, made history. *The Center Show* not only physically sidesteps the art world, it makes common cause with another culture on its own turf.

What kind of art will you find at the center? A stroll around the first-floor assembly hall heralds the diversity that's showcased throughout the building. This gargantuan room supported by a forest of cast-iron columns is both the largest space altered by artists and the first the viewers are likely to encounter.

In it are six artists' and two art collectives' wall-works: Leon Golub's torture victim seems to survey Nancy Spero's ritualistic procession of robed women and female nudes. Gran Fury's *Riot*, a play in Robert Indiana's *Love* icon and General Idea's updated AIDS version of it, seem a distant cousin to the Guerilla Girls' poster indictments of art-world sexism and racism hanging nearby. Graffitist Daze's blue mask of a woman and a smoking gun points at Barbara

Sandler's painting of Nijinsky and a wolf-headed nude flanking Cocteau's image of a hand strumming a lyre from *Blood of a Poet*. Jane Dickson's brushy monochrome figures face off on the room's glass-walled stairwells, Scott Tucker's collage of male imagery spanning four centuries culminates in a contemporary jack-off. (Kenny Scharf will install a work nearby in the coming weeks.)

Most of the show's thematic concerns and formal characteristics are visible in this representative sample. Sandler's dramatic homage to Cocteau and Nijinsky recalls an early modern moment in gay cultural history that helps bridge the century separating Walt Whitman from Stonewall. (Ilse Gordon and Rhonda Zwillinger invoke the pantheon of gay and lesbian cultural history from Michelangelo to Kate Millet, while Group Material's bathroom cum '70s disco evokes an already historic pop-cultural era.) Historical consciousness-raising remains an effective minority strategy for reclaiming a nearly invisible past.

Nancy Spero's pictorial body language points to the female form as site of cultural conflict. Images of the physical body recur throughout the center, but Spero, surprisingly, offers some of the show's few representations of women, and along with Judy Glantzman's, virtually its only images of the female nude. (Generally sexualized, male nudes populate the works of Arch Connelly, Arnold Fern, Luis Frangella, Glantzman, Keith Haring, Douglas Keeve, David Lachapelle, Stephen Lack, Rick Prol, and Gary Speziale.)

The scarcity of images of woman is not a matter of insufficient affirmative action on the part of the organizers; 21 of the 51 artists and group participants are women. How can the feminist critique of art's objectification of the female body be reconciled with the empowering value of seeing one's self represented? And what about the value of actually *doing* the representing?

The experience of making and viewing art in this space is brought home by an encounter with Golub's painting across a crowded roomful of light fixtures and ceiling fans. Up close, the intrusive molding that cuts a horizontal swath across the subject's neck comes into focus. Golub neatly turned the limitations of the crudely finished physical setting to his advantage. The raw site seems to function as a metaphor for the real-world contingencies that weigh on artists, while otherworldly white gallery spaces promote the illusion that art exists apart from society at large.

Gran Fury's appropriation of an appropriated painting requires a bit of insider information: knowledge of General Idea's *AIDS* painting based on Robert Indiana's ubiquitous *LOVE* image familiar from the postage stamp. This witty one-liner is also one of the few evocations of AIDS in the show. (Marcus Leatherdale's chamber of photographic *memento mori* is another.) Some may find it a problem that our community's preoccupation with AIDS is not at the heart of *The Center Show*. Robert Storr places the epidemic everywhere at the periphery of our vision and consciousness by peppering the center with dozens of inconspicuous paintings of pink triangles—the Nazi symbol for gays appropriated by gay liberation and now identified with the AIDS-activist injunction that "Silence = Death."

If you never left the assembly hall you'd miss the sculptural installations, some of the most intriguing works in the show. Many of the installation artists have laid claims to tiny alcoves, restrooms, or landings along the center's five staircases. In these enclosed sites, they've created wraparound artworks that convert unused space into mood- and mind-altering dreamscapes.

Doreen Gallo's eye-popping tile and found-object mosaics transform a vestibule into a neo-Byzantine homage to Grandma Prisby's Bottle Village. A theatricalized boudoir, or crypt, is evoked by Colette's seductively draped landing. Rhonda Zwillinger's elaborately decorated ensemble of chairs, mirrors, and heroines in name or portrait refashions a ladies' room into a lounge of feminist history.

Not all the installations are so decorative. (The embellish-the-earth approach is a frequent, and frequently successful, approach to installation making.) Marcia Salo's structuralist inquiry into the position of the female film viewer presents photographs of the artist with images of *Vertigo* stars James Stewart and Kim Novak projected onto her face. Visitors confront a text that asks, in part, "When you watch the film *Vertigo*, are you Scottie wanting Madeline, or are you Madeline wanting Scottie to want you? Or both?" Arch Connelly covered an entire third-floor chamber with gay-male porno imagery. Unlike Salo's work, his mini-*lusthaus* incites, rather than interrogates, desire. But that depends on who you—the audience member—are.

For the 3,000 persons who use the center weekly, *The Center Show* is public art. Like many public works, a few have already proved controversial, especially Keith Haring's exuberant restroom wall work in praise of polymorphous perversity. One anonymous middle-aged man irately said, "There's no safe sex there, it's just pornography...Why should we alienate funders over this?"

Public art has alerted us to the hypersensitivity of non-art-world audiences of any kind. For some people—especially seniors and stuff members—the center is a virtual second home. Kevin Dziadual, a jewelry designer and maintenance worker at the center, has become an informal docent and center art maven. I heard him conducting numerous impromptu tours and discussions of the artworks during the week before the show opened. "This comfortable old shoe [of a building] has become a high heel," he observed. "And most people simply don't like to be disturbed...But what they need to consider is whether things should be allowed to happen more freely here than on the outside."

By the time you've traipsed through the center's well-worn halls and stairwells, the cumulative effect of so much art is exhilarating: it makes you want more. The size and diversity of the show is the consequence of Barnett and Sahlman's open-ended invitation to artists to "address any concerns...in keeping with the spirit of the center" and the informal networking that such projects invariably entail. Many artists, including Jenny Holzer, Barbara Kruger, Mike Bidlo, and Tim Rollings, were invited to participate, but declined. Others heard about the show from artist-friends and submitted unrequested proposals. The looseness of the process might be regarded as an emblem of the center's inclusiveness.

Exclusions occurred, too. After Mark Kostabi's astonishingly homophobic remarks in June's *Vanity Fair*, he was bounced from the show (Good riddance). Of genuine concern is the absence of black and brown faces on the walls, save for Grace Graupe Pillard's multiethnic portrait cutouts, which triple the multi-racial

population of the center's administrative offices. Only the Guerilla Girls' agitprop posters actually evoke the malignant realities of
racism.

Some will criticize the exhibition for not being more politically
pointed. In fact, these—and many other-up-front representations
of gay sexuality and lesbian history—are decidedly political. Others
will reasonably observe that only half the artists involved truly dis-
tinguish themselves, but try to recall the last group show you saw
that offered two or three dozen evocative works.

When a savvy video artist from San Francisco (of all places!)
recently asked me what Stonewall was, I knew that I wanted to see
this show deal more directly with its historical *raison d'etre*. Only
two artists—Mimi Smith and Thomas Lanigan-Schmidt—invoke the
birth of gay liberation in their works. Smith's *Twenty years ago*
features a handless clock and articles from local papers about
the night the drag queens fought back on Christopher Street. Lanigan-Schmidt's work offers a paradigm of socially and emotionally
engaged art-making.

Titled *Mother Stonewall and the Golden Rats*, his two-part installation occupies a small room near the first-floor assembly hall
and a rooftop of a west-wing staircase landing. (Maps are available, I am happy to report.) The first-floor site brings us a cage-like
construction, golden rats, lots of the artist's signature tinsel and
glitz, and a batch of ecumenical quotations ranging from "Why is
this night different from other nights?" to Oscar Wilde's "A cynic is
a person who knows the price of everything and the value of nothing." His rooftop floor space is inhabited by adorable golden rats.
An autobiographical text gives additional meaning to both sites.

Lanigan-Schmidt participated in the riots at the Stonewall
Inn. His text describes forsaking a job on a ditch-digging crew to
head for the Big City to live as a "street rat" in "cheap hotels, bro-
ken-down apartments, abandoned buildings or on the streets."
Stonewall was a place for dancing, where you needed an empty
beer can to convince the waiter you'd bought a drink. For Lanigan-Schmidt it was also "the art that gave form to the feelings of
our heart beats...of finally being HOME." When the police invaded

the crowded bar "it was not only a raid, but a bust. Mother Stonewall was being violated."

Lanigan-Schmidt chronicles those events with affection, but without sentiment. His examination of historical causation and meaning is wonderfully apt. He coolly notes the working-class origins of the participants—"this wasn't a 1960s student riot"—and observes that "nobody thought of it as history, herstory, my-story, your-story or our story. We were being denied a place to dance together...Our Mother Stonewall was giving birth to a new era and we were the midwives. That night the 'Street Rats' shone like the brightest gold...the mystery of history happened again in the least likely of places."

Lanigan-Schmidt's work brilliantly marries the personal and the political and gives meaning to the Latin entreaty *"Sursum Corda!"* he's inscribed on the wall. It means "lift up your hearts." His deeply felt work helps get it up.

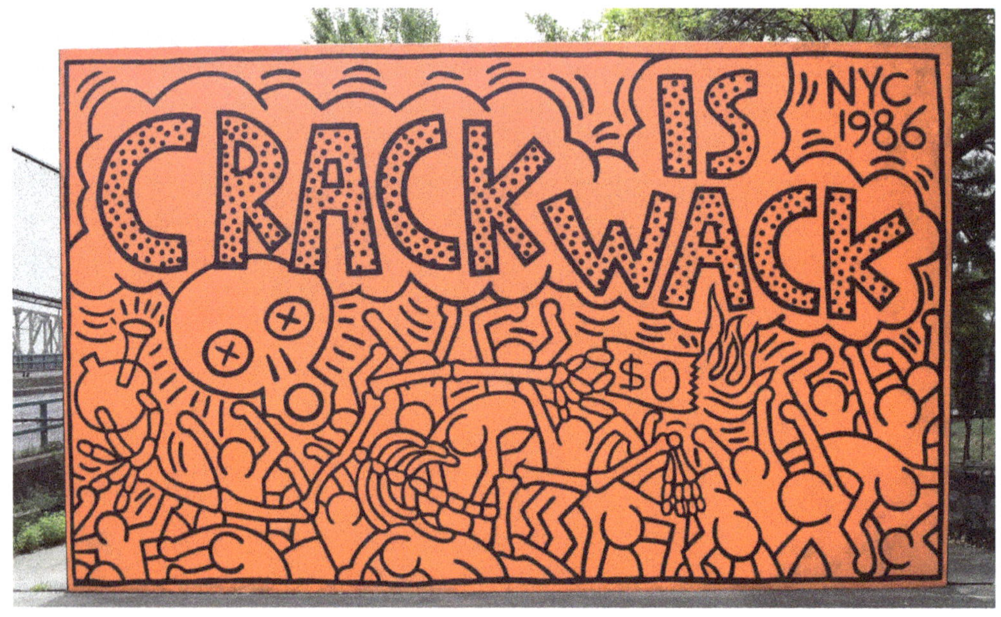

Keith Haring: Crack is Wack

KEITH HARING

Keith Haring: A Tribute

Contemporanea, September 1990, pp Page 32-34

For many of us, last season's most significant event was Keith Haring's death on 16 February 1990. It wasn't simply that AIDS had decimated another brilliant talent but that the world's best-known artist had come to embody the vitality and public spirit that flourish in contemporary New York. Haring's death by extension seemed emblematic of deepening social malaise. Goodbye eighties, hello *fin de siècle*.

Haring's intertwined art and life suggest much that is central to contemporary culture. Andy Warhol's heir, Haring made art that successfully bridged the once-gaping divide separating high art and popular culture. Although Andy yearned to make his art accessible, he thought of accessibility in terms of headline-hugging content rather than price tags. When Keith first opened his Pop Shop in 1986, it was to make art affordable and to keep his designs from being ripped off. He viewed the shop's mostly two-dimensional wares as art: subway advertising spaces, t-shirts, posters and canvas were all the same to him.

Haring had his first New York solo show in 1981, and by the time he had appeared in simultaneous exhibitions at the Tony Shafrazi and Leo Castelli galleries in 1983, he was a star. His timing (and luck) had been remarkable. He came to New York in 1977, at the moment when the late modern order was crumbling. Graffiti, hip-hop, and street culture, a lively club scene, nascent art-world internationalism, budding neo-expressionism, and the transformation of ethnicity into something that would come to be known as multiculturalism, were all components of the emerging eighties. The decade would nourish many young artists, none more than Haring.

Starting in the early eighties, Haring and the downtown scene led parallel lives, growing together from the streets and club-cum-galleries of the Lower East Side and the East Village; to the glitzy, Wall Street-fueled, Warhol-Palladium period of the mid-eighties; to the reemergence of activism about AIDS, the environment, and homelessness that has become such a conspicuous feature of today's art world. It is difficult to avoid constructing narratives about Haring, the art and media star. One alternative is to trivialize a body of art that has survived its fifteen minutes of media glare, to dismiss it as merely of sociological interest. But this is no longer possible in the media age—the distinctions between an artist, an artwork, and their social milieu have collapsed.

When Haring began drawing in the subway in 1981, he was already the veteran of two exhibitions that had helped define New York's so-called "New Wave": the *Times Square Show*, a circuslike extravaganza held in a decaying, midtown massage parlor; and *Events*, an exhibition organized by Fashion Moda (the Bronx alternative space) for the New Museum of Contemporary Art. The attention that he got in the subway for his chalk images of crawling babies, dogs, flying saucers, and TV sets was instantaneous. It never died down.

At first, that attention came from the art press. A snippet of a review of Haring's debut at Shafrazi suggests the seriousness and intensity with which his work was initially scrutinized: "Females are seen at birth, or as icons...the emotional climate is euphoric, totally unmediated." Semiotics, calligraphy, and *art brut* were frequently invoked by New York's leading critics in conjunction with Haring's work. From 1982 to 1984, the graffiti bandwagon spiced an art discourse hopelessly mired in international Neo-Ex.

But starting in late 1983, press attention began to come almost exclusively from the general media. Why had the art press moved on? Some critics, of course, had never liked the work, while others mistook Haring's simplicity for simplemindedness. The spotlight had shifted, and the basic Haring story (in which the pot-smoking, small-town boy who had learned cartooning from his father left commercial art school after seeing a Pierre Alechinsky retrospective and reading William S. Burroughs) had already been plotted.

Other astute art observers sensed that Haring had actually stopped being a gallery artist—despite the certification of well-placed collectors and museums. Exhibitions were regularly staged, including Haring's first foray into fabricated steel sculpture, presented at Castelli on Greene Street in 1986. Such works, however, lacked the site-specificity that had become so crucial to Haring's work.

Haring had always painted on everything, especially the walls of the clubs, galleries, and museums hosting his exhibitions. This cover-the-earth sensibility was both his art and this trademark; with it, he could transform even art objects of traditional format into environmental installations. Haring's decorative exuberance was most recently displayed in New York in the virtuoso celebration of polymorphous sexuality that he painted for a 1989 exhibition commemorating the twentieth anniversary of gay liberation at the Lesbian and Gay Community Center.

Haring's real calling was as a community artist. In 1982, he printed and distributed 20,000 free posters for the 12 June antinuclear rally in Central Park. One third of his sixteen-page, single-spaced resume is devoted to "special projects." A few excerpts from 1988-89: Artist-in-residence for the Chicago and Iowa City public schools; designer of a logo and t-shirts for "Young Scientists' Day" at Mount Sinai Medical School; painter of the "Easter at the White House" mural donated to Washington Children's Hospital; designer of a first-day cover and lithograph for the United Nations' "International Volunteer Year;" designer of a poster for a New York Public Library Literacy Campaign; painter of a permanent mural on the exterior wall of San Antonio church in Pisa.

This list certainly attests to Haring's concern for children and his long-standing desire to be a positive role model for them. It fails, however, to convey the cultural and racial inclusiveness that was second nature to him—this he expressed in works about South Africa, his relationship with a non-White lover, the "Crack is Wack" murals targeted at people of color and his gay and AIDS activism. He had been donating t-shirt and poster designs to ACT UP since 1988, and his sculpture *Totem* garnered $70,000 at the group's fundraising auction on 3 December 1989.

New York Mayor David Dinkins acknowledged these political activities at Haring's memorial "tribute," an elaborately staged affair held at the Cathedral of Saint John the Divine on 4 May. This "tribute" was oddly impersonal, showcasing performers such as Jessye Norman, Jock Soto and Heather Watts of the New York City Ballet, Haring-chum Melissa Fenley; as well as estate-plumping pontification from too dealers and art historians. Some moving moments did come from Keith's sister Kay and friends Kenny Scharf, Ann Magnuson, and Fred Brathwaife.

A few references were made to the conjunction of the memorial with what would have been Haring's thirty-second birthday, but too few to the significance that Keith's birthdays had held for him. It was his habit to let loose with elaborate birthday bashes that featured performances by friends such as Madonna, John Dex, and Grace Jones. Birthday parties and memorial services are, of course, quite different. Memorials are a form of portraiture, and this final likeness seemed largely official.

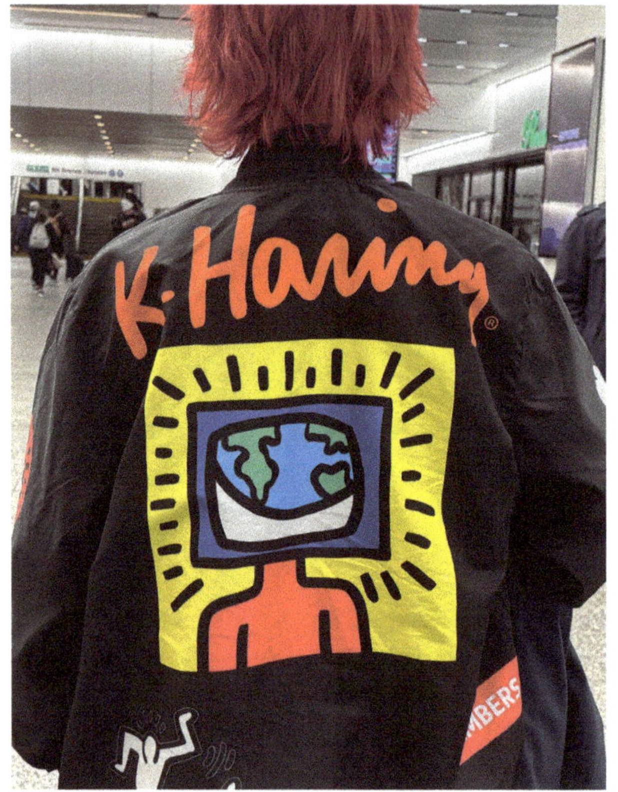

The Strange Case of Keith Haring

Art in America, 2009

"There are people that are trying to write me out of history also. I mean there are a lot of books and exhibitions that are supposed to be exhibitions of what happened in the eighties...that I'm not in."

-                    Keith Haring, interviewed by Jason Rubell, three weeks before his death on February 16, 1990

Has any artist received the posthumous exposure that Keith Haring has since his death nearly two decades ago in 1990? During the past two years alone, he has been the subject of new books, well-documented exhibitions including some recreating site-specific works, and the sole attraction at a commodious museum devoted to him in Japan. And yet the reputation of the object of so much affection remains unsettled; he is still—as suggested by his remarks to Jason Rubell quoted in the exhibition catalog, *Against All Odds: Keith Haring in the Rubell Family Collection*—a lightning rod for critical discord and hyperbole.

According to various observers he is either one of the best or worst artists of our time. The newly published *Keith Haring*, for instance, contains an encomium-of-an introduction by Julia Gruen, executive director of the Keith Haring Foundation, and Haring's former studio assistant. In it, she asserts hyperbolically that "In the almost two decades since Keith Haring's death, his reputation as an artist has risen to remarkable heights, the value of his work has soared and his legacy endures and thrives." By contrast, curator Mark Coetzee's introduction to the catalog of *Against All Odds*, published at the same time as *Keith Haring*, pleads for a better and deeper understanding of Haring's output in order to "contradict the stereotypical view of Keith Haring as simply a Pop artist who created nothing more than fun, vacuous, commercial icons that were cute, colorful and gimmicky."

So which is it? Is Haring an artist central to our understanding of the recent past? Or a once trendy art maker whose fifteen minutes ended long ago? But perhaps it is less productive to debate this question than to consider why the eighties—of which Haring is surely an emblem—remains so resistant to historical consensus. Put another way, it seems that every observation about Haring discloses at least as much about the observer as the observed.

Ironically, little is in doubt about Haring's short career—his upbringing and education, the artists, associates and social causes that mattered to him. The standard Haring narrative begins with the pot-smoking, small-town boy from Kutztown (actually Reading), PA, who learns cartooning from his father, leaves commercial art school in Pittsburgh after a month of classes and exposure to a show of Pierre Alechinsky's art at the Carnegie Institute, then, in 1978, heads to New York. He makes another brief stab at art school (this time at SVA), parties with artist-friends such as Kenny Scharf,

Jean-Michel Basquiat and Anne Magnuson and curates their work at Club 57 and other downtown venues. In 1980, he participates in the legendary, New Wave extravaganza, *The Times Square Show*, where he meets graffiti "writers" who tag subway cars. This spurs his eye-popping embellishment of Manhattan subway stations with chalk drawings of crawling babies, dogs, flying saucers, and TV sets. The attention that he got for them was instantaneous and never died down. In 1985 Haring's meteoric rise to pop-cultural stardom of the previous three years was ratified by simultaneous solo shows at the Tony Shafrazi and Leo Castelli galleries.

He continued to work in the subway until then, despite his growing frustration with collector-fans who stole the removable black paper on which he drew. His motivation, notes Jeffrey Deitch in his introduction to *Keith Haring*, is explained in a well-known, manifesto-like journal entry of 1978: "The public has a right to art / The public is being ignored by most contemporary artists / Art is for everybody." If the rest is, as they say, history, it is surprising that, as with Deitch's essay, the narrator of Haring's history has usually been Haring himself.

An opinionated lot, art critics (and historians) are rarely so deferential to primary sources. Nor are Haring's journals—which were not published until 1996—likely ever to be compared to Vasari's Renaissance writings. Their virtues include Haring's curiosity and unsentimental regard of himself, but they are also suffused with youthful naivete and artless charm. Little changes about the depth of Haring's insights as recorded throughout his brief life, whether describing a "blue moment" at age 20 in the first published entry, or the Tower of Pisa as "really major...every time you look...it makes you smile," in the final entry eleven years later. Unfortunately, the benign reaction to the journal entries is often accorded to Haring's *oeuvre* in its entirety, no matter how harrowing the subject matter of some works and how innovative their formats and venues.

In 1992, the first biography called *Keith Haring: The Authorized Biography* was published by John Gruen, Julia Gruen's father. It proved shockingly unrevealing. Gruen mimicked the memorable "oral biography" style of Warhol "superstar" *Edie Sedgwick* by Jean Stein and George Plimpton, who collaged a compelling portrait of the original It Girl from the words of those who knew her. The quoted stories and anecdotes about Haring came from too many boldface names like Timothy Leary and Princess Grace seemingly intended to establish Haring's social status and the reach of his art, while those of then-young fellow artists, boyfriends, and celebs like Madonna, are among the few that provide some more welcome commentary. Gruen's published interview snippets from 1992 were also repurposed—although not attributed to him on the title page—as the primary text of *Keith Haring*, the lavishly produced, 544 page volume published in 2008.

The table of contents of *Keith Haring*—arranged by chronology and subdivided by theme or event—resembles nothing so as the jumping off point for an outline of a biography. Instead of narrative- or critical texts, the majority of the book is devoted to more than 600 pictures of Haring's milieu. The lower East Side is seen here only as a tasty bouillabaisse of dance, dope and sex, graffiti, club and bar life, and illustrated by numerous photos of Keith pressing the flesh with celebs ranging from Dolly Parton to Pee-Wee Herman. The chaotic democracy of New York in the eighties, when the old modernist order in art and life was crumbling, seems the ideal subject for a CD-rom in which music, dance and video from that day might be animated by then-new digital technology. The affinity with, or disdain for, a new order memorialized by new technology might be an indicator of sympathy or antipathy for Haring's boundary blurring art. It's easy to forget the novelty and importance of Haring's accomplishment: the blurring of boundaries that formerly separated high and low art, or artists who made works on public streets *vis-à-vis* those who showed theirs in galleries. But for every 20 pictures of graffitists and break dancers, celebs and society types on the D.L., there are only a few images in *Keith Haring* of artists other than the very extroverted eponymous Haring or his collaborators

By contrast, *Against All Odds: Keith Haring in the Rubell Family Collection*, recently on view at the Palm Springs Museum of Art, travels a far more conventional art historical route. Including a small selection of work by Basquiat, George Condo and Francesco Clemente, among others, it demonstrates how snugly Haring's art fit within the gallery-oriented mainstream of the late eighties. Coetzee's intentions, however, were multiple: Not only to debunk the "stereotypical view of Keith Haring as simply a...[producer of] commercial icons" but to enlarge it with a recognition of the artist's abilities as draftsman. The quality of Haring's sometimes exquisitely limned drawings hardly seems at issue, to this viewer at least. The centrality of drawing to his practice was apparent to Haring: "Art for me is a record of a state of being or a moment of living," he told Jason Rubell in 1990. "...Everything around you is coming together in that one action of making, of creating, and usually in my case of drawing. Even when I'm painting...I'm drawing." (The catalog also contains Robert Hobbs's essay, "Keith Haring and Fernand Leger: Democratic Art, Popular Culture and Semiotics," which although lucid, historicizes Haring's art so fully it seems frozen in time: the moment in 1978 when Haring studied semiotics at SVA with Bill Beckley.)

The essential uniqueness of drawing, the sureness and speed of Haring's line, is a feature of that identifies his art but has received too little focused attention. (Although many commentators sadly described Haring's loss of hand-eye coordination, as his death approached.) It is the lack of Haring's signature, uniquely drawn line, which explains why the Day-Glo orange, green and hot pink mural re-created in 2007 on Houston Street near Bowery is unconvincing. The breakneck speed at which Haring and his boyfriend Juan Dubose painted the 500 foot long mural—it took just two days to complete—helped account for the spontaneity and sheer pleasure that seemed embodied in the relatively simple composition of fluidly drawn figures surrounded by atoms and three-eyed creatures.

That the A-list Rubell Collection is the show's organizer (and owner) of the works in *Against All Odds*, is merely a reminder of their economic value. (Although the museum's PR tartly notes that the Rubells were early collectors of Haring's work.) The ultra corporate Jeffrey Deitch Gallery represents the artist's estate and, as I've suggested, the Haring-related collaborations of Julia and John

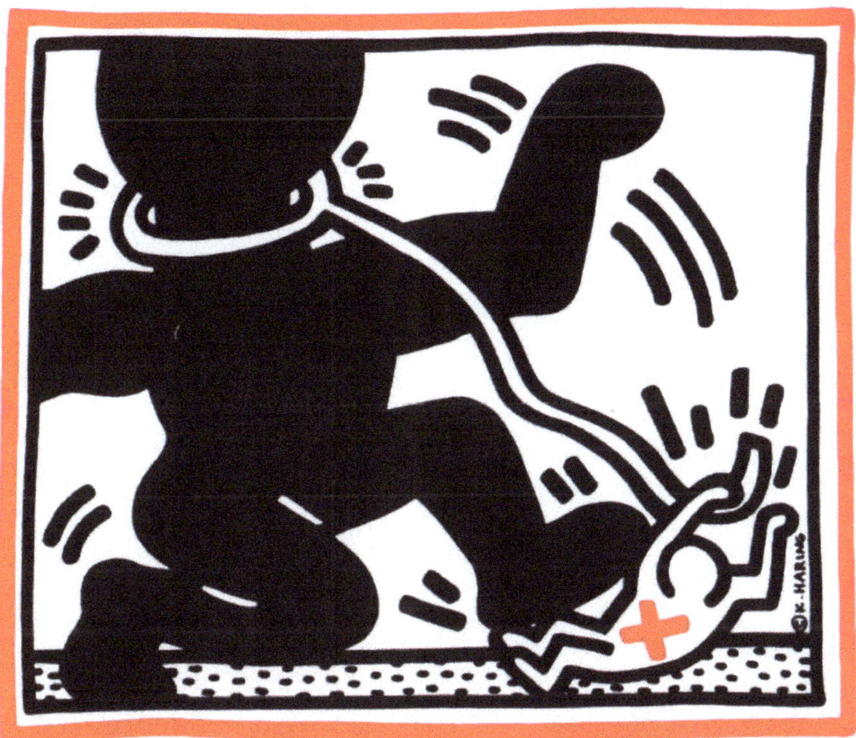

FREE SOUTH AFRICA

Gruen are too-familial. Why? Pointing out the diminutive nature of this group is not to suggest any legal impropriety so much as to assert that it poorly serves Haring. Together these organizations should initiate a robust conversation about the unique nature of Haring's artistic m.o. A fraction of the mega-budget for the glitzy *Keith Haring* book might have been better spent on commissioning essays from critics and historians with diverse views about the artist and the character of his work. He is too large an artist for so small (and unimaginative) a group to be in charge of his memory.

Even a cursory glance at a list of exhibitions and collections of which Haring is a part, makes it clear that he is held in far higher esteem abroad than in the United States. Is it due to the critics who stopped writing about him in 1985? To the lead-footed Puritanism of an American art culture that too-quickly dismissed the entirety of his *oeuvre* as lightweight? Or to the overly public nature of his output which seems to suggest little concern for conventional art world manners and mores? Last year, 2008, would have been the artist's 50th birthday. Major anniversary exhibitions were staged at the Museum of Contemporary Art of Lyon and in the poetic design of the new home of the Nakamura Keith Haring Collection, in Kobuchizawa, Japan, but nowhere in the US. The Japanese museum dedicated to Haring's work also published user-friendly materials intended to combat the spread of HIV through safer sex and clean needle use. Ironically, AIDS remains Haring's problem: Had he lived beyond his 31 years, his work is likely to have influenced more artists and created a clearer context of its meaning and usefulness to them. No artist, after all, can be said to have been far apart from—much less ahead of—his time.

DISCUSSED IN THIS PIECE: Keith Haring, Jeffrey Deitch, Suzanne Geiss & Julia Gruen with contributions by Kenny Scharf and Geroge Condo in association with the Estate of Keith Haring, NY: Rizzoli International Publications, 2008; 544 pages, $100

"Against All Odds: Keith Haring in the Rubell Family Collection" at the Palm Springs Art Museum, Nov 8, 2008 – Jan 18, 2009

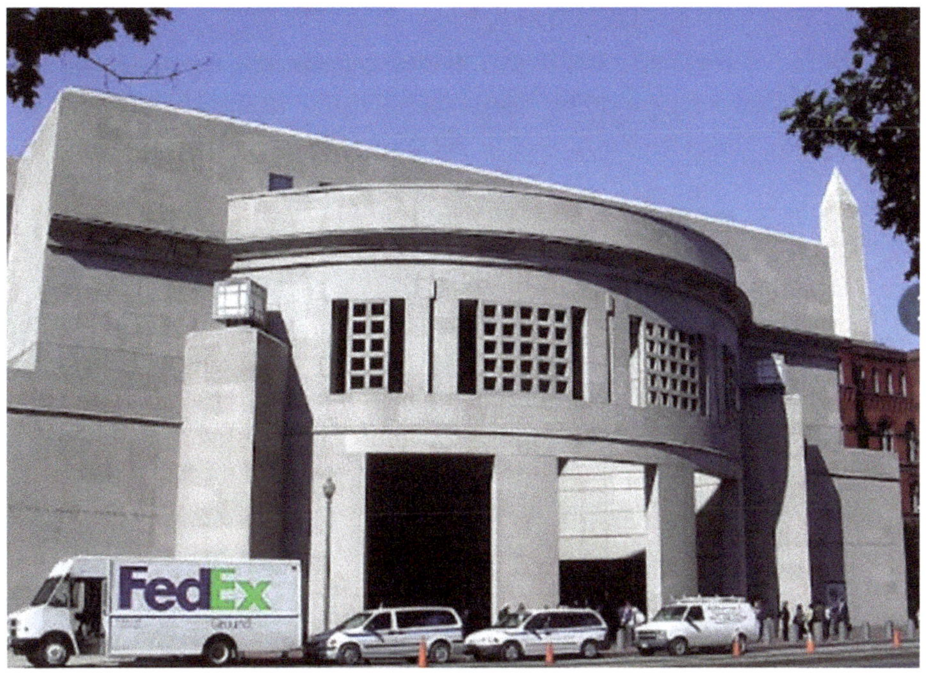

United States Holocaust Memorial Museum opened to the public the week of the March on Washington

Politicking in D.C.

Village Voice, 1993, PAGE 12-16 (3)

Queer Eyes/Queer-ize"—the Arts Contingent for the March on Washington's slogan—resonated with me and my chums. (*Queer-ize* as in *revolutionize, terrorize,* or—remember this one—*Martinize?*) Queer eyes in D.C. were simultaneously trained outward on lawmakers and media, and inward on our own communities. Events that ran the gamut from a group wedding at the IRS and the all-day dragfest, to ACT UP's hands-around-the-Capitol demo and reunion of African-American vets made the weekend a joyful celebration of homo life and a ringing call for equality. The arts, not incidentally, were at its center.

The Arts Contingent for the March on Washington (ACMOW)—like so many other groups—lobbied furiously during the days preceding the April 25 march. On April 22, a small ACMOW-organized delegation met with National Endowment for the Arts's acting chair, Anna Steele, deputy director of programs A. B. Spellman, and support staffers. Participants characterized the meeting in positive terms ranging from Roberto Bedoya's "Okay" (he's president of the National Association of Artists Organizations) to ACMOW co-coordinator (and veteran lesbian lobbyist) Shannon Thomas Kennedy's "It was the best Washington meeting I've had in the last two years." What matters, of course, is the NEA's follow-through. Steele heeded a suggestion to send a letter to the upcoming ACMOW town-hall meeting on the day of the march (it was a far warmer missive than Bill Clinton's arms-length message to marchers.) More important, Spellman said he had "no problem" recommending that a policy panel consider revamping the Expansion Arts Program's definition of multiculturalism to include not just ethnicity but sexual orientation.

On April 23, ACMOW held an unprecedented briefing session (that I sat in on) with Rocco Claps, the gay/lesbian liaison to the Democratic National Committee. Claps cheered the group when he noted that DNC staffers report to the White House and astonished us with the news that the DNC had never before met with an arts delegation. "It's an important sign that the DNC is paying me to be here," he commented. Claps, in turn, heard about the centrality of queer-art concerns to any progressive agenda. (The Clinton justice department's incomprehensible pursuit of the NEA 4 appeal, for instance, threatens every American's First Amendment rights.) The fundamental lesson of the week's politicking began to emerge: Despite an infrastructure of well-funded, national (mainstream) arts organizations, arts priorities are as marginalized as gay and lesbian concerns in Washington.

This lesson was played out at the ACMOW town-hall meeting of about 100 enthusiastic artist-citizens at the Corcoran Gallery of Art on the morning of the march. No consensus emerged for organizing a new (and expensive) national queer-arts organization—nor was one sought. Instead, participants opted for bringing our concerns to existing gay and non gay networks and organizations. As Kennedy noted, "art can no longer be the gap in gay lobbying."

NEA 4 pro bono attorney Mary Dorman—part of the legal team facing a June deadline in the government's appeal—proclaimed to tumultuous applause that "we're the cutting edge of advocacy and the struggle for the freedom of expression...Clinton is doing nothing for the arts."

The key role that the arts play in gay culture was reflected in the organization of the march-day rally—a nonhierarchical showcase of intertwined high, popular, and political cultures. British actor Ian McKellen followed tennis great Martina Navratilova and Teddy Kennedy; the late poet Audre Lorde (on film) preceded singer Holly Near and Jesse Jackson.

The arts and political components of many of the weekend's exhibitions and events were just as tightly knit. The *Gay & Lesbian Histories Exhibit* at the Stables Art Center featured artifacts from 11 organizations including the Gene Autry Western Heritage Museum and the Lesbian Herstory Archives. If the show's homo zeal is sometimes excessive, the One in Ten group that organized it certainly deserves encouragement for its new and daunting enterprise: the creation of a national, queer history museum. (One in Ten can be reached at 202-319-7208.)

Every regular newspaper reader knows that the United States Holocaust Memorial Museum opened to the press and glitterati during the week before the march (and to the public the day after). This state-of-the-art history museum exhaustively tells its tale not through artifacts, but primarily through video, film, and photo blowup. Coupled with the brilliantly expressive, industrial-looking architecture, this sense of technological reproduction—and endlessly reproducible death—is overwhelming.

But there are problems, among them the scant attention paid to homosexuals exterminated by the Nazis. (Others include the sometimes banal exterior architecture, the ponderously decorative, commissioned artworks by Ellsworth Kelly, Sol LeWitt, et al., and the unacknowledged rip-offs of installation artists like Christian Boltanski and architect Maya Lin for the museum's most visually striking exhibits.) During my three-hour visit, I counted a mere 13 lines of text—out of thousands—devoted to homosexuals. This issue was addressed at a candlelit "Holocaust Remembrance Ritual" across the street from the museum at sunset on April 23. Museum staffer Rabbi Michael Berenbaum acknowledge the "inadequacy" of the museum's portrayal of gays and lesbians, but attributed it to ongoing homosexual persecution and to the related lack of documents and artifacts. (So why not post this explanation on the wall?) Klaus Muller—a German research consultant at the museum—presented six, sometimes very sketchy portraits of gay and lesbian Holocaust victims that also belied Berenbaum's assertion. The sketchiest of them was Elsa S. "We know nothing about her," Muller told the hushed crowd. "Except that she was a waitress, a lesbian, and that she was sent to the camps when she was 26."

Contemporary causes of death, too, were present throughout the weekend. Recently completed panels from the *NAMES Project Quilt* were displayed on the mall, along with a new format for preserving handwritten messages about the deceased on cloth panels. Washington Project for the Arts hosted a festive April 23 benefit for the Whitman-Walker Clinic inside its wide-ranging, 26-artist show, *Beyond Loss: Art in the Era of AIDS*, and for me, the march weekend's most moving event was one staged in a cemetery.

Congressional Cemetery, the first national burial ground, was the site of the Never Forget foundation's April 24 tribute to illustrious homos past and present. It's where out servicemen and AIDS spokesman Leonard Matlovich is buried (his tombstones reads: "They Gave Me a Medal for Killing Two Men/And a Discharge for Loving One") and it's where a memorial to Harvey Milk will stand. Architect Joseph Mancuso's competition-winning design for the memorial was unveiled at the end of the program. Subtly evoking a closet, it will bear—after the necessary $100,000 is raised—the slain San Francisco supervisor's words: "If a bullet should enter my brain, let it destroy every closet door."

Foundation cofounder Ken McPherson also announced that an Audre Lorde memorial is next on Never Forget's agenda. (McPherson vividly described the organization's mandate as "in your face in stone.") Past and future were coupled again in a moving tribute to San Francisco Supervisor Roberta Achtenberg—the designate for deputy secretary of Housing and Urban Development, who will be the nation's highest un-closeted official. But, oddly enough, that drizzly afternoon lingers in the memory like a scene painted by Norman Rockwell. As a color guard of gay American Legionnaires and vets marched briskly beneath the flowering dogwood, time seemed to stop.

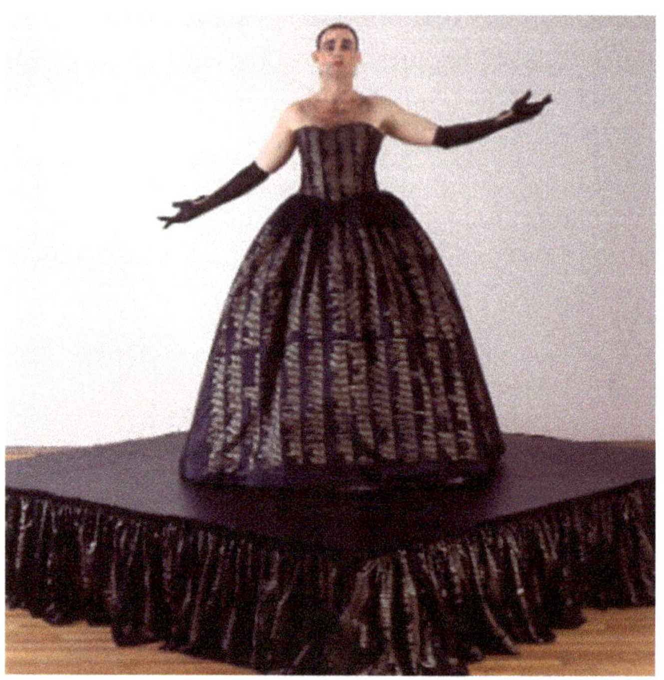

Hunter Reynolds: Patina de Prey's Memorial Dress

Queer For You

Village Voice, 1994

When the not-to-be-trifled-with queers at the Stonewall Inn resisted police harassment 25 years ago, there wasn't much overtly gay or lesbian art being made. The art world had only just begun to realize that giddy promise of '60s liberation, as the exuberantly varied *1969: A Year Revisited* show at NYU's Grey Art Gallery (33 Washington Place, 998-6780) demonstrates. That year marked the exhibition debuts of Conceptual Art and Process Art, along with the birth of the alternative space movement and Judy Chicago's Feminist Art Program, two events that would bear directly on queer art of the future. But if the nascent pluralism of the era allowed many things, being out and gay in your art wasn't one of them.

Civil rights and later liberation struggles are a reminder that no one gives us permission to be free: we take it. Not many career-minded gay and lesbian artists came out during the '70s; it wasn't until the mid '80s that AIDS finally emptied the art-world closets. Thomas Lanigan-Schmidt was an exception. His 1969 environment, *The Summer Palace of Czarina Tatlina*, invokes the East Village installation cum apartment he inhabited during the time he participated in the Stonewall riots. Dressed in drag as collector Ethel Dull, complete with Frank Stella earrings fashioned from the pages of *Artforum*, Lanigan-Schmidt led visitors through his brilliantly colored maze of gauzy hangings and faux liturgical objects wittily contrived from foil and paste jewels.

Lanigan-Schmidt's drag-queen exoticism seems familiar because he operated within a tradition he's helped raise from the underground. His late, lamented contemporaries in the enterprise were the filmmaker Jack Smith and the theatrical diva Ethyl Eichelberger, three of whose gown-creations—one with foam-rubber breasts—are currently visible in their own closet at the Leslie-Lohman Gay Art Foundation. Lanigan-Schmidt also paved the way for the current crop of East Village-bred drag queen artists, such as Rupert Goldsworthy and Paul Gehers, who are featured in *Stonewall 25: Imaginings of the Gay Past—Imagining the Gay Future* at White Columns (54 Christopher Street, 924-4212). Their faux-naif sensibility is only one of the many approaches curator Bill Arning presents. *Imaginings* mainly showcases work by thirty-something neo-Conceptualists with an almost uniformly deft and deceptively light touch. For Arning, pop culture and found objects are in; theoretically oriented painting is out. *Imaginings* is, incidentally, the best queer group show I've seen in New York.

Why? It's sexy. And because this is 1994, it means dykes are even hotter than fags. Witness Patricia Cronin's gorgeously Turneresque watercolors of faceless women-in-close-up eating pussy and playing with dildos, or Elizabeth Stephen's huge photos of a photographer shooting Annie Sprinkle and getting, shall we say, involved with her subject/object. Sex provides powerful inspiration for men, too. Andy Fabo's *Man Handling Matisse Suite* is a virtuoso installation of sometimes parodic, always erotic images etched into small black chalkboards, while Eric Rhein's exceedingly refined silver-, brass-, and gold-wire penis portraits slyly avoid a thousand potential pitfalls.

Imaginings demonstrates not only that the personal is political, but how. It's crammed with queer cultural history that functioned for many of the artists (and the rest of us) as an adolescent escape route from the closet. In word and image, exhibition visitors meet James Baldwin, Radclyffe Hall, John-Boy Walton, Pier Paolo Pasolini, André Gide, and Walt Whitman, among many others. Found photos become the screen onto which many of the exhibitors project their personal—and our collective—histories. Cary Leibowitz appended the closet-busting title *Celebration the Day After Stonewall* to a black-and-white publicity still of Rex Reed, Bobby Short, and Tallulah Bankhead (who oddly wears a sash that reads "Bette Davis"). For *Natural Nature*, Steven Evans couples a stylized, foliate motif from Beardsley and an early-twentieth-century photo blowup of a tattooed hunk with his arm on his androgynous-looking buddy's shoulder. The (against) nature theme is even mirrored in the greenhouse studio backdrop and the hunk's forestry company T-shirt, helping to make this one of the most resonant and allusive works in the show.

Happily, *Imaginings* is no sugar-coated, apolitical vision of queerdom. Cony Smith's moving *After the Wall* installation, devoted to Radclyffe Hall's landmark lesbo-novel, *The Well of Loneliness*, includes a reference to a 1928 letter from a young woman who asked Hall if tolerance of the "third sex" would ever come. "I could not help visualizing the many stony miles that her feet must tread," Hall noted. In his exhibition essay, Arning writes with similar ruefulness about his uncertainty in dealing with AIDS in the celebratory exhibition context he devised. Keith Mayerson's stirring artist book, *A Patriarchy's Nightmare*, and Stuart Netsky's bittersweet tableau of a swish sickroom/boudoir, with three medicine cabinets and a chaise for watching *Dark Victory*, should have allayed Arning's concerns.

Nineteen ninety-four marks the 13th year of the AIDS epidemic and, not surprisingly, the ongoing crisis holds center stage in a number of shows. ***Absence, Activism & the Body Politic***, at the

Fischbach Gallery (24 West 57th Street, 759-2345), is an effective and elegiac tone poem of an exhibition that might simply have been called *Absence*. From Mary Patten's whited-out address book at the gallery door, to a wall of spectral and poetic presences by Bill Jacobson, Daniel Goldstein, and Ross Bleckner, curator Joseph Wolin sustains his fugue.

Other noteworthy AIDS-related shows are the Organization of Lesbian and Gay Architects and Designers' *Design Legacies* (Gallery 91, 91 Grand Street, 966-3722) and **Patina du Prey's** *Memorial Dress*. The former is a tribute to 23 spectrum-spanning designers including Perry Ellis and William Oliver Johnston Jr., who was part of the Silence=Death Project. The latter is Hunter Reynolds's performance sculpture, sponsored at 45 Greene Street (966-2929) by Creative Time and the Contemporary Art Institute of New York. A site of mourning, the dress bears the names of 25,000 AIDS-deceased. In a ritual of healing, Reynolds/du Prey publicly dresses and silently addresses "her" audiences. Coincidentally, both shows provide vehicles for inscribing the names of those who have been lost. As Millie Wilson poignantly observed about gay mens' lives in her text work for *Absence, Activism & the Body Politic*: "The more they vanished, the more they were represented."

If there's a single standout exhibition-event among the very mixed bag of 40 or so Stonewall-season shows, it's *Becoming Visible: The Legacy of Stonewall* at The New York Public Library (Fifth Avenue and 42nd Street, 221-7676). Composed of hundreds of historical artifacts supplemented with photographs and the occasional painting or etching, this gargantuan and intelligent endeavor examines a century of queer activity and identity in New York. Curators Mimi Bowling, Molly McGarry, and Fred Wasserman wrest fascinating tales of social, amorous, and political attachments from placards and posters, political buttons and pop cultural icons (Gay Bob is packaged in his own doll-closet). The first major American exhibition of lesbian and gay history—three have been organized over the last decade in Europe—*Becoming Visible* is an especially meaningful embrace coming from our premier institutional symbol of equity and access.

Unfortunately, some of the exhibition's contextual meaning resides in the (current) lack of funding for a catalogue, the National Endowment for the Humanities' rebuff of the library's application for a planning grant for the show, and the near total indifference of local art institutions to lesbians and gay men this month. (The Caribbean Cultural Center's *Transcending Silence: The Life and Poetic Legacy of Audre Lorde* [408 West 58th Street, 307-7420] is a notable exception.) I'm willing to write off the elite-as-God Metropolitan Museum this year, but what happened to the New Museum, The Alternative Museum, the Studio Museum, El Museo del Barrio, the Jewish Museum, or any of the dozen other spaces whose programming derives almost exclusively from identity politics? Denying the complexity of identity (and eschewing coalitions) signals irrelevance, whether you're in Soho or Sarajevo.

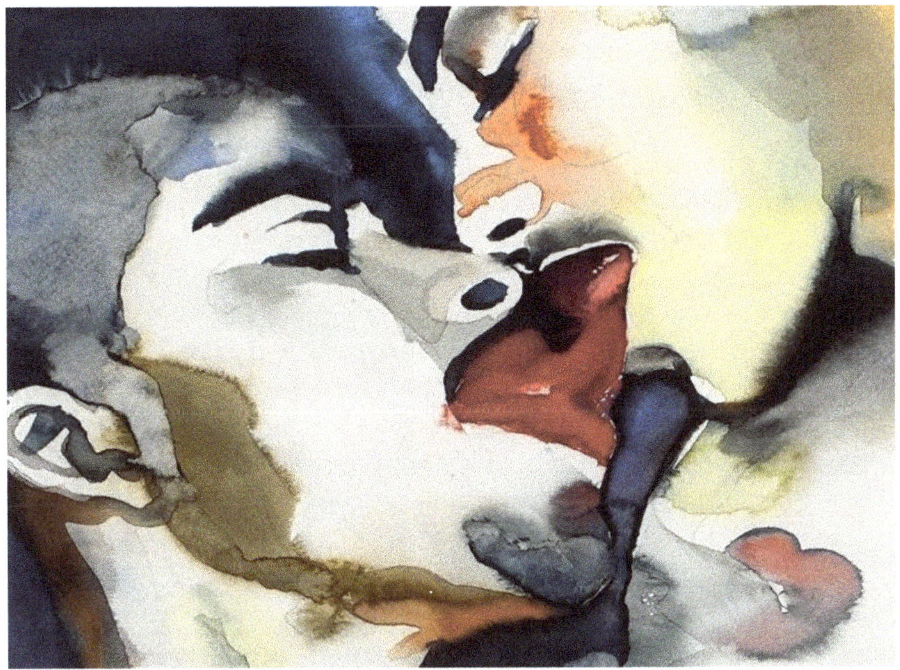

Rinaldo Hopf: Kiss

Lesbian & Gay Whatzis,

Village Voice, June 1995

It's Lesbian and Gay Pride Month. Or is it Gay and Lesbian History Month? You wouldn't know it by looking around the art world. As usual, there's plenty of work in local galleries by gay men and a smidge by lesbians. Some of it is overtly homo. But precious little is advertised as queer-made; only one press release touting Lesbian & Gay Whatzis has crossed my desk. Is this a hopeful sign that the art world's gone post-ghetto? Women's History Month, after all is not exactly *de rigeur* in Soho. Gender parity surely lurks just over the horizon, as the Guerrilla Girls periodically remind us.

Let's face it, June is the worst month of the season to show art. Every year the summer-heralding group shows and works on paper arrive a tad earlier. Art-wise, we'd be better off if those Stonewall girls had rebelled a month earrlier (but at least this year we don't have to endure another mismanaged Stonewall 25-style arts festival): May's Gay & Lesbian Whatzis would have included solo shows—many of them major, some at museums—by Matthew Benedict, Ross Bleckner, Paul Cadmus, Patricia Cronin, Steven Evans, Felix Gonzalez-Torres, Lee Gordon, Keith Haring, Robert Mapplethorpe, McDermott & McGough, Claude Simard, Andy Warhol, and Joe Ziolkowski. For an even more impressive roster, factor in the just-closed New York Lesbian & Gay Film Festival, where videos by artists Robert Blanchon, Shu Lea Cheang, Marlon Riggs, and Jocelyn Taylor, among others, were screened.

You can take it for granted that the contemporary film- and video-makers in the film fest are happy to identify themselves as queer professionals; it's gotten them onto the lesbian/gay festival circuit. The situation's different in the art world. Today's sophisticated homo artist doesn't necessarily want to be pegged as such, just as Georgia O'Keeffe detested being considered a *woman* artist. Identity-related adjectives attached to the noun *artist* always demean. An artist friend (I suppose it's okay the other way around) recently articulated the current posture of choice among out queer men: "I'd be in a show called 'Faggotry,' but not one called 'Faggots.'" (A lesbian artist friend later responded: "Hell, there are so few dyke shows I'd be happy to be in any of them.") How do we chart the boundaries of identity? Looking at this male friend's self-portrait, it seems obvious to me that he's gay. But that doesn't necessarily make his art identity-related.

As with feminism and liberalism, identity-related art has been demonized by conservatives; it's become synonymous with agit-prop. (If the 1993 Whitney *Biennial* could singlehandedly discredit identity-oriented art, why hasn't the current *Biennial* discredited painting?) By this problematic—or any—criterion, John Paradiso's in-your-face photo-based works are the virtual embodiment of identity politics. Paradiso's subject is sex in the age of AIDS. I braced for trouble when I entered the gallery through a door framed by the commercial yellow tape that blares "CAUTION, CAUTION, CAUTION" and appears wrapped around the artist's bod in several self-portraits. Paradiso attaches equally obvious sentiments to assemblages employing clocks and porn imagery (at

234

Artopia, 24 West 57th Street, though June 17).

By contrast, Robert Blanchon's small and satisfying solo show (at White Columns, 154 Christopher Street, though June 30) is all nuance and telling gesture. His untitled photos portray the bandanna-like hankies that still protrude from some gay men's pockets to signal specific sexual tastes. Blanchon's black-and-white prints have been hand-colored to resemble the real, color-coded things: yellow signifies urine, navy blue stands for anal intercourse, and so on, as the nearby wall label explains. The pictures resonate because the color has been meticulously applied to the entire image, including the pushpins used to splay the hanky against the wall for photographing. Inattentive viewers may miss this artifice and its meaning: these hanky signifiers are in drag, where they've become wily metaphors for the mutability of appearance and sexual interest itself.

Queers are such prodigious art makers because we've spent so much time looking for signs and reading between the lines. The survival-oriented queer obsession with layered meanings is an artistic advantage at this moment when neo-Conceptual complexity is hot. There are no fixed values in art: subtlety is in but obviousness rarely is. Does it come as any surprise that there are so few queer Neo-Expressionists?

Ironically, Rinaldo Hopf's black-and-white poster-series is too subtle for its own public-art good. The German artist's compelling photo images of a man with a shaved head sometimes paired with images of schools of swimming sperm can't compete with the visual cacophony of its streets-of-Soho location. But Hopf's wonderfully decorative sperm "wallpaper"—his term, not mine—and watercolors would fit right into *The Moderns*, one of two current, must-see, group shows. (The other is *Phallic Symbols*, dealer Hal Bromm's surprisingly fresh cornucopia of dick by artists such as Carolee Schneemann, Lynda Benglis, Nancy Spero, as well as many of the usual suspects-at 24 Hours for Life Gallery, 318 West 22nd Street, through July 7.)

Curated by Tony Payne, *The Moderns* (at Feature, 76 Greene Street, through July 28) is a quasi-installation of 59 works by artists "searching to articulate their desire." You may have noticed that *desire*—as buzzword—often has little to do with sex anymore: one of this show's standout works is Jim Isermann's exuberant flower mobile, which presides over the space like a benign Aquarian deity. But don't climb these gallery stairs looking for theory; there isn't even a curator's statement on the wall. There are, however, intriguing works by little known artists such as Robert Flack, Lovett & Codagnone, and Jeff Burton. (A solo show of Burton's photos of homosex captured in fugitive reflection is up at Casey M. Kaplan, 580 Broadway, through June 17.)

The Moderns also offers work by artists we see too infrequently, particularly Californians like Keith Mayerson and Judie Bamber. If you didn't make it to Berkeley for *In a Different Light*, this year's premier queer show, *The Moderns* brings you a taste of that exhibition's vivacious installation style and emphasis on so-called queer sensibility. Partly a generational reaction against identity-politics, this commercially sanctioned approach favors attitude over the artist's sexual orientation. (Work by ostensibly non-gay Mike Kelley, for example, is key to it.) At Feature, clever jokes, bourgeois baiting, and delicious outrage share gallery space with oblique ironies, dated dandyism, and perverse stupidities. Subversive feminist icons may be central to this aesthetic, but lesbian artists rarely are.

The most gratifying show of this Whatzis moment is Leone & Macdonald's (at Fawbush, 76 Grand Street, through June 30). Their work is predicated on resisting simple identities—like "lesbian"—in favor of complexity and dualism. Since the opacity of language is often their point of departure, it's more than apt that this show opens and closes with a readymade commercial sign: a rustling illuminated box reading "Ladies Entrance" on one side and offering four, fat cartoony butts on the other.

Last year Leone & Macdonald transformed all their clothes into handmade paper bearing an androgynous figure of a watermark for *Double Foolscap*, their disquieting installation at the Whitney's Philip Morris branch. For this show, they've forsaken their labor-intensive signature style for a number of smaller, discrete pieces. Dualism, their most frequent *leitmotif*, is embodied in a pair of champagne goblets joined at the rim and more ominously in *Handmade Straight Jacket*: two large knit garments with fused arms. There's no room for hands here—and perhaps none for straightness, either. Leone & Macdonald tend to operate where the meaning of language and image diverge. Their allusive piece, *Such as We*, will make some of us nod knowingly. But it's also a slyly inclusive gesture aimed at every gallery-goer. Why not give into its charms?

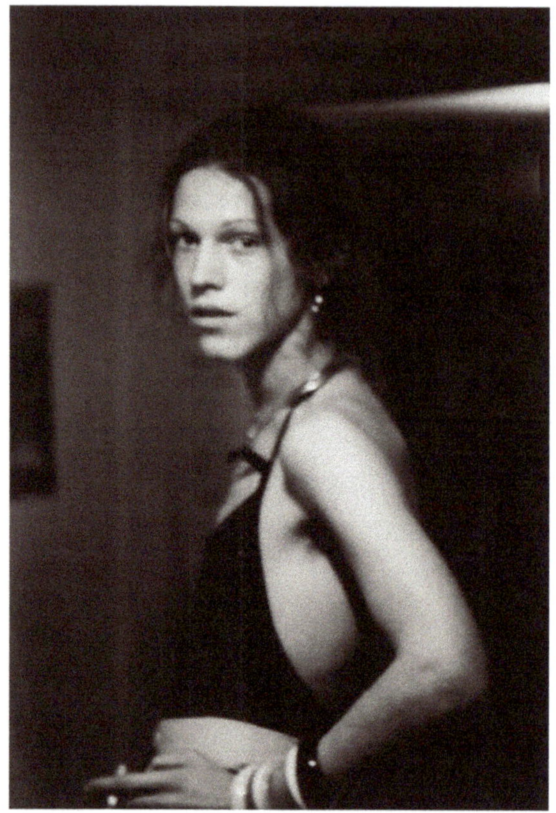

Nan Goldin: David at Grove St, Boston, photograph (1972)

Very Queer Indeed

In A Different Light; University Art Museum, Berkeley

Village Voice, January 31, 1995

BERKELEY—When a British court branded Oscar Wilde a pervert, it also gave birth to the modern homosexual. Homosexual acts were transformed into homosexual identity. At Wilde's trial, the prosecution cited *The Picture of Dorian Gray.* I like to imagine a mincing barrister in a powdered wig quoting Wilde's novella: "But I know that as I worked at it every flake and film of color seemed to me to reveal my secret. I grew afraid that others would know of my idolatry. I felt, Dorian, that I had put too much of myself into it…" Wilde's real crime, of course, was to be out—in both his life and work. For this transgressive queer artist, the personal and the political were synonymous.

The London court pilloried Wilde precisely a century ago. This symbolic event—and Wilde's generative influence—apparently escaped the organizers of *In A Different Light*, an impressive yet problematic show about queer art at Berkeley's University Art Museum. (Co-curators Larry Rinder and Nayland Blake don't even mention Wilde in their catalogue essays.) More than 200 contemporary and historical objects make this exhibition the biggest overtly queer show ever mounted by a major museum in this country. *In A Different Light* at once offers compelling and beautifully installed works, oddly subjective readings of twentieth-century art and gay history, and a simplistic assault on identity politics. It's a show that should travel to New York (but won't).

The exhibition is best regarded as a curatorial project-cum-artwork in the more-is-more style of Group Material. (This collective showed its *AIDS Timeline* at the University Art Museum in 1990.) Like Group Material, Blake and Rinder combine artworks with popular cultural artifacts, contextualize contemporary art with a dollop of historical art, and hang the objects salon-style. But that's where the resemblance ends. If Group Material were to mount a queer show, it would likely proceed differently: from the social to the aesthetic, by tackling an issue such as homophobia.

In A Different Light is, instead, largely about queer sensibility. It intends to explore "the resonance of gay and lesbian experience in twentieth century American art, focusing primarily on works made during the past thirty years." The work of non-gay artists as well as lesbian and gay artists' work is included; nobody's sexual interests are discussed. Much of the art, the curators aptly observe, "has little to do with representing gay and lesbian views of the world."

The exhibition itself is easier to read than these curatorial pronouncements. It is divided into nine sections that "move toward ever greater degrees of sociability": "Void," "Self," "Drag," "Other," "Couple," "Family," "Orgy," "World," and "Utopia." "Void," for instance, juxtaposes 18 works that range from John Cage's score for silence (*4 minutes 33 seconds*) and an album cover for Richard Hell and the Voidoids to a vagina-flower drawing by Judy Chicago and an aerial photo of Washington D.C., by Zoe Leonard. The "Void" category evokes vagina, anus, death and nothingness. This curatorial free association works—sometimes brilliantly—because the level of old-fashioned connoisseurship is so high. (The last Whitney *Biennial* failed for this reason, not ideological ones.) Eye candy is the exhilarating order of the day: the most bittersweet of Collier Schorr's plasterized baby-dresses-with-unsettling-texts-inside hangs just a few feet away from an unusually washy and ethereal canvas by Ross Bleckner.

Happily, the thematic curatorial m.o. doesn't pigeonhole the often allusive works, but it doesn't allow them to resonate much either. The two most effective thematic sections -"Drag" and "Other"-refer more pointedly to gay and lesbian rather than universal experience. "Drag" addresses, in part, the juicy issue of "appropriation as mask." One of the show's best passages consists of Robert Morris's famous biker-in-chains poster, Sherrie Levine's appropriation of a Walker Evans portrait of a bearded subject in glamorously abstracting negative, Amy Adler's photo of her own drawing after Levine's appropriation of Evans's portrait of his nude son, and Judie Bamber's photorealistic, graphite drawing of a pony bit that resembles some gynecological instrument out of a David Cronenberg flick.

"Other" showcases some of the most moving and historically rich works in the show. On a single wall Robert Indiana's gargantuan homage to Marsden Hartley's German officer *inamorato* hangs alongside Hartley's image of a phallic landscape in Mexico. Next to it, Millie Wilson's five-foot-high, all right, phallic-wig wittily flanks Donald Moffett's photo light-box of a reclining male nude. Emblazoned with the words "you, you, you," Moffett's male odalisque jacks off, providing one of the few literal erections or vaginas in the show. In *In A Different Light*, homosex is out; indirectness and irony, metaphor and perverse gesture, the dandyish and the cocquetish are in. Mike Kelley is represented, but not Patricia Cronin, Felix Gonzales-Torres, Robert Greene, Leone & McDonald, Frank Moore, or Julia Scher.

Of course, too much effective queer art has been produced over the past five years to be encompassed by a single exhibition, especially if that exhibition defines queerness in a way that skirts the issue of sexual persuasion. *In A Different Light* confusingly bills itself as the "work of gay, lesbian, and 'queer' artists." Blake asserts that Duchamp's practice "more than any other artist opened a space for queers to formulate points of resistance to the monolithic structure of 'culture'." In fact, Duchamp's gender play and twisted language operate squarely within the deconstructive, anti-essentialist tradition of the *flaneur* and dandy that Wilde and fellow "decadents" like Aubrey Beardsley paraded on an international stage. (Both of us are right, of course.)

Blake's search for queer ancestors might have benefited from more research. Was there really no room in a catalogue largely devoted to (reprinted) fiction and essays by writers like Dennis Cooper and Kathy Acker for an essay about lesbian and gay art history? Surely such gay father figures as F. Holland Day and Baron von Gloeden, Jean Cocteau and Francis Bacon, Minor White and Jess warrant a catalogue nod in passing. And what about George Platt Lynes and the other creators of the Mapplethorpe-ish iconography that is queer art in the eyes of most Americans?

The women of the Stonewall era come off decidedly better than the men. (Stonewall plays so small a role in *In A Different Light* that the curators fail even to note that artist Thomas Lanigan-Schmidt participated in the riots, which inspired the golden rats that are on view.) Feminist imagery garners more curatorial respect than overtly lesbian or gay imagery, which Blake terms "essentialist" and "retrograde." So the gendered but not particularly lesbian imagery of Harmony Hammond and Judy Chicago is seen alongside the gendered but not particularly heterosexual process and subject matter of artists like Eva Hesse and Ree Morton. Although information about the artists' lives and sexuality has been concealed, at least their work is visible.

By not exhibiting the overtly gay photo conceptualism produced in the '70s by male artists such as Duane Michals, Arthur Tress, and San Franciscan Hal Fischer, the record is falsified: these are some of the artists who created the psychological space necessary for the post-boomer generation of artists to operate freely. It's ironic that lesbian and feminist art historians are righting the historical record about feminist and process art, while Blake and Rinder sometimes seem to be erasing our gay art history.

In A Different Light explicitly rejects identity politics in favor of a return to a pre-Wildean era of homosexual acts rather than identities, of polymorphous perversity (and, I guess, punishment). Blake admiringly writes that "much of what queer artists are doing these days is questioning the value of identity politics," and Rinder comments in print that "this exhibition has been developed through poetics rather than polemics." Perhaps the irony escapes them that this show's nearly total lack of appeal to corporate or foundation funders has everything to do with polemics and nothing to do with poetics. Has any exhibition at a public institution ever been funded by so extensive a series of auctions and galas? One of the show's quasi-openings is a $250-per-ticket fundraiser on January 26—it's called "Fabulous."

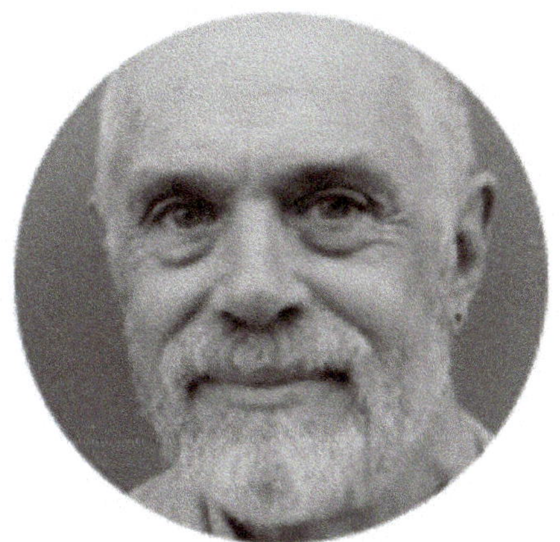

James M. Saslow

Queering the Art Historical Canon

James M. Saslow: Pictures and Passions: A History of Homosexuality in the Visual Arts

Art in America, May 2000, p 40-46

When I was an undergraduate, reading H.W. Janson's *History of Art* reminded me of reading the *Old Testament*: Both are authoritative and authoritarian texts that comprise fragmentary, tribal narratives in need of exegesis. I found the *History of Art* so dense that it seemed accessible only through rote learning. (I recently came across a yellowed flash card that reads: Velasquez, *Las Meninas*, Spanish, 1656, self portrait & dwarf). But mainly I kept reading because I liked looking at the pictures.

Pictures and Passions: A History of Homosexuality in the Visual Arts by James M. Saslow, like the fabulously illustrated *History of Art*, is an epic that transports us from the distant to the recent past. *Pictures and Passions* has many virtues: It is a product of both careful looking and (primarily) synthetic scholarship. It is an admirable corrective to Janson's early gender-challenged editions which implied that artists' lives rarely extended beyond court and cathedral. Straightforwardly, sometimes stylishly, written, Saslow's book connects desire and social circumstance, the play of the personal and political. At its best, it manages to create a panorama of art and cultural history, that elusive cross-disciplinary blend so much on the lips of academics but still so rare.

Saslow's primary interest is the relationship of art and (homo)sexuality, rather than the creation of an all-star line-up for the hetero or homo team. Nevertheless—and not surprisingly—an enlarged queer canon does result from Saslow's broader definition of homosexual outlook and emotions, as delineated in his introduction:

This book widens the scope of what counts as homosexual relations. Older scholars minimized homosexuality by limiting it to behavior, not feelings. But what matters for us today is less "who did what to whom" than who wanted whom—not just physical acts, but the nature of same-sex desire itself: how it feels, how it may combine or conflict with heterosexual passions, blossom or wither in various social climates. "Homosexuality" here embraces a continuum of emotions between people of the same sex, from homo social friendship to homoerotic intimacy to genital passion, whether or not they culminate in sexual union.

Two of his three previous books—*Ganymede in the Renaissance: Homosexuality in Art and Society* (1986) and *The Poetry of Michelangelo: An Annotated Translation* (1991)—make Saslow, a Renaissance scholar at Queens College in New York, an authority on homoerotic imagery and coding. In *Pictures and Passions*, he briefly sketches the congruence of Michelangelo's torment about his own homosexuality and the insidious workings of the closet—the connecting link between the social and the personal, between censorship and self-censorship. Art historians have their own part to play in this roundelay. Saslow, for instance, points out that the bevy of Greek nudes in the background of Michelangelo's *Doni Tondo* is frequently (mis)interpreted to represent moral progress from paganism to Christianity. Surely—primarily?—the lounging figures also represent what Saslow terms the artist's "irresolvable dilemma" of his simultaneous love of Christ and his sexual love of men.

Michelangelo's dilemma seems strikingly up-to-date. The (homo)eroticism of his work hardly went unnoticed by his contemporaries. The genitals of his statue of *David*, perhaps the hunkiest rendition of the biblical hero in history, also prompted the invention and application of history's first fig leaf. At the same time, homosexual and bisexual behavior became marks of sophistication among those pursuing the sixteenth-century *Dolce Vita*. Benvenuto Cellini wrote in his autobiography of a 16-year-old male model in drag he took as his date to an artists' ball. The Sienese artist Gianantonio Bazzi—dubbed "Il Sodoma" or The Sodomite—kept a retinue of boys and was later chastised by the chronicler Vasari for his brazenness. When one of Bazzi's horses won a race, the artist-owner insisted that he be announced by this unflattering nickname, an incident that Saslow describes as "arguably the first 'coming out' in Western history." (Less funny is Bazzi's narrow escape from stoning by the crowd.) Saslow notes that by around 1525, this alarming same-sex libertinism emanating from Rome led to the adoption of sodomy and censorship statutes throughout Western Europe. *Plus ca change...*

Pictures and Passions is divided into eight sections including an introduction, and seven chapters covering Classical Greece and Rome; the Middle Ages; the Renaissance, Asian and Islamic art; the rise of modernity; the modernist, pre-Stonewall twentieth century; and post-modernism. Not surprisingly, the Renaissance material makes for the book's most engaging and elegantly shaped section. But by the time World War II rolls around there is too much information, both art historical and social, for the author to deal with convincingly. It feels as if Saslow has run out of steam. (H.W. Janson solved this problem in the early editions of *History of Art*, by making World War II his cut-off date.) Andy Warhol, for instance, deserves more than three paragraphs devoted to a rather cliched discussion of whether or not the artist-emperor is wearing clothes. In fact, *contra* Saslow, scholars are finding Warhol's pioneering attitudes toward making gendered domestic products like wallpaper, increasingly resonant.

No art historian can master the entirety of art history and

Saslow's ambition is praiseworthy. The book's vast breadth is its strength, and weakness: this might have been a three-volume study. Saslow rightly tips his hat to high and low art, (for example Alice Austen's snapshot of women in drag or macho gay erotica from Tom of Finland) and to pioneering exhibitions and events such as the World Conference on Lesbian and Gay Culture in 1998. (A surprise to this reader.) But *Passions and Pictures* is still a rather old-fashioned book in its chronological approach and picture-by-picture interpretive style. Writing a survey may be a losing proposition akin to curating the Whitney *Biennial*: every commentator knows how he or she would have done it—invariably differently. Not the first work of its kind, it is the best. And it is surely a masterpiece compared to another recent LGBT-art overview, Emmanuel Cooper's *The Sexual Perspective: Homosexuality and Art in the Last 100 Years in the West* (Routledge & Kegan Paul, 1986). Alas, Cooper's work is long on kitschy male nudity, short on any sort of thesis.

Although the images in *Pictures and Passions* are well selected and reproduced, there are only 150 of them. Isn't it time such survey-works were produced in hybrid, print and online formats featuring thousands of images? Consider a print prototype from the early eighties: Peter Selz's *Art In Our Times*. This relatively inexpensive and little-noticed landmark, published by Abrams and arranged in thematic, non-chronological double-page spreads, contains thousands of images. It should have been be repurposed as a modern-art database on a disk, a CD-Rom documenting the final chapter of the analog era. (This, in fact, was Abrams' plan but the cost of reproduction rights rendered such visual abundance out of reach.).

Ultimately Saslow's book, too, is modern in its outlook rather than contemporary: It is the first such survey to appear after the emergence of the new disciplines of queer- and cultural studies as embodied in cross-disciplinary anthologies like *Queer Representations: Reading Lives, Reading Cultures* (1997), edited by Martin Duberman. Despite similar originating interests in private activities, *Pictures and Passions* doesn't reflect this recent coinage. A larger question *Pictures and Passions* inadvertently raises is How do we as gay and lesbian artists and critics move from the margins to the mainstream—that is, to the status of subject within a *History of Art* that encompasses our lives? When I was an art history graduate student in the seventies struggling to come out and to write a masters' thesis about Francis Bacon, this book might have provided personal and professional succor. Despite the plethora of queer films and novels of the past decade-and-a-half, I doubt that the need for such an affirming resource has diminished one iota.

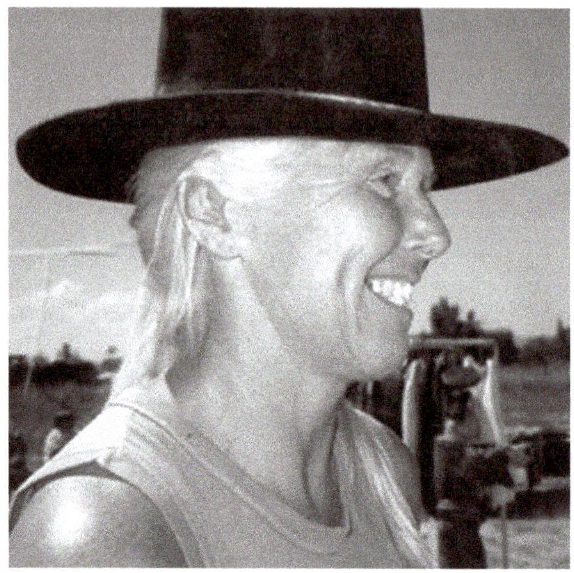

Harmony Hammond

The Rest of the Story

*A review of **Harmony Hammond: Lesbian Art in America**, Rizzoli International New York, Rizzoli International, 2000, $50*

Art in America, May 2001

Harmony Hammond's *Lesbian Art in America* is messy, fragmentary, overly ambitious and completely compelling. It's exactly the sort of account we need to counteract the exclusionary tendencies of the mainstream gallery-and-museum system. Hammond's sprawling book is less a work of conventional art history than a fervent report by a well-known lesbian artist, activist and player in many of the events she describes. Her ambitions for the book are extraordinarily large: "to document lesbian visual art since 1970 in relationship to gay and woman's liberation, lesbian feminism, mainstream art, feminist art, ethnic-based art movements, queer activism and theory, media attempts to commodify and consume the lesbian (and her art) in a chic spectacle...and to resist this appropriation and further a dialogue situated within feminist discourse and the history of visual production."

It's a tall order and, as with Hammond's art, she's balanced a focus on both overall form and close-up. The book is divided into three parts, each corresponding to a decade; within each part, she's integrated four to seven artists' profiles (performance and video artists are excluded.) So the first section "Representing the Lesbian Nation: The 70s," devotes 25 pages to feminist/lesbian social history and 10 pages to artist profiles of Kate Millett, Louise Fishman, Joan Snyder and Fran Winant. The social-history section brings us fascinating material about pioneering journals (e.g., the "lesbian issue" of *Heresies*) and events (e.g., the famous "battle of the sexes" debate in 1971 that pitted Norman Mailer against Jill Johnston, Germaine Greer and Jacquie Ceballos). The profiles offer not only biography but also the discussion of still-contested art-issues such as the possibility of lesbian content within abstraction.

If the '70s seems intriguing but distant to those readers who weren't around then, the book's '80s and '90s sections rehearse the familiar modern-to-postmodern shift embodied in the move from representations of the lesbian body to active, queer interventions. Although lesbians (and gay men) found little place in the art world's straight, male-dominated Neo-Expressionism of the '80s, some—like Nicole Eisenman and Catherine Opie—became quite prominent in the '90s. How did this happen? Who were the dealers, curators and collectors who helped? Did it have anything to do with the media's 1993 "Lesbian chic" boomlet (insufficiently discussed by Hammond despite prods like a *New York* magazine cover story), and Clinton's election over George Bush and the Pat Buchanan crowd (?). And how can social history of the last five years be written from so recent a vantage point? Hammond's dismissal, for example, of inclusive queer, versus lesbian, linguistic strategies during the late '90's—she wrote "The quick antiquity of Queer was inevitable"—seems premature and wrong.

Her m.o. is broad and anthropological. She's refreshingly unconcerned with canon building, in contrast to the arbiter-of-taste role many overview-book-authors unthinkingly adopt. It's simplest to see *Lesbian Art in America* as a collage or archive-in-distilled form. Like an archive, though, it's sometimes difficult to navigate.

The book's profiles, for instance, are interspersed with the historical text, and even printed on identical paper in identical type, making it hard to tell where one ends and the other begins. The confusing design functions almost as an emblem of the subjectivity of the art-historical enterprise, however, especially when the author is so intimately involved with her subject. Still, I was sorry to read in the notes that a timeline describing lesbian art events (in perhaps the most objective of all narrative formats) was axed from the book due to considerations of space. It's a shame, but *Lesbian Art in America* is a brilliant beginning for a field that demands more such contributions. Hammond's liberation-minded work will help make that needed study possible.

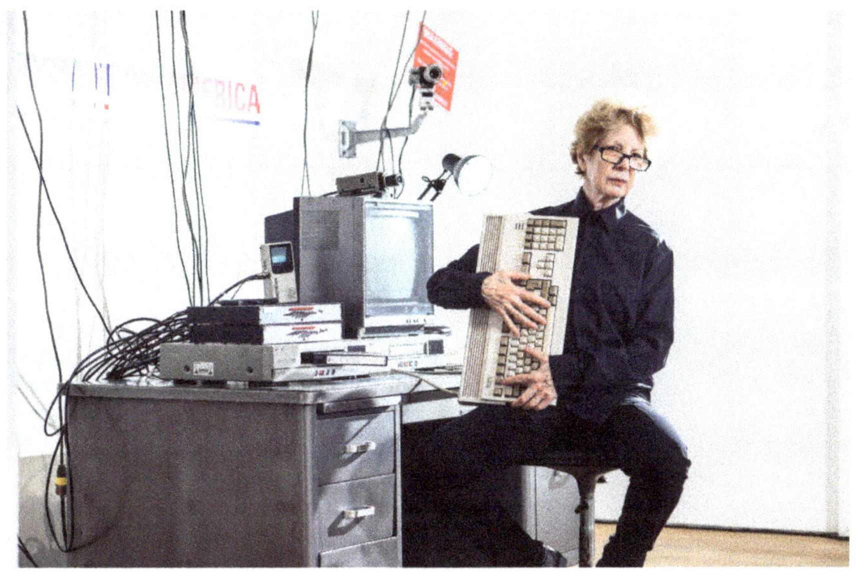

Julia Scher ponders dystopia in her studio

Julia Scher: Watching the Detectors
World Art, 1995 #2

When Julia Scher learned that the *Musee de l'Art Moderne* had mistakenly returned six borrowed works to Pat Hearn's Soho gallery instead of her studio, she made a mental note to pick them up. No big deal. The xerographic prints were part of last year's "Winter of Love" show and some portrayed the artist in S/M, uniform-drag. After she opened the crate containing the works, she found that all of the 11" by 14" prints were rumpled and dirty. Their leit-motif is bondage and one photo depicts Scher presiding over a nearly-nude woman, gagged and tied to a chair. "That's the one the guards refused to guard," Scher sighed, although she's unclear whether the prints were damaged during the show's run or in shipping. "The curators told me that the guards objected to the uniform," Sher said, "They apparently regarded it as an insult to their profession." Intended to challenge conventional ideas about authority, Scher's imagery frequently does more than just evoke ambivalence, it elicits highly visceral responses. But rarely that visceral.

*   *   *

Many writers also find Scher's work hard to resist. Her resume lists 82 articles and reviews devoted to her art. Scher came to many New Yorkers' attention (including mine) with two proto-typical installations that riveted viewers at a pair of 1989 group shows. For that year's Whitney *Biennial*, she installed a guard in a hot pink, Security-By-Julia uniform next to the ticket seller in the lobby, (Scher is a certified security specialist who operates a company called Safe & Secure Productions.) She also sited six surveillance cameras throughout the museum, and put their linked video monitors inside a phone booth by a restroom. Her contribution to the simultaneous "Dark Rooms" show at Manhattan's Artists Space comprised a narrow entryway featuring a uniformed guard at work, as well as banks of cameras and monitors. The monitors projected real-time images of the staff at work or fictional footage of a threatening figure with a gun or the like.

Critics describe Scher's work as a Foucault-inflected evocation of postmodernist dystopia—that recently-arrived, post-1984 era in which only money counts, nature is replaced by technology, the corporate state controls everything, image saturation is complete, and the un-fragmented self and unmediated consciousness are artifacts of a by-gone era. Although her work does embody these concerns (often brilliantly), this laundry list of contemporary malaise can replace—and obscure—its highly experiential quality. Such rote interpretations are often coupled with inventories of the installations' mechanical components. (The oddly literal effect is comparable to describing Rouen Cathedral as one of Monet's blurry paintings of a church.) Let me tell you about one of Scher's recent works and you can tell me how you'd describe it. (We'll con-

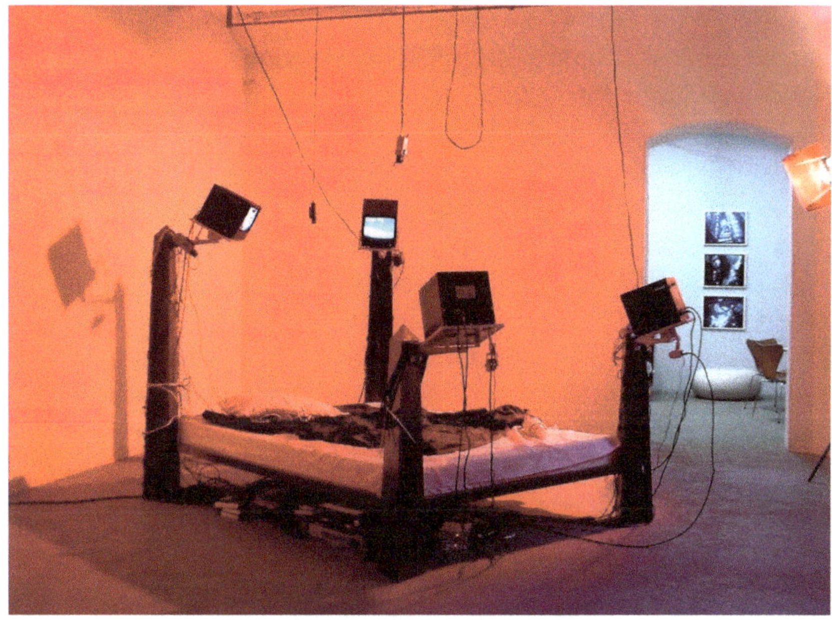

*Julia Scher **Always There** (1994)*

sider this your take-home midterm.)

Always There, shown at New York's Andrea Rosen gallery in November 1994, mainly comprised a bed. A surveillance camera and a black and white video monitor were attached to each of the bed's four steel posts allowing the consumer—the term *viewer* seems too limited in Scher's voyeuristic universe—to survey both this private domain and herself on the screen. (Goodbye anachronistic distinctions between private and public.) Reality exists primarily on screen, for Scher. "What other visible signs of life are there?" she asks. A sort of techno soundtrack played in the background; occasionally one heard the artist faintly intoning futuristic sounding directions: "Please do not leave until the sensors have completely absorbed you," or "For the highest security, please enter now." Outside the gallery door, a sign anounced that "this area is under video surveillance." Even from my thumbnail sketch, it must be apparent that Scher's interests in the watched and watching body, the state of security and the security state, have not diminished over the past five years.

Always There both invited and repelled interaction. Its meaning derived from the visitor's experience of the surveillance equipment and the sensation of the bed dwarfed by the cavernous space it inhabited and the prosthetic imaging devices. Its crisp, flowery sheets—which no bodily fluids would ever soil—exuded pathos. Are we at liberty to romp on Scher's bed? DO NOT TOUCH.

Consider instead the positions of the camera(s). You could insert your hand into its stationary gaze as if it were a beam of light, but all you got in return was a black and white image of your hand. The work seemed sexy, especially with the potentially porno-inflected thrill of real-time imaging on the video monitors, but they actually purveyed only a crude mechanical responsiveness masquerading as interactivity, cock-teasing masquerading as genuine (electronic) communication. Why can't my computer be transformed into a home cash point? YOU ARE NOT IN CONTROL.

Scher's tone is wry and dry and likely to elicit giggles of appreciation. Seeing her or her art reminds me of the pre-adolescent discovery, derived from the stained glass in church, of what Adam and Eve were doing in the Garden of Eden that warranted their expulsion. The emotions elicited range from pleasure to despair, embarrassment to recognition, dis-inhibition to tears of laughter. Her work is paradoxically impersonal. She never targets specific governments or corporations or herself. And no matter how disturbing, its m.o. is gentle, mimickiing the sublimely seductive onset of techno-social control that's washed over us. Her deadpan pose is not a mask for neutrality, however, but precisely the opposite. As Scher tells me, "Two hundred years ago I'd have been a *trompe l'oeil* painter. I'm not talking about the realism of it," she explains,,."it's the perversity."

*   *   *

Scher came of artistic age in the mid-seventies' heyday of information-oriented, video- and media- art. (She recenty compiled a glossary of security industry neologisms ranging from access mode to zoning.) As a painting student at UCLA, she couldn't take the film production classes she wanted to. She was, however, exposed to performance, installation, and video art by the likes of the Kipper Kids, Paul McCarthy, Vito Acconci, and video subject-object-manipulator Bruce Nauman, with whom she would later be compared. At the time she was doing "these kind of mutilated landscape-feminist fantasy, performance-paintings with titles like *Busted Cherry Candy* series," the garrulous artist recalled. "I got in touch with my exhibitionism, but I had to stop using candy because I ate so much of it."

The one-time political science major also credits her countercultural distrust of authority as a definer of her sensibility. It took a while, though, until the mid-eighties for Scher to find her form. After receiving an MFA from the University of Minnesota in 1984, she started a cleaning service that prompted *Hardly Feel It Going In* (1985), her first surveillance camera piece, which was surreptitiously shot while she cleaned a gym. A year later she produced *Softly Tapping the Wires* (1986), a riff on the fetishization of tools and hardware. That year she also moved to New York and began to offer security services for women. While she was far from the first artist to merge her art and business into an often invisible entity (Les Levine, Iain Baxter, and Bonnie Sherk offer precedents from the seventies), Safe & Secure Productions seems less precious than many such enterprises: it is an actual business that sprang first from economic necessity. Although Scher takes on only a few jobs now, she keeps her company on the tax rolls. "Occasionally if friends are having trouble with someone pissing in their elevator I'll do the job, but basically I just like the tradeshows," she quips.

A product of seventies'-style pluralism, Scher's love of words and hybrid, conceptualist modes remain a constant in her work. A 1990 "event" for the Walker Art Center is typical. Participants in a cocktail-hour, bus tour of Minneapolis surveillance sites, not only visited Honeywell House and the local convention center's security control areas, but were transported to them in a bus equipped with surveillance and imaging systems. The printed itinerary invited participants to "Feel free to help yourself to your own image."

Within her installations, Scher's droll language may be read or heard. Texts often appear on screens and monitors that provide real-sounding options: Step right up for urine detection whips, regression chemistry, or the interrogation and bio-merge center. Sometimes these phrases are audible, as in *Always There*. Whether seen or heard, their distancing irony and ersatz user-friendliness cut across the impersonality of the mechanically-articulated environments. Equally important, this strangely compelling newspeak synthesizes psychoanalytic and biomedical lingo with technologies designed to monitor space. You are where you are, Scher's work proclaims. Put another way, YOU ARE COMPLETELY OBJECTIFIED.

*　　　*　　　*

Watch for this stand-uppish shtick—Scher's term—to be released on audiotape or compact disk. (She is currently working with Canadian musician Mark Bell.) But don't wait to see Scher in performance; she's no longer (formally) doing it. "I loved performing [at UCLA]," she recalled, "and I quickly learned that you could get lots of people to look at photographs, but not many to come to a performance." It's too bad because she's magnetic: her open face and genuine solicitousness are no preparation for her very smart, very fast talk. Cast Debora Winger in the movie version of her life.

Scher galvanized an October 1994 audience at a New Museum panel called "The Submissive Moment: Pleasure and the Politics of Pain," held in conjunction with Bob Flanagan's and Sheree Rose's *Visiting Hours* exhibition. Her energetic, 15-minute presentation covered a lot of ground: it opened with a ritualistic tying up of the moderator's hands, generously paid homage to Flanagan and Rose, considered S/M as a fact of (teenage) life, and closed with a witty photo-meditation on American Home Products' annual report and its imagery of medical products shot from an incomprehensibly low-angled, downright submissive position. "I speak in *non sequiturs*," she breathlessly told her audience. But it's not really true.

"I can't handle straightforwardness," Scher tells me. "I value it, but I don't really try to overcome [my lack of it] because my technique points to that problematic. If duplicity is your subject matter shouldn't you be oblique?" Lucid if loopy? "We are talking about art institutions and the support Scher has received from so many of them. Her first museum encounter as a teenager with a Warhol Brillo box "disrupted and destabilized everything," she says, and her love/hate relationship with the art-institutional powers-that-be continues unabated.

"I play with institutions, I don't attack them directly. If we're talking about straightforwardness, take Hans Haacke's work. It puts a jolt into the system like a finger in a socket." Scher picks up two clips and attaches one to an electrical cord. "I'm putting on alligator clips," she affixes the other to her clothed breast, her voice rising in volume and pitch, "then running that current right through my body. Ouch!"

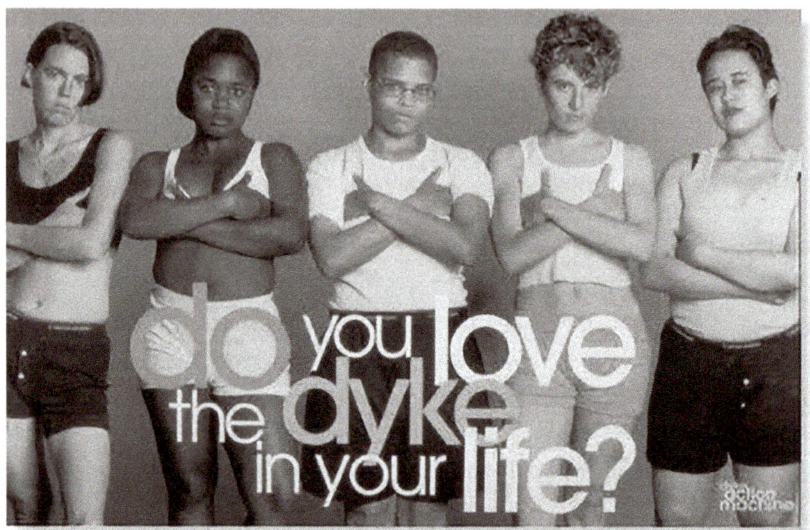

Dyke Action Machine!

Girls with Wheat Paste and Web Space

Media Channel website, 2001. an interview with DAM! (Dyke Action Machine), Adapted for "DAM! The Message," Straight to Hell, Yerba Buena Center For the Arts, San Francisco, 2002

Inspired by '70s sexploitation and action flicks, *Gynadome*—the latest work by the lesbian culture-jamming duo DAM!, or Dyke Action Machine!—takes place in a "remote biosphere" on another planet where "women are Women, men have been put out to pasture and computers are just Big Paperweights." Meet Marsha (code name Ditto, born deaf and left for dead on the Microsoft campus), RenČe (code name Womewaccka, the subject of a nefarious scheme to produce originals for cloning) and Crystal (code name Media, a shape-shifter with overly peaceful inclinations for the information-war era).

They're all characters in a "trailer" for the Webwork *Gynadome*, which is set to debut online in late June and will feature a Neo-Luddite chat room and a game where visitors will suffer surprising punishments for even mentioning technology. The project will also showcase videos by the GynaGirls going "back to the land" on Mother Earth and moderated discussion events with "scientists" and "celebrity lesbians." A marvel of flash animation and evocative sound, *Gynadome* manages to satirize simultaneously the contemporary technophile movement and the commune movement of the sixties counterculture. Who said progressive media art can't be funny?

A collaboration by photographer Sue Schaffner and painter Carrie Moyer, DAM! was originally a larger collective that was part of the gay and lesbian direct-action group Queer Nation. The two met at a meeting in 1991 after Schaffner saw (and admired) Queer Nation's "Absolutely Queer" poster campaign, which "outed" celebrities like Jodie Foster using the Absolut Vodka ads as a model. They conceived a project together parodying a Gap advertising campaign, then continued to work together after the larger group disbanded in 1993.

1993 was a watershed year in American media art. The social crises of the late '80s mainstreamed art about AIDS and multicultural identities. Artists like Barbara Kruger and the AIDS-activist collective Gran Fury employed the mass-media language of advertising and agit prop in the subversive posters and billboards they designed for the street. By the time Bill Clinton was inaugurated in 1993 and began to retreat from his left-leaning campaign promises, fickle art-world tastes had shifted away from artistic social engagement—or at least official support for it.

This change of zeitgeist hardly deterred DAM! Their campaigns directly targeted the inequities of the '90s political scramble to the middle-right, such as a ferociously funny project attacking the absurd "don't ask, don't tell" policy restricting the Constitutional right of American servicemen and women to speak about their sexual persuasion. (Reflecting their backgrounds in advertising and their political concerns, DAM! always refer to their projects as campaigns.)

The culture-jamming strategies of '80s artists who borrowed communications-industry tactics and took them surreptitiously to streets and billboards were altered by the widespread use of the Internet. DAM! augmented its street-works with a sophisticated Web site. By providing inspiration and example for activists everywhere, the Web may be radically altering the notion that all politics, art and action is local.

Robert Atkins: In the '90s, did you work with other activist groups besides Queer Nation?

Sue Schaffner (SS): I went on to be a part of the Lesbian Avengers, where I was in charge of the distribution—all right, wheat pasting—of propaganda. I was also involved with the Lesbian Avengers video team. We traveled the streets posing as a crew from MTV and asked people at tourist sites to explain to us what a "Lesbian Avenger" was. I have always loved this idea of disguising a socially conscious message with humor. I went on to produce and direct some spots for Dyke TV in the mid '90s.

Carrie Moyer (CM): I was also involved in the Lesbian Avengers, where I became a sort of Minister of Propaganda. I also did years of agitprop for the Irish Lesbian and Gay Organization. Plus pro *bono work* for the New York Gay and Lesbian Anti-Violence Project.

RA: This reminds me how much was cooking in the realms of activism and agitprop then. Where has that energy gone? Has it simply dissipated or is culture jamming a better arena for getting out progressive messages now?

CM: Culture jamming is a good strategy now for trying to reclaim public and virtual spaces from the encroachment of corporate sponsorship. In addition, DAM! injects images of people—dykes—who are never represented within the visual culture that surrounds us each time we step outside or turn on our television sets.

SS: The evolution of our culture jamming has been influenced by the notion that effective advertising has to constantly reinvent itself. So we've targeted commercial spaces normally occupied by product marketers and motion picture publicists. We have also jammed spaces in our very own gay community by placing our work next to ads that are now directly targeting us. We want lesbians to consider the price we pay for assimilation into consumer society.

RA: Has any of your output been co-opted by advertising and the media? Do you think pointed critique always cycles into toothless pop culture?

CM: To my knowledge, our work has not yet been directly co-opted by advertising. I did see a picture of lesbians at the WTO protest in Seattle with the caption "Dyke Action" in Newsweek last year. Yes, you've pinpointed a problem with this work. The tone of bravado always gets absorbed by the voracious machine of pop culture. Many art directors are smart and highly attuned to what is happening on the so-called margins of society. However, our projects still work for the lesbian-on-the-street or -Internet. We get tons of fan mail from people saying how great it is to see themselves and their feelings represented in the world.

SS: Our early work was a mostly reactive critique. Even later as we became less reactive our style changed with every campaign. Although we have revised historical forms and at the same time developed new visions, we rarely push the same design style more than once. We do constantly employ irony and references to popular culture and lesbian identity. In that, we are the co-opters of the slick ad agency. I think it would be quite difficult to co-opt something that is already riffing and constantly changing. Is the marketer today more interested in the outside vantage point of Dyke Action Machine! than they were in 1991? We'll let you know when dyke becomes a household word.

RA: Can you talk about the early ad-based works about queer families? What sort of response did they get?

CM: We have generally gotten very enthusiastic responses to our work, especially from the gay community. We started veering away from direct appropriation of existing mainstream ad campaigns in 1994. It started to get kind of tired just inserting images of lesbians into existing campaigns. This strategy was a pretty simplistic and even innocent means of becoming visible. Even though there are still virtually no representations of lesbians in visual culture, the solution is not to simply use images of dykes to sell yet more products. Our "Gay Marriage: You Might As Well Be Straight" campaign was probably the most controversial one we've done. A lot of gay people are really into gay marriage, so they were angry that we were questioning it. At the same time, people have asked us for posters to give their gay friends as wedding gifts!

SS: The "Family Values" campaign that posed a pregnant lesbian couple was unique for its day in 1992. It received a very positive response from the gay community and a "polite" response from others. I'm not sure the straight community knew what to make of it at the time. They had not yet been programmed by the mass media, which would soon bring them celesbians such as Ellen and Anne, and Melissa and Julie in baby-land bliss. The "Gay Marriage" campaign definitely got people riled up, which becomes a bigger challenge every year. As long as our audience feels that we are critiquing someone else, then they're entertained by our message. With "Gay Marriage" some people felt personally attacked and offered pretty negative feedback. Whereas some amusing responses came from straight people who seemed confused, thinking that gay marriage is what we all want and now don't know our minds.

RA: Are you now giving up your object works—print posters, etc.—for an entirely digital practice?

SS: We are constantly evaluating the Net audience against the audience of the street. Right now the urban scape of New York is overflowing with messages, and the locals are somewhat cooled to street messages. The Net is still a relatively new frontier with an audience that may be a better target for something with shock value. Although our online output does allow us to reach a far wider audience than our street campaigns, there is something incredibly satisfying about actually seeing (and greeting) the end user of our art. A virtual world does not allow you to walk down Fifth Avenue with a bunch of dykes that have plastered *Gynadome* tattoos all over their very real bodies. Ephemera's qualities of collectability and nostalgia aren't relevant yet to digital works. I don't think we will ever give up the object work.

CM: The object has been important to us. We give them out free to people who request them from us. I've often had the pleasant experience of going to somebody's home, [somebody] whom I don't already know, and seeing one of our posters there. So these cheap, ephemeral objects have a life long after the street installation comes down. We feel having a street presence is important to our history. Partly in response to Giuliani's "quality of life" dictates, there are fewer and fewer locations to wheat paste, so our forthcoming project *Gynadome* will have a billboard component to augment the Web site. We think it will be funny to see a billboard advertising nothing for this neo-Luddite site which critiques the

Internet explosion. Last year dot-com billboards seemed to be taking over the public space of New York City. Let's see what happens now that the NASDAQ is in the dumps.

RA: In an increasingly conservative era, identity politics has been increasingly marginalized by the art world and the media. What strategies can we use to combat this?

CM: Tough question. As you may surmise, DAM! has struggled long and hard to be "seen" by the art world. The fact that we always use overt lesbian content somehow precludes our work from being "art" in the minds of many curators [and] magazine editors and therefore not of interest to the general public—whoever that is! Fortunately, some curators and writers have been able to situate DAM!'s work within the continuum of political and conceptual artwork produced in the past decade. Sometimes I've wondered if we really need a project with a more overt "lesbian agenda." I think we're using such a strategy now with *Gynadome*, where the lesbian viewpoint is implicit. The sci-fi/superhero narrative is shown through the lens of '70s separatism, essentialism, and "back to the land" movements. This is a tactic that a lot of gay artists are using right now, probably as a means of making sure their work gets seen and appreciated. Sometimes it feels like a bit of a cop-out, though, because it re-inscribes how "progressive," "tolerant" and "comfortable" our culture has become with queers. Ha! At the same time, we have been doing this for 10 years, and we want to try different strategies and keep growing as artists. I don't know that you can be truly radical if irony is one of your primary strategies.

SS: The work needs to be evaluated on more than the basis of identity politics, and this is something that we have been struggling with for a long time. There have been some recent breakthroughs like the Studio Museum of Harlem featuring gay content in a non-gay show with Glenn Ligon and John Bankston. One of the ways we combat this is by strategic publicity. We become the distributors and the presenters of the work when we publish on the Net or the street. We create our press releases and help the media position us in a way that favors less marginalization and more content.

CM: Or least we hope they'll position us that way.

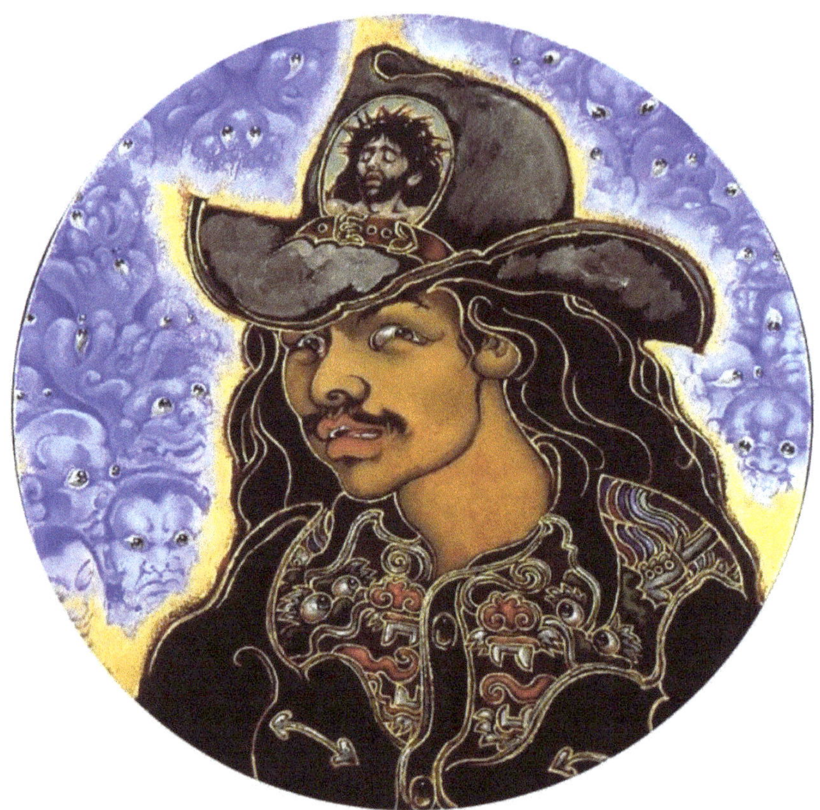

Martin Wong: **Self-Portrait**

Martin Wong: East as Eden

SquareCylinder.com November 20, 2017

Martin Wong's paintings depicting tenements, people of color, prison cells, gated storefronts, constellations labeled in gold, firemen (the fetishized objects of his affection) and dialects ranging from American Sign Language to visual poetry, are remarkably resonant. They infuse the Berkeley Art Museum (BAMPFA) and the Anglim Gilbert Gallery with the pungent flavor of the street. Wong's deceptively simple art encapsulates a culturally seminal place and time—the East Village of the 1980s— as fully as any artist's output. Between the BAMPFA's comprehensive offering of paintings (*Martin Wong: Human Instamatic* on view through December 10) and Anglim Gilbert's exhibition devoted to Wong's, post-student years as craftsman and draftsman (*Martin Wong: California Years* on view through December 9), it is unlikely that a more comprehensive view of this artist's work will again be available to viewers.

Born in Portland in 1946 and raised in San Francisco, Wong studied ceramics at Humboldt State University in Eureka, beginning in 1964, and in 1970, mosaics in Afghanistan. During the 1970s, he split his time between San Francisco and Eureka, producing poems on scrolls in stylized calligraphy, and sets for the gender-bending theater troupes, the Angels of Light and the Cockettes. (A photo at BAMPFA shows Wong with Divine, the bicoastal drag-queen-star of John Waters' films and the Cockettes' psychedelic extravaganzas.) Wong playfully advertised his services in Northern California as the "Human Instamatic," an artist available to produce portraits priced according to their size. Wong's cheeky gesture tips its hat to Andy Warhol, who famously announced his desire to be a machine, and capitalized on the Polaroid Instamatic camera's capacity for party-ready spontaneity and documentary verity. It's not an especially apt moniker for Wong, however. He was an artist who paid obsessive attention to labor-intensive detail and devotion to fact, rather than to any brand of realism or naturalism, as conventionally understood.

The Years is nearly monochromatic, consisting of small ceramic plaques, many with texts and glitter; a handful of graphite self portraits in a Gothic psychedelic style; a cartoonish drawing, *Instamatic 314* (1970) that suggests signage; a delicate cityscape of North Beach; and—mainly—words: Words in the forms of poems, texts and "fairy tales" (Wong's term) rendered in florid, graffiti-like script. Yet he employed so large a variety of eccentric styles for his words that they might have been limned by more than one artist. Sometimes it was the appearance of words that seem to have primarily interested Wong. The often over-written scrolls tend toward the indecipherable, while the short texts on conventional square or rectangular formats are the easiest to make out. Looking sometimes beats reading, though, as with the undated, *Untitled (Love's Sweet Residue)*, which notes with a Shakespearean sentimentality: "Love's sweet residue lingers on and on immune to time itself."

Of the two shows, *Martin Wong: Human Instamatic* is clearly the main event. Apart from a few early works, archival documents and a must-see video portrait of Wong by the artist Charlie Ahearn, the exhibition presents dozens of paintings created during the last two decades of Wong's life: a decade-and-a-half in New York and his final five years in San Francisco, preceding his death in 1999 from HIV-related causes. New York was Eden for him as evidenced by the letter he sent his parents immediately upon his arrival. Illustrated by a drawing of the Brooklyn Bridge it announces his delight with his new nabe downtown and describes the Museum of Modern Art—with its then-inexpensive artist's membership—as a "drop-in center for artists."

He reveled in downtown's bohemian, multi-ethnic, multi-gendered population. Paintings produced the year of his move such as the droll *Tell My Troubles to the Eight Ball* (1978) employ some or all of the new strategies that quickly came to characterize his practice. He retained words and signs but jettisoned visual poetry and the scroll format. He turned to painting friends and neighbors, rather than portraits for hire, which allowed him to explore a greater range of feelings. One perpetual characteristic of his sensibility was his attachment to materiality: it was expressed in his ceramics during the seventies, and later, in his paintings by the carefully rendered *faux-*wood borders and the eccentrically shaped and ornate frames he sometimes appended to them. The effort entailed in finding those frames reflected the artist's life-long passion for collecting.

The word passion, however, probably understates the savvy Wong brought to his obsession with collecting. His acquisitions ranged from a slightly battered Andy Warhol Brillo box to hundreds of kitschy salt-and-pepper shakers, which were showcased in *I M U U R 2*, Danh Vo's 2012 exhibition about collaboration at New York's Guggenheim Museum. Vo acquired them from Wong's mother, Florence Wong Fie, a collector who apparently passed on to her son a mania that explains the postscript to the initial letter

Wong sent to his parents from New York suggesting that she consult Sotheby's for an appraisal of a Mimbres bowl.

Wong was a pioneer of the mash-up, of synthesizing strategies, styles and visual idioms. *Sweet 'Enuff* (1987) is a large and paradigmatic example. The 6 x 11-foot diptych employs age-old tricks of the mural trade, evident in radically foreshortened figures, in rhyming curves of bodies and in parallel lines of architecture that contain and communicate his phantasmagoric vision of urban life. Wong combined many of his favorite motifs in this composition: A cityscape of dilapidated tenements and barbed wire inhabited by flying skateboarders, a sleeping convict (probably Wong's sometime lover and collaborator, the playwright Miguel Piñero) and a pair of firefighters beneath the umbrella of a black sky dotted with a golden map of stars and stylized images of hands signing for the deaf. It's Wong's way of suggesting that painting—like signing and astronomy—is yet another abstract and symbolic language.

Fact, wit and complex shifts of tone characterize his art, sometimes even within a single work. The tragedy of ruined neighborhoods, for instance, seen in crumbling brick walls and in iron-gated storefronts, is rendered bittersweet by Wong's loving depictions of them, the latter at almost actual size. Elsewhere, he casually fesses up to an infatuation with firefighters in two voyeuristic canvases from 1988: *The Big Heat*, which depicts two burly men in firefighter uniforms smooching, and what may be the smallest—and certainly the most crudely painted work in the show—*I Really Like the Way Firemen Smell*. Once they shower, the artist explains in text that fills most of the latter painting, it's only their unwashed uniforms that excite him. For this casual, diaristic work he shows himself in silhouette from the rear, wearing his trademark cowboy hat. It reappears in the *Self Portrait* (1993), an over-the-top tondo that depicts him as an unidealized, god-like figure surrounded by a golden aura. The cowboy hat is emblazoned with a psychedelic-looking Christ, a man of sorrows set against what first appears to be a star-studded sunset, but is actually a wall of indigo-colored Buddhist demons. It's a goofy riff on art and divinity,

Although this is an exhibition filled with charming, sensuous, and beautiful paintings, there's also something essential missing—a lack of context, of an understanding of Wong's identity and importance both within a community of artists and the continuum of history. I never thought I'd be troubled by a lack of information in a capacious monographic exhibition like this one. Wall-labels in many museums unfortunately instruct us in how to look at an artwork and what to think and feel about it. *Human Instamatic*, by contrast, largely ignores the East Village milieu in which Wong operated and which helped ensure his success.

I use the term *East Village*—rather than the exhibition labels' occasional references to the *Lower East Side*—as a cultural as well as a geographical descriptor. (*Lower East Side*, a/k/a Loisaida, takes in a larger geographical swath of Manhattan that includes the East Village but also extends south of Houston St.) When Wong arrived in New York in 1978, these adjacent neighborhoods were similarly down-at-the-heels; by time he left in 1994 NYU had occupied the East Village and made it unaffordable (and unappealing) to many of those who'd lived there 25 years earlier. But more important, *East Village* was not only common parlance—as in *East Village Art*, *artists*, or *galleries*—but a signifier that transcended geography to describe the tumultuous moment when Modernism went PoMo.

The 1980s marked the return of figurative painting following the Conceptualism of the 1970s and the embrace of commerce by artists who opened funky storefront galleries such as Gracie Mansion, Fun, Civilian Warfare, Semaphore and PPOW. (Wong first showed at Semaphore; his estate is represented by PPOW.) The most successful galleries helped usher in our era of global art commerce by opening branches across the pond or across the country. The consummation of the marriage of art, money and real estate was symbolized by events like the 1983 opening of the swanky, white-walled Pat Hearn Gallery on then-derelict Avenue B. (The architect Robert Venturi, in his 1966 book *Complexity and Contradiction in Architecture*, documents the messy "complexity and contradiction" arising from diversity of every sort, including the blurring of high and low art, and modernism and popular culture.)

The closest thing to an East Village style was the graffiti and cartoon-inflected work of Jean-Michel Basquiat, Keith Haring and Kenny Scharf. But there was no orthodoxy in operation. Jeff Koons exhibited his puzzling-looking amalgams of basketballs and aquariums; Peter Halley produced theory-laden geometric systems and Mike Bidlo pioneered appropriation for his paintings and performances, expertly mimicking the drip paintings of Jackson Pollock and others. The essence of the East Village approach was psychic rather than stylistic. Its validation of diversity and range of visions enabled a democratic expansion of art and foretold the era of identity politics ahead. By the end of the 1980s, however, the East Village art scene was decimated not only by gentrification, but by AIDS and drugs.

Wong's complexity extended, of course, to his personality, as well as his art. Judging from my casual interactions over a decade in New York, he was neither naïf, nor naïve, nor cynical. He was a romantic, but a clear-eyed one. As a gay Chinese-American with HIV he was, of course, an outsider. Yet within the East Village community of outsiders, he was a consummate insider. Paradoxical? It's a very Whitmanesque, very American contradiction. He and his inclusive work "contain multitudes" that enrich us all.

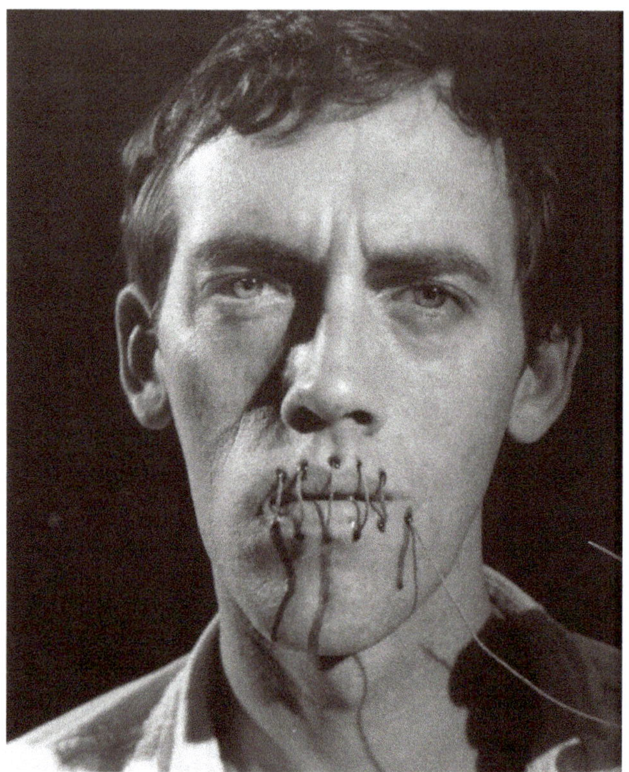

David Wojnarowicz, sewing action employed in photograph, performance and film, 1978-92

East Village Rimbaud

*A review of **Fire in the Belly: The Life and Times of David Wojnarowicz**, by Cynthia Carr, Bloomsbury USA*

Art in America, October 2012

David Wojnarowicz (1954-1992) was as full of contradictions as the changing East Village neighborhood he lived in during the 1980s. For nearly every quality of mind or personality the emblematic artist-activist possessed—his commitment to speaking truth to power, for instance—its opposite seemed to coexist within him. (In this case, a difficulty revealing intimate feelings to friends.) The heroic public persona he created was both a mask to disguise his psychic pain and a mirror that accurately reflected the impassioned artist. As his longtime friend Susan Gauthier told Cynthia Carr, author of the new biography *Fire in the Belly: The Life and Times of David Wojnarowicz*, the artist "wanted to be a puzzle nobody could figure out." Carr goes even further, insisting that "he never told everything." And yet her compelling and authoritative account is likely to answer any conceivable question a reader might pose about Wojnarowicz.

Like many people who grew up in the 1950s and '60s, Woznarowicz saw his early life documented in innocuous-looking snapshots, several of which appear in the book. These Ozzie-and Harriet-style photos are extremely incongruous, given Carr's stark descriptions of the artist's upbringing in a household devastated by alcoholism and physical abuse. Rivetingly awful, her account of Wojnarowicz's dysfunctional home is deeply relevant to his later life and work.

The family history begins with the marriage in 1948 of David's father, the then 26-year-old seaman Ed Wojnarowicz, and his mother, Dolores, an Australian beauty ten years Ed's junior. Of their three children—a girl and two boys—David, born in Red Bank, N.J. was the youngest. Violence—both real and vividly threatened—was a traumatic constant. Dolores divorced Ed in 1956, when David was two. Ed remarried and, in 1958, kidnapped the three children and took them to his native Michigan. A year later, for seafaring convenience, he moved the family back to ocean-adjacent New Jersey. In 1976, Ed hung himself, and two days later, on Christmas Eve, David came out to the family as gay.

Improbably, Dolores's performance as a mother—marked by a truly disturbing unpredictability—was little better. Just before Ed kidnapped the kids, Dolores boarded them out, moved to Manhattan, and did not see them again for five years. (Carr points out that this "boarding them out" is not synonymous with "putting them up" for adoption—but, either way, it sounds a lot like desertion.) Later, Dolores occasionally reached out to David—often by postcard at birthdays—and attended a couple of his early readings. But for the most part, she coyly discouraged contact, causing David's siblings to banish her from their lives for the first half of the 1980s. Yet David found Dolores impossible to excise from his life or consciousness—because, Carr believes, she (unlike Ed) remained alive, undercutting his impulse to recreate her for a romanticized version of the family history.

One hardly needs a psychoanalyst to connect the dots between David's behavior and his parents' instability: Ed's drunken bullying and beatings seem to have provided a model for David's high-decibel, often unjustified outbursts of temper and hurt; Dolores's controlling and withholding behavior probably set the pattern for David's exasperating on-again/off-again relationships with several female friends. Two of the most notable of these nonsexual connections were with the then unknown artist Kiki Smith and with Marion Scemama, a photographer from Paris. He and Scemama sometimes worked collaboratively, and their bond may have been the most intense of his adulthood.

In the male domain, the prime candidate for that designation was the photographer Peter Hujar, who was 20 years Wojnarowicz's senior. Briefly a lover, Hujar was far more essential as gay mentor and urbane art-world guide. In 1987, Wojnarowicz took 23 photographs of Hujar immediately after his death and thereafter continued to work with them, saying later, "Everything I made, I made for Peter." For the last seven years of Wojnarowicz's life, his lover was Tom Rauffenbart, a child welfare worker who was sexy, good-hearted, middle-class and "utterly dependable," according to Carr. He also operated from an emotional remove nearly as vast as Wojnarowicz's. The artist kept Rauffenbart and the majority of his friends so far apart that some were unaware of his existence until Wojnarowicz's imminent death.

Fire in the Belly deals with far more than psychology. Carr describes in minute detail Wojnarowicz's evolution from writer and fledgling rocker (he was part of the band 3 Teens Kill 4—No Motive) to visual artist, performer and neophyte video- and filmmaker, all set against the backdrop of the East Village and the AIDS epidemic. Writing was a far more constant element of Wojnarowicz's work than visual imagery or music, and the first work for which he received credit (and payment) was literary. A promiscuous boundary breaker, he relished the postmodernist dissolution of barriers between disciplines and often repurposed his Beat-inflected texts in his artwork or peppered his writing with visual art. This mix is strikingly evident in *Close to the Knives*, a selection of his short, literary nonfiction published in April 1991, a year before his death.

Knives originated when a very determined Random House editorial assistant named Karen Rinaldi encountered a Wojnarowicz text in a downtown gallery. (She would later acquire and edit Carr's biography, here under consideration.) Wojnarowicz, who thrived on the cultural density and ferment of New York, also loved nature and had itchy feet. For a starving young artist, he spent a surprising amount of time traveling to Paris, the Southwest and Mexico. It was in Teotihuacán that he shot the footage for the never-finished film *A Fire in My Belly*, which in late 2010, some 18 years after the artist's death, would cause a censorship dust-up fomented by the Catholic League and other organizations of the religious right. These groups objected when the National Portrait Gallery in Washington, D.C., included a brief video version of *Fire* in the gay-themed survey exhibition Hide/Seek: *Difference and Desire in American Portraiture*. As edited by the show's co-curators, the piece contains an 11-second sequence depicting ants crawling over a crucifix—a scene that League president William Donohue charged was blasphemous. The head of the Smithsonian Institution, fearing congressional defunding, peremptorily removed the video, and the incident created the sort of uproar that first brought Wojnarowicz national attention in 1989.

That was the year he wrote "Postcards from America: X-Rays from Hell," an incendiary catalogue essay for *Witnesses: Against Our Vanishing*, an exhibition of work by artists with AIDS, organized by the photographer Nan Goldin for the nonprofit Artists Space in New York. Dedicated to the still living of the downtown scene—though the participants were presumably to be soon deceased, given the futile treatment options for HIV at the time—the project had received $10,000 from the NEA. Wojnarowicz's essay was a rude, impassioned indictment of inaction and/or opposition to effective responses to the AIDS crisis. He targeted primarily local and federal government officials and the Catholic Church, personified by New York's Archbishop Cardinal John O'Connor, whom Wojnarowicz characterized as a "fat cannibal from the house of walking swastikas." As in the controversy over Andres Serrano's *Piss Christ* that same year, it was words rather than images that most offended censorious legislators in Washington. John Frohnmayer, the dithering chairman of the NEA, convened an expert panel, which found merit in the show's art—a judgment that incensed Senator Jesse Helms and his conservative cohorts and led to Frohnmayer's nonsensical decision to fund the show but not the catalogue.

In the process of covering the spectacularly messy events at Artist Space for the *Village Voice*, I spoke with Wojnarowicz on the phone daily—and periodically for my arts-politics column after that. (Disclosure: Carr and I were colleagues at the *Village Voice* from 1987-92, although I didn't know her well. I had similar relationships with many of the book's artists, gallerists and activists.) Despite the grim realities of the day, the only topic Wojnarowicz invariably raised during our numerous calls in 1989-90 was his anger at being used as a boogey man by the religious right, especially for fundraising purposes.

By the time of the Artists Space incident, the loss of the East Village to money and hype, pseudo-artists and real-estate developers, was ancient history. Commentators like Rene Ricard and Carlo McCormick had competed to announce its death years earlier, and a consensus developed among hipsters that the late-1983 arrival of non-artist Pat Hearn's posh new gallery on Avenue B signaled more than the beginning of the end. (Some 25 galleries had opened by this time, with another 150 or so on the way.) Wojnarowicz, remaining indifferent to money, never cashed in on the frantic commercial activity of the East Village during the mid-'80s, and he later rejected an invitation to do a Gap ad.

Fear of controversy—reinforced by a sort of informal blacklist—may help account for the fact that Wojnarowicz was the subject of only a single museum retrospective exhibition during his lifetime (and few since, most notably Dan Cameron's for the New Museum some 13 years ago.) Thanks to a suggestion from dealer Gracie Mansion, Barry Blinderman, director of the Illinois State University galleries in Normal, organized a large retrospective of Wojnarowicz's work, "Tongues of Flame," which opened in 1990, two weeks after "Witnesses: Against Our Vanishing" closed. At the time, I recall, it was noteworthy for the positive buzz and large audiences it drew during its year long U.S. tour. Now—thanks to Carr's prodigious reporting—I'm fascinated to learn that, despite his diminishing energy, Wajnarowicz struck up a long-term, nonsexual, mentoring relationship with Patrick McDonnell, an ISU grad student who helped him install the show in Illinois. Moreover, Carr points out, the formation of Normal's ACT UP chapter took place inside the university gallery, surrounded by Wojnarowicz's work.

I have only a few cavils with Carr. She occasionally falls for Wojnarowicz's self-presentation as a hustler-turned-unschooled-artist. (He was both, having peddled himself for sex in Times Square, yet how long can someone so sophisticated remain uneducated?) And she can be oddly reticent about interpreting some of his art. Referring to a Wojnarowicz work that includes the image of a Savarin coffee can, Carr doesn't recognize (or at least doesn't acknowledge) this as a signature motif of Jasper Johns, the superstar (and closeted gay) artist of the day, who had retrospectives at the Museum of Modern Art and the Whitney Museum during the late 1970s and '80s. More important—and surprising—Carr treats the so-called culture war a-historically, as though it emerged with the assaults on the work of Robert Mapplethorpe and Andres Serrano, rather than at least a century earlier in such forms as the Comstock laws. (Named after Postmaster General Anthony Comstock, these laws clamped down on "indecent" photographs and books, as well as abortion and contraception information and devices shipped by mail across state lines.)

Interestingly, *Fire in the Belly* arrives exactly two years after the publication of Patti Smith's *Just Kids*. Smith's National Book Award-winning memoir describes the coming-of-age she shared with Robert Mapplethorpe, like Wojnarowicz, a gay artist who lived in downtown Manhattan amid the censorship skirmishes and died before his time of AIDS. Yet how different are these artists and their art! While Mapplethorpe's photographs represent gay liberation, unitary identity and a late modern mode of representation, Wojnarowicz's wildly protean queer art anticipates current postmodern practice, with its shattering of representational norms and forms, its flickering focus and lack of resolution.

Carr's lucidly written and novelistic narrative sometimes feels like an existential contest to determine whether Wojnarowicz can heal himself, physically and psychologically, before he dies of AIDS. Although the artist entered psychotherapy late in his short life, he remained plagued by his dysfunctional background and constant depression, while the East Village body count from AIDS rose steadily. Nonetheless, the book's inevitable conclusion is devastating.

Fire in the Belly will surely prompt, among many things, a meditation on loss and possibility. Loss not just of unmade work by Wojnarowicz but also of the ideal of moral authority he came to personify. Yet larger than any individual loss was the tragic devastation of an entire community of artists, gay and/or needle using, in downtown New York. Some of those individuals, now obscured by time's haze or critical neglect, were once avidly talked about; others died too young to have reached—or even truly discovered—their potential. Perhaps Carr's book is a hopeful harbinger of the numerous AIDS-art-themed books and exhibitions currently in the works. If there is a God, their artist-subjects will receive the probing and insightful treatment Carr accords Wojnarowicz in this monumental biography.

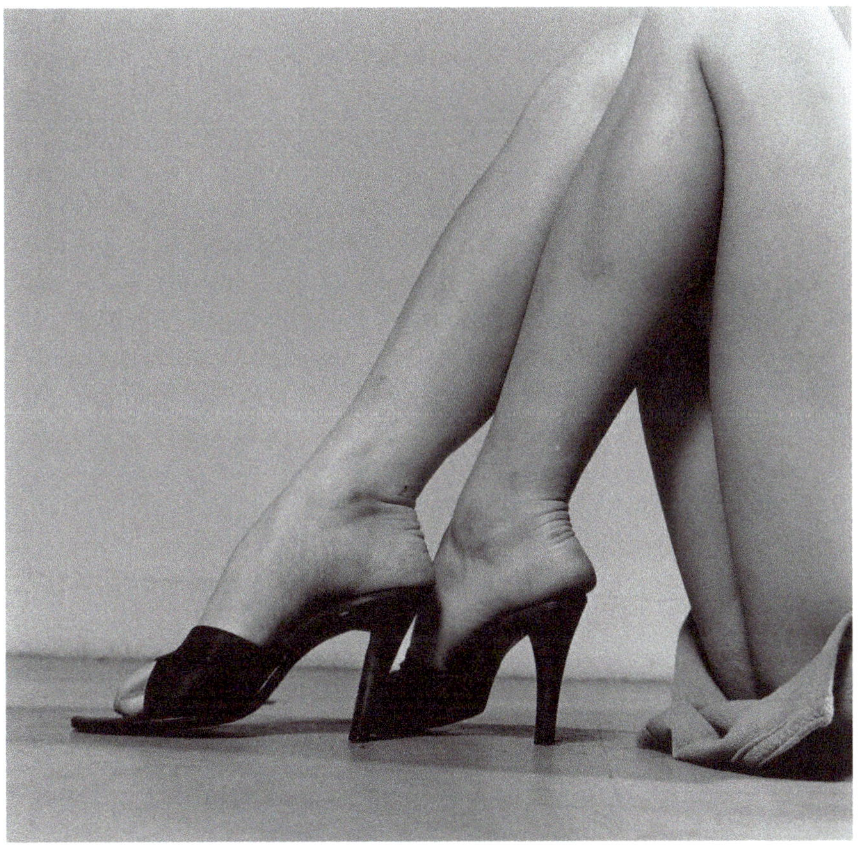

Peter Hujar: Greer Lankston's Legs (1983)

East Village Eye

SquareCylinder.com, September 2018

Some photographers are so closely identified with their moment and milieu that their pictures have become emblems of a particular time and place. It is difficult to think of nineteenth century Paris, for instance, without visualizing Atget's photographic *momento mori* of a pre-industrial past, or the U.S. heartland of the 1950s without filtering it through the ironic gaze of the Swiss photographer Robert Frank. Yet these photographs could hardly be further from anybody's notion of documentary "objectivity." So it is with Peter Hujar, whose retrospective exhibition *Speed of Life*, currently on view at the Berkeley Art Museum, evokes his East Village of the 1970s and '80s

Hujar is best known for his black-and-white portraits of artists, writers, drag performers and boyfriends. Although less romanticized than other representations of the downtown scene such as Jonathan Larson's rock-musical *Rent* (1994), in retrospect, the two share a vision of a Bohemian paradise lost. Only an occasional photograph of Hujar's, however, captures the grittiness of the East Village of that day, such as *Girl in my Hallway*—a picture of the derelict subject passed out on the photographer's doorstep. With the onset of AIDS a few years later, widespread misery reached epic proportions in Lower Manhattan and in 1987 the disease claimed Hujar.

Born in 1934, Hujar died during the heyday of the East Village scene. (Many observers pronounced its demise as early as 1983, with the opening of Pat Hearn's posh gallery on then out-of-the way Avenue B.) For newcomers, the decaying neighborhood seemed an alternative to the conservative juggernaut that gained momentum after the election of Ronald Reagan to the White House in 1980—characterized by the upward redistribution of wealth (a/k/a Reagonomics), the religiosity of right-wing politicians (a/k/a the culture war), and the public health crisis caused by the city's do-nothing response to AIDS. As the epicenter of the previous decade's hippie influx, the East Village continued to offer relatively cheap rents to a youthful populous bent on re-invention and acting out in public. A paradoxical mix of community and narcissism seemed to animate this neighborhood bounded by N.Y.U. and the East River, Houston and 14th Streets

Like his ostensible rival Robert Mapplethorpe, Hujar was by no means a photographic pioneer. He possessed a conservative, fashion-inflected sensibility—despite his unconventional treatment of some portrait subjects. (He also produced pictures of twins, cows and sheep, the abstract geometry of Manhattan architecture, infants breast-feeding and even subjects' legs, seen from knee to foot.) A quick turn around the show reveals Hujar's roots in mid-century New York photography: the oddness of Diane Arbus, who upon meeting Hujar bawled him out for appropriating her style; the narrative flavor of Irving Penn; the revealing detail caught on the street by Lisette Model; and the fashion aesthetic of Richard Avedon.

These varied influences also suggest that Hujar never quite found his groove, that his attention shifted frequently. Consider the contrast between two images of New York: *San Gennaro Street Fair at Dawn*, a wonderfully moody, nightlit picture of the annual festival's site to which the greasy smell of zeppoli seems to cling, and *From Rockefeller Center: The Equity Building*, one of Hujar's views of skyscrapers seen in raking angle, a compositional convention nearly as old as the turn-of-the-century "tall building" itself. Unfortunately, Hujar gave up the former approach and continued to pursue the latter.

Portraits comprise the heart of Hujar's output. Close looking underlines their complexity: They are intimate and clear-eyed, affectionate but unsentimental, and formally elegant. Despite the permissiveness of the time, Hujar rarely violated the tenets of good taste. Perhaps the closest he came was his portrait of the lithe, naked performer Bruce de Ste. Croix calmly seated, holding his sturdy erection in his hand. Set against the stark, studio backdrop Hujar employed in his portraits, the photograph was produced for a polemical show about the male nude staged at the Marcuse Pfeifer Gallery. Although it was discretely hung in Pfeifer's office, the nude turned out to be Hujar's second best selling photograph, after *Candy Darling on her Deathbed*. For this touching portrait of the transsexual actress and Warhol Superstar, Hujar dramatically lit its hospital room setting and placed its subject's face at the center of the composition. Heavily made up, the actress surveys us—and seemingly impending death—with both toughness and vulnerability from behind a whitened mask.

Hujar's crowning achievement was an extensive series of portraits of the actor and playwright Ethyl Eichelberger. An influential figure on the downtown scene, Eichelberger performed in more than 30 plays, often based on historical figures or classics. They included a vast array from Lucrezia Borgia, the characters conflated for his vision of *King Lear*, Abraham and Mary Todd Lincoln, and *Klytemnestra* (with Accordian). Hujar's portrait of *Ethyl Eichel-berger as Minnie the Maid*, presents the performer in signature stilettos, as a giddy blond, perched on a chair off which she seems to levitate. Like so many of Eichelberger's characters—as well as Hujar's portraits—she is witty and stylized rather than caricatured. Hujar ranged widely in his treatments of cross-dressing perform-ers, some of the best make no reference to drag at all. Tomata du Plenty, for instance, is portrayed nude and spiky-haired, as if he had just leapt from an Egon Schiele painting, while *John Hays with Orange Breasts*, brings us the subject in male street clothes augmented with protruding, citrus-fruit falsies. Inexplicably, the show provides no information about these and other public figures whose likenesses are on view.

Many of his subjects—such as the humorist Fran Lebowitz and cultural critic Susan Sontag—were friends, although not yet the household names they would become. His friendship with Son-tag resulted in the brilliant portrait of the writer photographed in profile reclining in calculated (and sensual) reverie. The reclining pose became a signature of Hujar's photographs—as seen in por-traits of the Beat writer William Burroughs and the gallerist Dean Savard, among many others. Sontag wrote the introduction to *Portraits in Life and Death* (1976), the sole monograph devoted to Hujar's work published during his lifetime. It appeared short-ly before the publication of Sontag's seminal collection, *On Pho-tography* (1978). Hujar was understandably piqued that she nev-er mentioned him by name in her essay, instead philosophizing about the relationship of photography and death.

During his lifetime, his work appeared in more than three doz-en shows in the U.S. and Europe. Many of those in New York were held at the Marcuse Pefeifer Gallery and the gay-oriented Robert Samuel Gallery, two pioneering photography venues, and at the hip Gracie Mansion Gallery, which featured art in all media. He was the recipient of a Fulbright Fellowship and several artists' fel-lowships from the National Endowment for the Arts. He was less successful in his own eyes, though. Fran Lebowitz's description of him as "One of the most difficult [and angry] people in the world...

He could never sell himself" was a view shared by many. But despite his bitterness, he was hardly a tortured outcast.

In 1980, he met the artist David Wojnarowicz and embarked on a complicated relationship. It began with a brief romantic fling but was cemented by their similar origins in emotionally abusive households. The conventional wisdom exaggerates its impact on their work. It suggests that Hujar mentored Wojnarowicz, who was twenty years his junior. Wojnarowicz—whom I knew—was single-mindedly dedicated to his art, supported by well-placed admirers and *en route* to professional success. Hujar mattered deeply to Wojnarowicz, as evidenced by his statement that "Everything I made, I made for Peter," as well as the pictures he took of the just-deceased photographer on his deathbed, then incorporated into his art. But the emotionally labile artist was also prone to infatuations, omissions, obfuscations and exaggerations. Hujar, in turn, was too old to have his work much affected by the younger artist's post-modern outlook.

Whatever Hujar's individual psychology, the sociological character of twentieth century New York was fixed: It enshrined the East Village as the latest creative hub in a century-old line dating from pre-World War I Greenwich Village, and on to the Harlem Renaissance of the 1920s and the post-war Beats. Each of these moments was promoted in the romanticized, ideological terms of a beleaguered avant-gardism. The East Village differed, however, in at least one, crucial way: The shocking deaths of so many young artists, writers, and curators during a single decade. It also coincided with the demise of the twentieth century, modernist photographic ethos of which Hujar was an exemplar, and was doomed in part for its inability to depict AIDS, a syndrome with no visual signs. The brilliant artistic production inspired by the plague fails to compensate, of course, for the heartbreak that accompanied it. Hujar's work brings it into sharper focus.

*In honor of Susan Sontag's production
of Waiting for Godot in wartime Sarajevo*

Between Eros and Intellect

*A review of Benjamin Moser's **Sontag: Her Life and Work**. New York: Ecco, 2019.*

Art in America. 2019

Susan Sontag (1933-2004), the subject of Benjamin Moser's authorized biography *Sontag: Her Life and Work*, has so far proven extraordinarily difficult to characterize. The virtual embargo David Rieff, her son and literary executor, placed on Sontag's still-not-entirely published journals and recently opened archives has doubtless limited the content presented over the past two decades, in two unauthorized biographies, a documentary film, and a pair of memoirs. Yet other factors also account for the inadequate analysis to date of the woman Moser calls our "last great literary star."

Telling Sontag's story demands grappling with sizable, sometimes daunting, intellectual challenges. The biographer must do at least three things well: examine a body of works so wide-ranging in references and varied in form that it unsettles the notion of a career; navigate Sontag's changing political views and moral sympathies during the tumultuous era that encompassed the Cold War; and avoid producing a gossipy tell-all account of a subject who knew—and did—everybody. Has Moser, the author of a respected 2009 biography of Brazilian writer Clarice Lispector, met these demands? In part, but at 800-plus pages his ambitious book is overlong and oddly lacking in psychological acumen.

Sontag was born Susan Rosenblatt in New York in 1933 to two American-born children of Jewish immigrants from Eastern Europe: Jack, a fur trader who worked in China; and Mildred, Susan's aloof and alcohol dependent mother. With her parents living abroad, the young girl was raised on Long Island by a nanny. (She would later employ the same woman to take care of son David when she moved to Oxford for graduate school.) Jack died of tuberculosis in 1938 and a few years later Mildred married Nathan Sontag in Tucson, where she had settled with her daughters, Susan and the younger Judith. In 1945, the family moved to Sherman Oaks in Los Angeles' San Fernando Valley. There the nerdy, gangly Susan became—what else?—an editor at The Arcade, the North Hollywood High School newspaper.

Nearly every biographical (and autobiographical) account singles out two key events from Susan's early years: Her first view of Holocaust photos, at age twelve, so disturbed her she described it as "bisecting" her life. Later she was shaken by a visit to one of her idols, Thomas Mann, the German émigré novelist living in Pacific Palisades. His failure to treat the 16-year-old as an equal irked her for decades, as evidenced in the short story, *The Pilgrimage* (1987).

By time of that visit, she had already graduated high school and was attending UC Berkeley while waiting to enroll in the University of Chicago, drawn by the latter's Great Books curriculum. In Berkeley, she met her first girlfriend, Harriet Sohmers, who introduced her to the local lesbian scene. In Chicago, she audited a course taught by the sociologist Philip Rieff, eleven years her senior; just ten days after meeting, they married. In 1952, David was born to the nineteen-year- old Susan.

Rieff is best known for *Freud: The Mind of the Moralist* (1959), an acclaimed examination of the context in which psychoanalysis originated. Moser asserts that the young Susan both researched and wrote the book, though there is no evidence of the latter. The jury is still out. Rieff demanded she renounce any claims to the book's authorship as part of their divorce decree in 1959, a concession she probably made in exchange for Rieff's eschewing a custody battle over David. More surprising, Moser offers no case for Herbert Marcuse's influence on the book's development. During the mid-fifties Rieff was teaching at Brandeis, while the Frankfurt School philosopher was teaching at nearby Harvard. Marcuse's wife died around the time of the publication of his seminal work, *Eros and Civilization: A Philosophical Inquiry into Freud* (1955). Marcuse spent a year as a guest in the Rieff house, where discussion of Hegel was so common that the three-year-old David used the philosopher's name in wordplay. Marcuse found Susan an intellectualizer ("She can make a theory out of a potato peel"), an opinion she likely shared given her burgeoning desire for the erotic liberation he advocated.

In 1959, the year she divorced, Sontag moved to New York, with its emerging 1960s cultural mélange. Most key witnesses to the first half of her writing life are deceased, including both Marcuse and Philip Rieff, as well as Roger Straus, her life-long publisher and financially supportive father figure. A number of early friends were lost to AIDS, among them the gay artist Paul Thek, with whom Sontag discussed having a baby and to whom she dedicated her first essay collection, *Against Interpretation* (its title derived from his many anti-theory remarks).

Sontag's bisexuality was expressed in long-term relationships with women (including Sohmers, photographer Annie Leibovitz, playwright Irene Maria Fornes, dancer-choreographer Lucinda Childs, and actress Nicole Stephane) and brief liaisons with men, such as Jasper Johns, Robert Kennedy, and Warren Beatty. Sontag came of age at a time when homosexuality was illegal and its exposure caused the ruin of countless lives. She never emerged from the closet. Ironically, the essay that first brought her public attention was *Notes on Camp*, a founding document of contemporary queer culture, published in 1964 in the *Partisan Review*.

Notes identifies over-the-top, camp taste as quintessentially homosexual, an idea that was already current in 1909, according to the OED, and described at length in Christopher Isherwood's *The World in the Evening* (1954). Sontag's purposes were dual: The essay endorses camp, but rather than assaulting the traditional canon, it pleads for a broadly inclusive engagement with high art, popular culture and gay taste alike. Sontag often seasoned her texts with striking aphorisms. Her observation that "the two pioneering forces of the modern sensibility are Jewish moral seriousness and homosexual aestheticism and irony"—one of her most memorable pronouncements—is a form of autobiography sited between the lines.

Over the next four decades, Sontag occupied a towering position in American culture as a cultural critic and essayist, filmmaker and novelist, playwright and director. She was known for provoking controversy,right up to her final essay, about Abu Ghraib, written just before her death from cancer. The influence of some of her boundary-blurring essays—republished in collections such as *Styles of Radical Will* and *On Photography*—is so ubiquitous as to seem paradoxically invisible. To radically abridge her curriculum vitae, she published many nonfiction books (including *Illness as Metaphor* and *AIDS and Its Metaphors*), wrote four novels (*The Benefactor, Death Kit, Volcano Lover,* and *In America*) and directed four films in four languages (*Duet for Cannibals, Promised Lands, Brother Carl* and *Unguided Tour*). Moser judges *Promised Lands*, a wartime documentary about Israel, the best of the films, but he misses its near-fatal flaw: It denies Palestinians a voice by employing a sympathetic Israeli to represent them.

Like such oversights, Moser's psychologizing can also be a problem. He relies too heavily on an Alcoholics Anonymous-derived model of intergenerational co-dependency to account for Sontag's insecurities and compensatory acting out. He also too trustingly takes Sontag's journals (of which we now have two of three projected volumes) at face value. Does her self-delusion make her the most truthful narrator of her life? Her haughty response to the plagiarism charges leveled against parts of *In America* was simply cringe-worthy. When it comes to the over-close relationship she developed with her son (and chosen editor) the comments of those who saw them together are far more persuasive than her obsessive rationalizing and narcissism.

Moser also over-examines the minutiae of her private life (she apparently had questionable personal hygiene) at the expense of her public accomplishments. The exception is his fascinating account of her production of *Waiting for Godot* in wartime Sarajevo.

One viable approach to discussing Sontag's diverse endeavors is to categorize the films, essays and books as her "textual" output, and the public activities as her "performative" production. Both should be considered her "work." The latter category included publicly questioning Norman Mailer about women's writing at New York's Town Hall; denouncing, in her role as president of the US branch of PEN, the *fatwa* against Salman Rushdie; helping to launch the New York Institute of the Humanities at NYU; turning up on TV talk shows and appearing, or being invoked by name, in Hollywood film fare including *Zelig, Bull Durham* and *Gremlins 2*. Sometimes the two modes overlapped, as did her role as a bridge between modernism and post-modernism. She was an impresario who introduced American audiences to writers like E.M. Cioran and Machado de Assis, and filmmakers such as Yasujiro Ozu, Hans-Jürgen Syberberg and Bela Tarr. Her finesse at media manipulation reminds us of the distinction between deserved fame then, and Kardashian-style celebrity now.

Detractors often dismissed her performative acts as publicity stunts. They were, however, far more than mediagenic interventions in the regular news flow. They also helped her craft the striking persona that at once reflected and galvanized the cultural zeitgeist. This m.o. functioned as an alternative to academia with its conventional decorum, male chauvinism, and rigidly defined disciplines. In this she resembled predecessors such as Hannah Arendt and Simone de Beauvoir. Her reputation was surprisingly unresolved at the time of her death, as suggested by the ambivalent portrait of her painted in *The New York Times* obituary titled "Social Critic with Verve."

Moser concludes, in a recent interview with Gary Indiana in *Interview* magazine, that "The world has never needed a Susan Sontag more than it does now," At least we have the little-known views about contemporary matters expressed in her final (and very fine) work, *Regarding the Pain of Others* (2003). Overlooked because of its proximity to her death, the extended essay grapples with issues of long-standing interest to her: the distancing effect of technology, the complex nature of images of violence and refugees; and the danger of diminished empathy. In 2019, the Metropolitan Museum evoked the former cultural icon, who had been absent from its programming. Instead of reminding us of the ongoing relevance of Sontag's work, the Metropolitan Museum coyly appropriated—really extracted—from her writing, a title for its glitzy, annual Fashion Institiute ball "Camp: Notes on Fashion."

I am indebted to Betti-Sue Hertz for the collaborative development of some theoretical modes for engaging with Sontag, in our role as co-directors of the *On Susan Sontag: Media, Modernity & Morality* project, sponsored by the San Francisco Art Institute.

About the Author

Robert Atkins is an art historian, writer and activist who studied at the London School of Economics and the University of California's Riverside and Berkeley campuses. A former staff columnist for the *Village Voice*, he has written about the intersections of art, politics and media for more than 100 publications including *The New York Times*, *Art in America*, (Japanese) *Esquire* and *Wired*.

Atkins has also written numerous books and exhibition catalogs. He is the co-author of *Censoring Culture: Contemporary Threats to Free Expression* (published by the New Press) and the best-selling gateways to contemporary and modern art: *ArtSpeak: A Guide to Contemporary Ideas, Movements, and Buzzwords* (Abbeville), and its prequel *ArtSpoke: A Guide to Modern Ideas, Movements, and Buzzwords 1848-1944* (Abbeville). Other books he has written include *From Media to Metaphor: Art About AIDS* (Independent Curators Inc.), the book accompanying the first international traveling exhibition devoted to AIDS-art.

He is a co-founder of Visual AIDS, the producers of *Day Without Art* and the *Red Ribbon*. He has taught and lectured widely, at such institutions as the Rhode Island School of Design, the Maryland Institute/College of Art, and the San Francisco Art Institute, where he co-organized *Susan Sontag: Media, Modernity & Morality*, a cross-disciplinary project of diverse institutions throughout the Bay Area. He has curated more than two dozen exhibitions at far-flung venues including *Between Science and Fiction* (which he co-organized for the *Sao Paulo Biennal*), *David Ireland* (for the New Museum) and *Fusion! Artists in a Research Setting* for Carnegie Mellon University, where he was a Fellow at the STUDIO for Creative Inquiry. He has created pioneering websites, including *TalkBack! A Forum for Critical Discourse*, sponsored by the City University of New York, *Artery: The AIDS-Arts Forum*, sponsored by the New York

Arts Alliance, and *ArtSpeak China*, the first "wiki" about contemporary Chinese art. He is also the former arts editor of *The Media Channel* and Vice-President/editor-in-chief of the *Arts Technology Entertainment Network* (a *New York Times Video* start-up).

Atkins is a former board member of the American branch of the International Art Critics' Association (AICA) and the recipient of awards for arts criticism and cultural commentary from the National Endowment for the Arts, the National Endowment for the Humanities, Manufacturer's Hanover Bank, Microsoft and the Penny McCall Foundation, among other foundations and government agencies.

www.robertatkins.net

www.ingramcontent.com/pod-product-compliance
Lightning Source LLC
Chambersburg PA
CBHW040729070726
47599CB00033B/1061